00820

ANCIENT ISRAEL'S CRIMINAL LAW

TO MY MOTHER

ANCIENT ISRAEL'S CRIMINAL LAW

A New Approach to The Decalogue

ANTHONY PHILLIPS, B.D., Ph.D.

Fellow, Dean and Chaplain of
Trinity Hall, Cambridge

OXFORD

BASIL BLACKWELL

1970

0 631 12280 X

PRINTED IN GREAT BRITAIN BY
WESTERN PRINTING SERVICES LTD, BRISTOL

PREFACE

This book has its basis in my dissertation entitled *The Religious Background to Israel's Criminal Law* submitted to the Faculty of Divinity in the University of Cambridge for the degree of Ph.D. in 1967. Although the book mainly reiterates the conclusions then reached, the text has been substantially rewritten. The manuscript was completed in January 1969.

I wish first to acknowledge my debt to the late Professor D. Winton Thomas who supervised my research, both for his guidance of my work and also for his personal kindness to me during my period as his research student and subsequently. I am also much indebted to Professors G. W. Anderson and P. R. Ackroyd for reading the original thesis, and offering their criticism and advice. Finally I should like to thank Dr. A. W. Marks and the Reverend G. W. F. Lang for their help in bringing this book into being, Mrs. B. F. Smith for all her kindness and efficiency in typing the manuscript, and the Reverend A. K. Jenkins for reading the proofs.

I dedicate this book to my Mother. She will know how indebted I am to her.

Cambridge, July 1970   ANTHONY PHILLIPS

CONTENTS

INTRODUCTION

In recent years considerable research has been undertaken on the problems of the Decalogue. Whereas once scholars were more or less unanimous in rejecting an ancient date for it, today opinion is much more open. Though many would question the Decalogue's connection with the Mosaic period, or even that it came into existence as a unity, yet there is a fairly general recognition that at least part of its contents come from Israel's ancient past.

It is, however, not my intention to provide any detailed discussion of this research: for that I must refer the reader who is interested in these problems to the relevant literature.[1] My purpose is rather to approach the Decalogue from an entirely different standpoint by considering what kind of law Israel understood the commandments to be. It will be my contention that in fact the Decalogue constituted ancient Israel's pre-exilic criminal law code given to her at Sinai. This code both brought Israel into being, and formed the very basis of her continued existence. Although some of the commandments were later expanded and reinterpreted, I shall show that no new crimes were added to her pre-exilic criminal law which could not be derived from the Decalogue.

My discussion will open with the contention that the covenant concept is based on the Hittite suzerainty treaty form. Yahweh is seen as the suzerain who imposes certain absolute stipulations, the ten commandments, on his vassal, Israel. Breach of any of these stipulations would result in action by Yahweh against the covenant community, and could even amount to the repudiation of the covenant relationship itself. Consequently it will be argued that Israel treated the covenant stipulations as her criminal law code, and, in order to propitiate Yahweh, imposed the death penalty for their breach. I shall show that

[1] J. J. Stamm, 'Dreissig Jahre Dekalogforschung', *TR*, N.F., xxvii, 1961, pp. 189–239, 281–305; H. Graf Reventlow, *Gebot und Predigt im Dekalog*, Gütersloh, 1962; J. Schreiner, *Die zehn Gebote im Leben des Gottesvolkes*, München, 1966; Stamm and M. E. Andrew, *The Ten Commandments in Recent Research*, SBT², ii, 1967; F. Nielsen, *The Ten Commandments in New Perspective*, SBT², vii, 1968.

in pre-exilic Israel it was only for breach of the Decalogue that execution was exacted, thereby indicating that the ten commandments have an inner unity of which both the Book of the Covenant and Deuteronomy take note.

But in order to isolate ancient Israel's criminal law it will be necessary to distinguish this from other types of her law, civil, customary, family and cultic. Indeed it is part of my purpose to show that pre-exilic Israel clearly distinguished between criminal and civil offences, that is between crimes and torts.[2]

After considering some general observations concerning legal status, the administration of justice, and liability, all of which naturally form the background to any discussion of ancient Israel's criminal law, I shall investigate in detail each of the commandments. It will be argued that the first five commandments were concerned to secure the permanent relationship of each individual Israelite to Yahweh, while the second five were designed to protect not his property, but his person. In each case an attempt will be made to isolate the original commandment, and to show why it was included in the Decalogue. Subsequent expansions of the commandment itself and of the crime which it created are examined.

Finally, in the light of my discussion of the individual commandments, I shall attempt to survey the history of the development of Israel's criminal law from the giving of the Decalogue at Sinai to the inauguration of the priestly legislation.

The only adequate definition of a crime is that conduct which the state prohibits. Thus there are as many criminal law codes as there are states to enact them. The criminal law of any one state is therefore peculiar to that state, and like any other national feature can indicate much about it, both concerning its political and religious ideologies, as well as the value it places on the individual within the state.[3] It is the realization of this fact which is the justification for this study.

[2] It is failure to recognize this distinction that has made recent studies of ancient Israel's law so ineffectual (cf. Z. W. Falk, *Hebrew Law in Biblical Times*, Jerusalem, 1964; E. M. Good, 'Capital Punishment and its Alternatives in Ancient Near Eastern Law', *Stanford Law Review*, xix, 1967, pp. 947–77).

[3] A comparison of the racial legislation of the Republic of South Africa with that of the United Kingdom would make this point clear.

PART I

THE BACKGROUND

CHAPTER ONE

THE COVENANT

It was G. E. Mendenhall[1] who first related the Decalogue to the Hittite suzerainty treaties, in which the vassal, consequent upon certain historical events enumerated in the prologue to the treaty, bound himself in absolute obedience to the Hittite king, but was left free to determine his state's internal affairs. While it was presupposed that the Hittite king would give to the vassal his protection, no specific obligations were laid upon him, and he was not a 'party' to the treaty.[2] It is Mendenhall's contention that it is in the light of these treaties that the covenant relationship should be interpreted. Yahweh is to be understood as fulfilling the role of the Hittite king, and the clans that of his vassal, who as a result of the exodus from Egypt, agree to enter into the covenant with him, and become absolutely liable in respect of the stipulations which he lays upon them, namely the commandments of the Decalogue. These both determine the clans' relations with Yahweh himself, and with those other clans who enter into the covenant, and to whom they are bound by sacral alliance. It is presupposed that in return for their absolute allegiance, Yahweh will give the clans his protection and help,[3] though he himself remains entirely free and exists independently of them. The covenant is not a contractual agreement between partners, but the granting of a particular status by Yahweh to a group of clans from whom certain obligations

---

[1] 'Ancient Oriental and Biblical Law', *BA*, xvii, 1954, pp. 26–46 and 'Covenant Forms in Israelite Tradition', ibid., pp. 50–76.

[2] Cf. parity treaties between equals (ibid., pp. 55 f.). In 'Covenant', IDB, i, p. 717, Mendenhall distinguishes two further covenant types which he designates 'patron' and 'promissory'.

[3] Cf. F. C. Fensham, 'Clauses of Protection in Hittite Vassal-Treaties and the Old Testament', *VT*, xiii, 1963, pp. 133–43.

are required. None the less, the fact that particular obligations are specified means that there can be no arbitrary exercise of divine power.[4]

Further examination of the Sinai pericope (Exod. 19–24), which is to be attributed to E, would seem to support Mendenhall's thesis.[5] Thus Exod. 19:3 ff. is to be understood as recording in the language of the Hittite suzerainty treaty form[6] the preliminary negotiations which resulted in the agreement to establish the covenant.[7] This is now set out in Exod. 20:2 ff., Exod. 20:2 acting both as the preamble introducing the suzerain, Yahweh, as well as the historical prologue. It will be argued that originally all ten commandments consisted of short apodictic injunctions, which together made up what is here termed the 'Sinai Decalogue'. The I-Thou style is entirely consistent with the Hittite suzerainty treaties, as is the basic demand for exclusive allegiance to Yahweh (Exod. 20:3). Further, like the obligations of the Hittite treaties, the covenant stipulations are designated 'words', Exod. 24:3 referring directly to Exod. 20:1, thereby indicating that the Book of the Covenant has been subsequently inserted.[8] This has resulted in the displacement of Exod. 20:18 ff., which would have preceded the Decalogue, to which in the preliminary negotiations the covenanting clans had already pledged themselves. Although sanctions are not specifically mentioned, they are implied by the absolute

[4] It will readily become apparent how much this study disagrees with the contention of J. Begrich, 'Berit', ZAW, N.F., xix, 1944, pp. 1–11, that the covenant was given to a passive recipient, and that only later were legal demands introduced into the covenant concept. Cf. further A. Jepsen, 'Berith. Ein Beitrag zur Theologie der Exilszeit', Verbannung und Heimkehr, Rudolph-Festschrift, Tübingen, 1961, pp. 161 ff., and the reply of W. Eichrodt, 'Covenant and Law', Interpr., xx, 1966, pp. 302–21. For an attempt to understand the form of the covenant from a Near Eastern source other than the Hittite suzerainty treaties, namely the Mari letter ii. 37 (ANET, p. 482b), cf. M. Noth, 'Old Testament Covenant-Making in the Light of a Text from Mari', The Laws in the Pentateuch and Other Essays, E.T., Edinburgh, 1966, pp. 108–17; H. W. Wolff, 'Jahwe als Bundesvermittler', VT, vi, 1956, pp. 316–20.

[5] Cf. K. Baltzer, Das Bundesformular, WMANT, iv, 1960; J. A. Thompson, The Ancient Near Eastern Treaties and the Old Testament, London, 1964; A. S. Kapelrud, 'Some Recent Points of View on the Time and Origin of the Decalogue', ST, xviii, 1964, pp. 81–90; W. Beyerlin, Origins and History of the Oldest Sinaitic Traditions E.T., Oxford, 1965.

[6] J. Muilenburg, 'The Form and Structure of the Covenantal Formulations', VT, ix, 1959, pp. 351 ff.; Beyerlin, op. cit., pp. 6 ff., 67 ff.

[7] Cf. E. Gerstenberger, 'Covenant and Commandment', JBL, lxxxiv, 1965, pp. 38–51, who fails to take this passage into account in arguing that the Hittite treaty document was the result of preceding negotiations and agreement to enter into a treaty relationship.

[8] A. Weiser, Introduction to the Old Testament, E.T., London, 1961, p. 119; O. Eissfeldt, Introduction to the Old Testament, E.T., Oxford, 1965, p. 213; Beyerlin, Origins and History, pp. 4 ff.

nature of the covenant stipulations,[9] breach of any of which could result in divine punishment, and if sufficiently widespread might even lead to the total repudiation of the covenant relationship itself. Thus the Decalogue implicitly contains both curse—that is divine rejection —and blessing—that is divine protection. There was therefore no need to conclude it with a list of curses and blessings like those found in the Hittite suzerainty treaties,[10] though Deut. 28 and Lev. 26 indicate that this formula was known in Israel (cf. Josh. 8:34).[11]

Clearly, as can be deduced from the Hittite suzerainty treaties, there must have been some method whereby the covenanting clans affirmed their obligation under the covenant (cf. Josh. 24:24).[12] This is the purpose of the two separate ceremonies recorded in Exod. 24, namely the blood rite at the foot of the mountain (Exod. 24:3–8), and the common meal at its summit (Exod. 24:1a., 9–11). These two accounts have generally been regarded as alternative versions of the way in which the covenant was ratified perhaps to be attributed to the sources J and E.[13] In fact both rituals appear to describe recognized methods whereby a covenant might be concluded and are used by the E compiler to illustrate the two different aspects of the covenant relationship, namely that between Yahweh and the individual members of the covenant community, and that between these individuals themselves.[14]

Thus the blood ceremony at the foot of the mountain emphasizes the God-man aspect of the covenant relationship. This ceremony, whereby half the blood is thrown on the altar representing Yahweh and

---

[9] Ibid., pp. 53 f.

[10] The absence of the curse-blessing formula is the chief reason for D. J. McCarthy's contention (*Treaty and Covenant*, Analecta Biblica, xxi, Rome, 1963, pp. 152 ff.) that the Sinai covenant was not based on the Hittite treaty form, which he alleges was only later used to describe Israel's covenant relationship. However, he still considers the Decalogue to be part of the covenant inaugurated at Sinai. On the other hand Gerstenberger, op. cit., pp. 38 ff., and *Wesen und Herkunft des 'Apodiktischen Rechts'*, WMANT, xx, 1965, severs the Decalogue from its connection with Sinai.

[11] Cf. Fensham, 'Malediction and Benediction in the Ancient Near Eastern Treaties and in the Old Testament', *ZAW*, N.F., xxxiii, 1962, pp. 1–9 and 'Common Trends in Curses of the Near Eastern Treaties and *kudurru*-Inscriptions Compared with Maledictions of Amos and Isaiah', ibid., N.F., xxxiv, 1963, pp. 155–75; D. R. Hillers, *Treaty Curses and the Old Testament Prophets*, Biblica et Orientalia, xvi, Rome, 1964.

[12] Even though the Hittite treaties refer to the oath of the vassal, this is lacking in the treaties themselves (Mendenhall, IDB, i, p. 715; Beyerlin, *Origins and History*, p. 62).

[13] Cf. the recent study of M. L. Newman, *The People of the Covenant*, London, 1965, pp. 37, 50.

[14] Beyerlin, op. cit., pp. 16 ff. ascribes both passages to E. Exod. 24:1a should be placed after Exod. 24:8. Exod. 24:1b–2 would appear to be a later theological insertion due to the desire to maintain that it was only Moses who ascended the mountain.

half on the people, is intended to bring into effect the covenant
between Yahweh and the people, who, by assenting to the covenant
law by what amounts to a solemn oath (Exod. 24:3, 8),[15] both corporately and individually acknowledge his absolute authority.[16] Thus
breach of the covenant stipulations would result in both individual and
communal liability to divine punishment.

But nothing is said in this rite as to the man-man element in the
covenant relationship. This is dealt with in the account of the covenant
meal when a delegation representing those who had taken part in the
earlier rite at the foot of the mountain is summoned to the top of the
mountain, and by partaking of a ritual meal in the presence of Yahweh,
whose absolute authority had already been acknowledged, bind themselves, and in consequence the clans whom they represented, to one
another (Gen. 26:26 ff.; 31:44, 54; Josh. 9:14 f.).[17] The obligations
to Yahweh and to one's neighbour were the twin elements of the
covenant from its inception. Thus Yahweh should not be understood
to have taken part in the meal, for the covenant between God and man
had already been formed.

The Hittite suzerainty treaty only came into effect on its committal
to writing by the suzerain, and the handing over of the written document to the vassal. Thus Exod. 24:12 ff. records Yahweh's promise to
give to Moses the tablets of stone inscribed by Yahweh himself, which
is fulfilled in Exod. 31:18.[18] It would seem that the Hittite treaties
were deposited in the shrines of the parties' deities. Clearly this is the
function of the ark (cf. Deut. 10:1 ff.; 31:9, 26), which also acted as
the throne of Yahweh, upon which he would manifest himself.[19]
Although it is only D and P which understand the tablets to have been

[15] Newman, op. cit., p. 36; cf. G. M. Tucker, 'Covenant Forms and Contract
Forms', *VT*, xv, 1965, pp. 487–503.

[16] Cf. W. Robertson Smith, *Kinship and Marriage in Early Arabia* (new ed.),
London, 1903, pp. 60 ff.

[17] J. Pedersen, *Israel: Its Life and Culture*, i–ii, E.T., London and Copenhagen,
1926, pp. 305 f.; Robertson Smith, *Lectures on the Religion of the Semites*[3], London,
1927, pp. 269 ff.

[18] This verse originally followed Exod. 24:15a as the conclusion of the E narrative
(Noth, *Exodus*, E.T., London, 1962, p. 247; Beyerlin, *Origins and History*, p. 18).
Only in Exod. 34:27 f. is it recorded that Moses wrote the 'ten words' on the tablets,
the significance of which will be adduced later (p. 173). The mention of writing in
Exod. 24:4 probably reflects the insertion of the Book of the Covenant at this point.
Certainly Exod. 24:7 interrupts the blood rite of verses 6 and 8, and is a doublet of
verse 3. Cf. Josh. 24:26. The tradition that the law was written on the stones of witness
is late, and is to be derived from Deut. 27:1 ff. (cf. Josh. 8:32).

[19] Mendenhall, *BA*, xvii, pp. 64 f.; Eichrodt, *Theology of the Old Testament*, i, E.T.,
London, 1961, pp. 107 ff.; R. de Vaux, *Ancient Israel: Its Life and Institutions*, E.T.,
London, 1961, p. 301; Beyerlin, *Origins and History*, pp. 56 ff.; Kapelrud, *ST*, xviii, p. 88.

placed in the ark, this object would never have been termed 'box' had it not from the first acted as a container. The practice of placing legal documents at the feet of a divinity is well known elsewhere in the ancient Near East. In this way the ark would have been regarded as the pedestal for Yahweh who guarded the covenant law at his feet. Indeed it would seem that the ark came to be understood as a portable Sinai.[20] The fact that tradition records that there were two tablets of the law is also due to the Hittite suzerainty treaty formula under which one copy was retained by the Hittite king, and the other was given to the vassal. But at Sinai both tablets were placed in the ark, thereby symbolizing the suzerain's (Yahweh's) permanent presence within the vassal community, provided, of course, that the latter obeyed the covenant stipulations. Thus the tablets are to be understood as identical, each containing the full Decalogue.[21] Consequently there is no need to distribute the stipulations over both stones.

It was usual for the Hittite suzerainty treaties to conclude with a list of witnesses, both divine and natural phenomena being cited. While Exod. 20:3 precluded any appeal to divine powers, the use of natural phenomena as witnesses is attested both in the prophets and psalms.[22] Further, it is possible that originally a single stone such as is found acting as a witness of the Shechemite covenant (Josh. 24:26 f.) was set up at Sinai, for in Exod. 24:4 *maṣṣebah* is in the singular, thereby indicating that 'twelve' is a later insertion reflecting the amphictyonic situation.[23]

The Hittite suzerainty treaties provided for their regular recitation before the vassal. Although there is no regulation concerning this in the Decalogue itself, Pss. 50 and 81 indicate that it was later recited in the cult at Jerusalem.[24] From Deut. 31:10 ff. it may be deduced that earlier such a public recitation of the covenant stipulations took place at the end of every seven years at the central shrine of the amphictyony.[25] Further evidence of this festival will be found when the law

[20] Newman, op. cit., p. 58.
[21] At the time of writing my original thesis I had not realized that M. G. Kline, *Treaty of the Great King. The Covenant Structure of Deuteronomy*, Grand Rapids, 1963, pp. 17 ff. had already come to this conclusion.
[22] H. B. Huffmon, 'The Covenant Lawsuit in the Prophets', *JBL*, lxxviii, 1959, pp. 285 ff.
[23] Beyerlin, op. cit., pp. 45 ff., 61 f.
[24] On the early identification of the Decalogue with the cult, cf. S. O. P. Mowinckel, *Le Décalogue*, Paris, 1927; A. Alt, 'The Origins of Israelite Law', *Essays on Old Testament History and Religion*, E.T., Oxford, 1966, pp. 123 ff.
[25] On the question whether this festival should be termed a covenant-*renewal*, cf. Mendenhall. IDB, i, p. 720; Hillers, *Treaty Curses*, p. 84. Mendenhall seeks to connect

B

of the release of the Hebrew male slave is examined (Exod. 21:2 ff.).[26]
It has been suggested that the reference to 'young men' in Exod.
24:5 visualizes the actual incorporation into the covenant relationship
of those who had now reached maturity.[27]

If then the covenant concept is to be understood in the light of the
Hittite suzerainty treaties, which during the fourteenth and thirteenth
centuries seem to have been the recognized international covenant
form throughout the ancient Near East,[28] it follows that exodus and
covenant become inseparable, for the latter must be dependent on the
former. Further, since the covenant would only have been entered into
while the exodus event was a living reality, it would therefore seem that
the Decalogue can be attributed to Moses, to whom both chrono-
logically and geographically the Hittite suzerainty treaty form could
have been known.[29] Accordingly the contention, based largely on the
so-called credos in Deut. 26:5 ff. and Josh. 24:1 ff., that the Sinai
and the exodus-conquest traditions were only later combined in
Canaan[30] must be rejected.[31]

On the basis of this hypothesis, can one then offer an explanation
as to how the covenant came to be inaugurated?[32] It was once assumed
that the clans which escaped from Egypt adopted a nomadic existence,
but it cannot be supposed that these ex-slaves from an urban environment with no experience at all of desert life would have maintained
such an existence any longer than was absolutely necessary. Indeed

---

the three annual appearances at the agricultural feasts (Exod. 23:14 ff.) with the recitation of the covenant, but these were not celebrated at the central amphictyonic
shrine, but locally (Noth, *The History of Israel*[2], E.T., London, 1960, pp. 97 f.).

[26] See below, pp. 73ff.   [27] Beyerlin, *Origins and History*, p. 39.

[28] Ibid., pp. 51 f.; Kapelrud, *ST*, xviii, p. 85.

[29] Beyerlin, op. cit., pp. 145 ff. Thus it seems that the question whether the later
suzerainty treaties preserved the same form as the earlier Hittite treaties, particularly
in relation to the historical prologue, need not be investigated here (cf. Mendenhall,
BA, xvii, pp. 56 f., IDB, i, p. 715; D. J. Wiseman, 'The Vassal Treaties of Esarhaddon',
Iraq, xx, 1958, pp. 27 f.; J. A. Fitzmyer, 'The Aramaic Suzerainty Treaty from Sefire
in the Museum of Beirut', *CBQ*, xx, 1958, pp. 444–76; McCarthy, *Treaty and Covenant*, pp. 98 ff.; Thompson, *Ancient Near Eastern Treaties*, pp. 14 f.; Huffmon, 'The
Exodus, Sinai and the Credo', *CBQ*, xxvii, 1965, pp. 109 f.; McCarthy, 'Covenant
in the old Testament: the Present State of the Inquiry', ibid., pp. 227 ff.).

[30] G. von Rad, 'The Form-Critical Problem of the Hexateuch', *The Problem of the
Hexateuch and Other Essays*, E.T., Edinburgh, 1966, pp. 1–78.

[31] Weiser, *Introduction*, pp. 83 ff.; Beyerlin, *Origins and History*, pp. 167 ff.; Kapelrud, *ST*, xviii, pp. 83 f.; Huffmon, *CBQ*, xxvii, pp. 101 ff.; Newman, *People of the
Covenant*, pp. 20 ff.; E. W. Nicholson, *Deuteronomy and Tradition*, Oxford, 1967, pp.
40 ff.; Th. C. Vriezen, *The Religion of Ancient Israel*, E.T., London, 1967, pp. 126 ff.;
R. E. Clements, *God's Chosen People*, London, 1968, pp. 55 ff.

[32] For a review of recent work on the covenant concept, cf. McCarthy, *Der Gottesbund im Alten Testament*, Stuttgart, 1966.

the legends of their survival in the desert seem to testify to the fact of their ignorance of life there. It seems therefore reasonable to suppose that these clans would have settled and become resident in the first suitable place which they encountered. Tradition supports the view that this was Kadesh (Judg. 11:16 f.; Exod. 15–18), situated in the vicinity of Sinai (Deut. 1:2).[33] Here it would seem that the covenant was inaugurated and the clans formed into a new community based on the covenant stipulations of the Decalogue. Thus from its inception the covenant community would have been resident as a pastoral society in a defined locality.[34]

The result of Mendenhall's thesis is to confirm that the community, which later came to be known as Israel,[35] can no longer be thought of as descended from a single ancestor, for it was the covenant itself which both created and defined the people of Yahweh, and the covenant stipulations which determined their character.[36] It is this creative nature of the Decalogue which Mendenhall holds has not been fully recognized.[37] It was no racial or political bond that united the clans, but their common adherence to Yahweh.[38] From its inception the covenant community was a mixed sacral union of which any person or clan could become a member, provided they complied with the covenant stipulations. Indeed an example of such incorporation is provided by Exod. 18:10 ff., though since the narrative had not yet recorded the making of the covenant, this could not be specifically referred to there. Thus Exod. 18:10 f. recounts how the Midianite Jethro is led to acknowledge Yahweh consequent upon his historical act in effecting the exodus from Egypt. After the necessary sacrifices have been made, the clans of Jethro and Aaron, who had thus independently and at different times bound themselves to Yahweh, take part in the communion meal before Yahweh, thereby signifying that they are also bound to each other (Exod. 18:12). Thus one can recognize both the God-man and the man-man elements of the covenant relationship.[39]

[33] Beyerlin, op. cit., pp. 145 ff.; Kapelrud, op. cit., pp. 88 ff. Cf. R. Brinker, *The Influence of the Sanctuaries in Early Israel*, Manchester, 1946, pp. 136 ff.; J. Gray, 'The Desert Sojourn of the Hebrews and the Sinai-Horeb Tradition', *VT*, iv, 1954, pp. 148 ff.

[34] Cf. Mendenhall, 'The Hebrew Conquest of Palestine', *BA*, xxv, 1962, pp. 68 f.

[35] It would seem that the name Israel was first applied to the tribal amphictyony based on Shechem (Noth, *History*, pp. 3 ff.).

[36] Mendenhall, *BA*, xvii, p. 62, xxv, pp. 85 f.   [37] Ibid., xvii, p. 28.

[38] J. Bright, *Early Israel in Recent History Writing*, SBT[1], xix, 1956 pp. 113 f.

[39] Though the question of the Kenite origin of Yahwism does not materially affect this study (cf. K. Budde, *Religion of Israel to the Exile*, London, 1899, pp. 1 ff.; H. H.

In spite of the evidence which has here been briefly summarized, Mendenhall's thesis has failed to win universal acceptance,[40] though his critics should perhaps remember that the Sinai pericope is only a narrative *about* the inauguration of the covenant and the covenant ceremonies, and while it does contain the covenant stipulations, it does not pretend to set out the covenant text itself. Nonetheless Mendenhall's argument would be immeasurably strengthened if it could be shown that the ten commandments themselves possessed an inner unity which throughout the history of the covenant relationship differentiated them from all other legal enactments, and of which both the Book of the Covenant and Deuteronomy took note.[41] It is the purpose of this study to show that this can in fact be done by recognizing that for Israel the Decalogue is to be understood as her criminal law code, and that although certain crimes were expanded and reinterpreted, no new crimes were added to her law while she understood her existence to be dependent upon the covenant concept, that is throughout the pre-exilic period. Thus it will be argued that the covenant stipulations were deliberately chosen, the first five being particularly concerned with relations with Yahweh, while the final five dealt with relations between individual members of the covenanting clans, being offences against persons and not property. Since all those individuals who entered into the covenant relationship were in effect Yahweh's vassals, naturally they were to be protected.[42]

A crime is a breach of an obligation imposed by the law which is felt to endanger the community, and which results in the punishment of the offender in the name of the community, but which is not the personal concern of the individual who may have suffered injury, and who has no power to stop the prosecution, not derives any gain from it. Although the prosecution may be privately instigated, it is in the name

---

Rowley, *From Joseph to Joshua*, Schweich Lectures 1948, London, 1950, pp. 149 ff.) it would seem that Exod. 18:10 ff. does not necessarily point to this conclusion (T. J. Meek, *Hebrew Origins*[2], New York, 1950, pp. 94 ff.; Chr. H. W. Brekelmans, 'Exodus xviii and the Origins of Yahwism in Israel', *OTS*, x, 1954, pp. 215–24); for whether Jethro already knew of Yahweh or not, the narrative's concern is to show how Jethro entered into the exclusive covenant relationship with Yahweh, and so became part of the Hebrew covenant community.

[40] Cf. the views of Gerstenberger, *JBL*, lxxxiv, pp. 38–51, and *Wesen und Herkunft des 'Apodiktischen Rechts'*; Stamm and Andrew, *The Ten Commandments*; Nielsen, *The Ten Commandments*.

[41] The maintenance of this contention would effectively answer the view of C. F. Whitley, 'Covenant and Commandment in Israel', *JNES*, xxii, 1963, pp. 37 ff. that the Decalogue was the work of the Deuteronomist.

[42] On relations with co-vassals under the Hittite suzerainty treaties, cf. Mendenhall, *BA*, xvii, p. 59.

of the state, and any fine inflicted will be paid to the state and not to the injured party. The latter must sue for damages under the civil law of tort, where the case will be between the individuals themselves as plaintiff and defendant, and will be of no direct concern to the community.

From the point of view of Yahweh, the Decalogue was Israel's constitution, and any breach of it amounted to an act of apostasy which could lead to divine action both against the individual offender and the community, and might even result in Yahweh's repudiation of the covenant itself. But it is the contention of this study that Israel herself understood the Decalogue as her criminal law code, and that the law contained in it, and developed from it, was sharply distinguished from her civil law. Thus breach of a commandment was not only regarded as an offence against Yahweh, but also, since it endangered the community, as an offence against the latter, in other words a crime, for which prosecution must be undertaken in the community's name. While an individual who was wronged by the act of the criminal may have acted as the prosecutor on behalf of the community, he derived no personal benefit from this prosecution, as he would from an action in tort. Following the conviction of the criminal, immediate execution was inflicted by the community, for the criminal could no longer be regarded as part of the covenant people. Outside breach of the Decalogue, the death penalty was never exacted.

Thus the significance of the blood rite contained in Exod. 24:3 ff. now becomes apparent, for this is to be understood as constituting a self-imprecation.[43] Those who have the blood sprinkled upon them thereby undertake to obey the covenant law, or to pay for their act by a similar shedding of their own blood (cf. Gen. 15:9 ff.; Jer. 34:18). Consequently the execution of the criminal at the hands of the community followed automatically on his conviction for breach of the covenant stipulations. It was therefore propitiatory, being a plea by the community that no divine action might be taken against them. In

---

[43] Thompson, *Ancient Near Eastern Treaties*, pp. 25 f. Cf. the similar practice referred to in 1 Sam. 11:7 and Judg. 19:29 (G. Wallis, 'Eine Parallele zu Richter 19: 29 ff. und 1 Sam. 11:5 ff. aus dem Briefarchiv von Mari', *ZAW*, N.F., xxiii, 1952, pp. 57–61). The slaughter of an animal to conclude a covenant may have provided the technical Hebrew expression כרת ברית ('cut a covenant'). Cf. W. F. Albright, 'The Hebrew Expression for "Making a Covenant" in pre-Israelite Documents', *BASOR*, cxxi, 1951, pp. 21–2; Mendenhall, 'Puppy and Lettuce in Northwest-Semitic Covenant Making', ibid., cxxxiii, 1954, pp. 26–30; Noth, *Essays*, pp. 108 ff.; Hillers, *Treaty Curses*, p. 20. R. Kilian, 'Apodiktisches und kasuistisches Recht im Licht ägyptischer Analogien', *BZ*, vii, 1963, pp. 189 ff. discusses the Egyptian practice of breaking pots on which proscription texts had been written.

enforcing the execution, the community showed its willingness to continue to obey the covenant stipulations. Thus the execution itself made
good the breach of the covenant. But there was never any suggestion
that a substitute should suffer the death penalty in order to secure this
propitiation (Deut. 21:1 ff.).

Modern theories of punishment are therefore totally inapplicable
when considering reasons why ancient Israel executed her criminals,
for the punishment was not looked at from the criminal's point of view.
This extreme penalty was not designed to deter potential criminals,
nor as an act of retribution, but as a means of preventing divine action
by appeasing Yahweh's wrath. On the other hand, in distinction from
human punishment, divine punishment was always understood as an
act of retribution, which by virtue of the covenant relationship itself
could fall on either the individual or the community. Thus the attempt
to differentiate between 'covenant' and 'law' in the discussion of the
Decalogue is unnecessary, for, from the first, breach of the covenant
stipulations could result in both divine and human punishment.[44]
Further, there is no need to abandon the Decalogue's place in the
covenant formula in order to recognize that Israel understood it as a
code of law.[45] It is because the Decalogue constituted the covenant
stipulations that it was treated as Israel's criminal law code.

But it is not only Israel's criminal law which is to be understood in
relation to the Hittite suzerainty treaties, but also her civil law. While
these treaties regulated the external relations of the vassal state, they
did not seek to interfere in its internal affairs. It is in this light that one
is to understand Israel's civil law, which, since it did not involve any
infringement of the covenant stipulations, did not necessitate any recourse to Yahweh. Thus in contrast to the religious background of
Israel's criminal law, that of her civil law was secular, and therefore
could incorporate foreign material. Further, its breach did not involve
the community as a whole in any action, but merely resulted in a suit
between individuals. Thus where injury to persons or property
occurred which did not constitute a crime, the injured party himself
sued the tortfeasor for damages, which were awarded on the basis that
the plaintiff ought to be restored so far as possible to the position he
was in before the injury. Exceptionally in cases of theft of personal
property fixed punitive damages were provided as a deterrent.

Much attention has been paid to the contrast between the apodictic
and casuistic law in the Old Testament, and it has been argued that

---

[44] Cf. Mendenhall, *BA*, xvii, pp. 26 ff. and W. Zimmerli, *The Law and the Prophets*,
Oxford, 1965, p. 51.   [45] Cf. Nielsen, *The Ten Commandments*, pp. 128 ff.

while the latter was inherited from Canaan, the former was distinctively Israelite.[46] This can no longer be maintained, for a mixture of apodictic and casuistic laws as in the Book of the Covenant have been found over a wide area of the ancient Near East, not only in the third person as in the Laws of Eshnunna, the Code of Hammurabi, the Middle Assyrian Laws and the Neo-Babylonian Laws,[47] but also in the second person as in the Hittite treaties[48] and the West Semitic inscriptional curses.[49] Accordingly this distinction can tell one nothing about the foreign or indigenous origin of Israel's laws.[50] Nor should it be held that the apodictic law must *necessarily* reflect a nomadic background, being collections of clan laws.[51] The real difference between apodictic and casuistic law is a matter of scope, the former dealing with a certain area of activity, the latter with a particular concrete case. The reason that the apodictic rather than the casuistic form was used in the Decalogue was that absolute obedience to Yahweh was to be ensured over certain wide areas of activity, rather than in specific cases.[52] Later it sometimes proved necessary to define more clearly whether particular occurrences fell within that area, for example whether certain action constituted murder or merely assault (Exod. 21:18 ff.). These definitions naturally used the casuistic form.

Thus it is the contention of this study that Israel's law can only be examined on the basis of its *content*, and not of its form. It is through ignoring the former and concentrating on the latter that the distinctive nature of the Decalogue as Israel's pre-exilic criminal law code has not hitherto been recognized.

[46] This distinction was first made by Alt, *Essays*, pp. 81 ff., and has been followed by Albright, *From the Stone Age to Christianity*[2], Baltimore, 1946, pp. 204 f.

[47] B. Landsberger, 'Die babylonischen Termini für Gesetz und Recht', *Symbolae ad iura orientis—Paulo Koschaker dedicatae*, Leiden, 1939, p. 223; Meek, *Hebrew Origins*, pp. 72 f.; ANET, p. 183b; R. Yaron, 'Forms in the Laws of Eshnunna', *RIDA*[3], ix, 1962, pp. 145 f.

[48] Mendenhall, *BA*, xvii, pp. 29 f.

[49] S. Gevirtz, 'West Semitic Curses and the Problem of the Origins of Hebrew Law', *VT*, xi, 1961, pp. 140 ff.

[50] Cf. for further discussion I. Rapaport, 'The Origins of Hebrew Law', *PEQ*, lxxiii, 1941, pp. 160 ff.; D. Daube, 'Some Forms of Old Testament Legislation', *Oxford Society of Historical Theology*, 1944/5, pp. 36 ff.; J. van der Ploeg, 'Studies in Hebrew Law', *CBQ*, xii, 1950, pp. 416 ff.; Mendenhall, IDB, i, p. 720; Kilian, *BZ*, vii, pp. 185 ff.; Falk, *Hebrew Law*, pp. 16 f.

[51] Gerstenberger, *Wesen und Herkunft des 'Apodiktischen Rechts'*, pp. 110 ff. He redefines apodictic law to include only those prohibitions and commands which have no stipulation of the legal consequence (pp. 23 ff.).

[52] Similarly this explains why the apodictic form was also used in the Rechabite code (Jer. 35:6 f.) for it was designed to prohibit absolutely those activities which would jeopardize the nomadic way of life.

CHAPTER TWO

GENERAL OBSERVATIONS

(i) *Legal Status*

Initially only free adult males were subject to Israel's criminal law, for only they could have entered into the covenant relationship with Yahweh. It was to them that the covenant stipulations of the Sinai Decalogue were addressed. No technical term was evolved to cover these persons, reliance being placed, where it was needed, on רע, whose basic meaning indicates a person with whom one is habitually associated, whether this is through friendship (Exod. 33:11), geographical location (Exod. 11:2), engaging in battle (Judg. 7:22) or legal obligation (Exod. 20:16 f.).[1] There can, however, be no doubt that where this word appears in legal enactments, it is to be restricted to the Israelite legal community.[2] The fact that רע is only used in the final two commandments indicates that the sixth and probably the eighth commandments were absolute, giving protection not only to adult male Israelites, but also to their wives and children. Since the seventh commandment was specifically directed at sexual intercourse with the wife of one's neighbour, it is possible that the term רע, which is actually expressed in Lev. 20:10 (cf. Deut. 22:22), has been omitted through the influence of the surrounding commandments.

It was with puberty that an Israelite boy became an adult and consequently a full member of the covenant community, being able to take part in religious duties, marriage, law and warfare.[3] At the same time he would have been circumcised.[4] Originally this rite was con-

---

[1] J. Fichtner, 'Der Begriff des "Nächsten" im Alten Testament', *WD*, iv, 1955, pp. 23 ff.   [2] Cf. Lev. 19:17 f. and 34.

[3] L. Köhler, *Hebrew Man*, E.T., London, 1956, pp. 87 f.

[4] Thus Gen. 34:18 ff. does not merely recount the assassination of the able-bodied men, that is the warriors capable of engaging in battle as E. A. Speiser, ' "Coming" and "Going" at the City Gate', *BASOR*, cxliv, 1956, pp. 20–3 maintained, but as verse 29 indicates by its reference to women and children only, of all adult males who had reached the age of puberty, and consequently had been circumcised (G. Evans, ' "Coming" and "Going" at the City Gate—a Discussion of Professor Speiser's Paper', ibid., cl, 1958, pp. 28–33). The expressions 'to go out of' or 'go in by' the city gate applied to a person indicate a full citizen. Cf. the status of an elder, pp. 17f.

nected with initiation into marriage (cf. Gen. 34:14 ff.; Exod. 4:25),[5] but since this coincided with entry into membership of the covenant community, it early became a sign of this status among the Israelites themselves, though because all other people with whom Israel came into contact, other than the Philistines, practised circumcision, it could not be used to distinguish the covenant community from other nations. Thus it was not made a provision of the Sinai Decalogue.[6]

But women did not enter into the covenant relationship, and were therefore outside the scope of the criminal law. They had no legal status,[7] being the personal property first of their fathers and then of their husbands. Thus injury to a woman was a tort against her father or husband, to whom damages would have been paid (Exod. 22:15 f.; 21:22), and who may himself have been liable for his daughter's or wife's torts.

As a man generally married within his clan, his marriage would have been with a daughter of a fellow member of the covenant community.[8] This explains why the Sinai Decalogue prescribed that a son was to treat his mother in the same way as his father, and why it was unnecessary to legislate against foreign marriages. Even in the period of the judges, foreign marriages did not constitute a problem, and virtually could only have been contracted with members of the Canaanite city states which held out against the spread of Yahwism, or the Philistines. The ceremony whereby a woman captured in war could renounce her country of origin (Deut. 21:10 ff.), and so become eligible for marriage, may date from this period.[9] Thus since pure foreign marriages would have been exceptional (Judg. 14:3), there was still no need to prohibit them. However with the establishment of the monarchy and the entry of Israel into international affairs, foreign marriages came to be contracted with women who were not required to renounce their nationality, and therefore their gods. There is, however, no means of knowing how widespread such marriages were among the general populace, nor can the situation under the early monarchy be judged by the polemic of later legislation.[10]

Whatever was the exact position, later generations held that the

---

[5] Köhler, op. cit., pp. 37 ff.; de Vaux, *Ancient Israel*, pp. 47 f.; H. Ringgren, *Israelite Religion*, E.T., London, 1966, p. 203.

[6] Rowley, 'Moses and the Decalogue', *BJRL*, xxxiv, 1951/2, pp. 115 f.

[7] Köhler, op. cit., pp. 84 f.; de Vaux, op. cit., pp. 39 f.

[8] Ibid., pp. 30 ff.

[9] It may, however, have been part of the Deuteronomic revolutionary legislation whereby women were made members of the covenant community (see below).

[10] Josh. 23:12; Judg. 3:6 reflect the later Deuteronomic legislation. Cf. Deut. 7:3 f.

political foreign marriages of the Judaean and Israelite kings had resulted in the rejection of the principles of the Mosaic covenant. Hence arose the necessity of banning all such marriages in order to recover the primitive position under which members of the covenant community would have married within that community itself. This was achieved by the Deuteronomist's revolutionary legislation whereby he made women equal members of the covenant community with men, and so liable for breach of the criminal law, the covenant stipulations of the Decalogue being understood to have been addressed to adult members of both sexes. As a result of this legislation neither an Israelite male could take a foreign wife, unless she renounced her country of origin and its gods (Deut. 21:10 ff.), nor could an Israelite female be given to a foreign husband, for she too was part of the covenant community (Deut. 7:3; Josh. 23:12; Judg. 3:6).

The only other reference to foreign marriages in the pre-exilic legislation is contained in Exod. 34:16. This is in fact not a prohibition of such marriages, but a caution against them, and it only concerns Israelite males. Exod. 34:16 has generally been considered part of the Deuteronomic expansion to the so-called ritual Decalogue. When the history of Israel's criminal law is considered a different interpretation will be put forward.[11]

There is no need here to discuss further the effect of the Deuteronomic legislation, for in examining the individual commandments reference will be made to a variety of measures whereby the Deuteronomist effected his purpose. But in spite of their new status women still remained entirely under the authority of men, damages for tort being paid either to the father (Deut. 22:29) or presumably the husband. All the Deuteronomist did was to bring women within the scope of the covenant community, and therefore of the criminal law. The prohibition of foreign marriages was to form an important element in the reconstruction of post-exilic Israel (Ezra 9 f.; Neh. 10:30; 13:23 ff.).

Another major class of persons who did not possess legal status in Israel were slaves. Initially, however, such persons would not have been found among the covenant community. This is not to be attributed to economic factors,[12] but to theological, for the clans which gathered at Sinai made freedom from slavery the basis of their covenant with Yahweh (Exod. 20:2), and instituted the sabbath to remind them of this.[13]

---

[11] See below, pp. 168ff.
[12] L. Wallis, *Sociological Study of the Bible*, Chicago, 1912, pp. 51 f.
[13] See below, pp. 66ff.

But later, as the Book of the Covenant testifies, slaves were found in Israel, and included members of the covenant community themselves (Exod. 21:2 ff.). Even if all men start with equal opportunity, there will be those that fail and fall into debt, which in the ancient Near East was the chief cause of slavery.[14] By entering into this state, whether by self-sale or through seizure, the slave became the personal property of his master, and thus lost his status as a free Israelite and member of the covenant community. However, a remedy was devised for this loss of status in the right of a Hebrew male slave to his release prior to the seven year covenant festival.[15]

It was not until the exilic or post-exilic period that legal status was conferred upon the גר ('resident alien') (Deut. 1:16; Lev. 20:2).[16] Like the widow and the orphan he had to rely on the good nature of the covenant community, having no legal redress for wrongs committed against him (Exod. 22:20; 23:9.).

(ii) The Administration of Justice

Initially it was the local community upon whom the responsibility for bringing the criminal to justice rested (Deut. 21:1 ff.),[17] and who would first suffer divine punishment if this was not undertaken. Thus the trial of the criminal took place in the gate of his town before the elders. It has been suggested that this term covers all adult male citizens.[18] זקנים would then indicate all those capable of growing a beard (זקן), that is all males who had reached the age of puberty, and so entered into the covenant relationship. But it would, however, seem that legal status and the office of elder should be distinguished,[19] and that the term 'elder' denoted the senior male member of each house, who would act as its spokesman in the community's affairs. Thus the office of elder was tied to ownership of property, the elder being the houseowner.[20] When a son left his father's house to establish his own house, he would thereby constitute himself an elder. Consequently the community's affairs were administered on a democratic

---

[14] I. Mendelsohn, 'Slavery in the Ancient Near East', *BA*, ix, 1946, pp. 78 ff. Cf. *Slavery in the Ancient Near East*, New York, 1949, pp. 1 ff.

[15] See below, pp. 73f.

[16] Cf. de Vaux, *Ancient Israel*, p. 75. Cf. Exod. 12:49; Num. 9:14; 15:15 f., 29 and the discussion on pp. 55f. of Lev. 24:10 ff. Cf. further Lev. 19:17 f. and 34.

[17] Cf. C. H. Gordon, 'An Akkadian Parallel to Deuteronomy 21:1 ff.', *RA*, xxxii, 1936, pp. 1 ff.; BL, i, pp. 110 f.

[18] C. U. Wolf, 'Traces of Primitive Democracy in Ancient Israel', *JNES*, vi, 1947, pp. 99 f.

[19] Evans, *BASOR*, cxliv, pp. 32 f.

[20] Cf. J. L. McKenzie, 'The Elders in the Old Testament', *Bibl.*, xl, 1959, pp. 522 ff.

basis, each family being represented in its deliberations. It will, in fact, be argued that the purpose of the original tenth commandment was to guarantee the democratic nature of the administration of justice in Israel by prohibiting seizure of one's neighbour's house.[21]

In spite of the establishment of the monarchy, the administration of justice, apart from cases of alleged unintentional murder,[22] remained the concern of the local community, though social classes now appear among the elders themselves. Thus Naboth was tried by the elders and חרים of Jezreel (1 Kgs. 21:8 ff.), which term would appear to indicate the upper classes.[23]

But while there is no further definite information concerning the administration of justice in the northern kingdom, 2 Chr. 19:5 records that Jehoshaphat appointed judges in all the fortified cities of Judah. Since the Book of Kings makes no mention of this reform, and Deut. 16:18 ff. contains a similar provision, the historicity of the Chronicler's account has been questioned.[24] It would, however, seem that in this respect the Chronicler's account can be upheld.[25]

In the first place it should be noted that the royal judges were specifically appointed to the fortified cities, that is those towns in which soldiers would have been quartered. Secondly, Isa. 1:21 ff. describes the administration of justice in Jerusalem as in the hands of corrupt שרים and looks forward to the restoration of a former system of justice. The שרים, who are not to be restricted to Jerusalem, could therefore be understood as Jehoshaphat's royal judges (Isa. 32:1; cf. Mic. 3). This makes very good sense for the שר, a term which basically indicates someone who is in a position to command[26] and is particularly applied to royal officials, appears to have possessed not only judical, but also military authority.[27] It can therefore be deduced that Jehoshaphat abolished the local jurisdiction of the elders, and instead

---

[21] See below, pp. 151 f.

[22] See the discussion of the cities of refuge on pp. 99 ff.

[23] Van der Ploeg, 'Les chefs du peuple d'Israël et leurs titres', RB, lvii, 1950, pp. 57 f.

[24] Thus R. H. Pfeiffer, Introduction to the Old Testament (Rev. ed.), London, 1952, p. 793 repeats the view that the Chronicler chose Jehoshaphat as the institutor of this reform because of his name, 'Yahweh is judge'.

[25] Albright, 'The Judicial Reform of Jehoshaphat', Alexander Marx Jubilee Volume (Ed. S. Lieberman), New York, 1950, pp. 61–82. Albright does not, however, bring any concrete evidence from the Old Testament to support his contention. It will be argued on pp. 151 f. that the present version of the tenth commandment resulted from this reform.

[26] Van der Ploeg, op. cit., pp. 40 ff.

[27] McKenzie, op. cit., p. 528; R. Knierim, 'Exodus 18 und die Neuordnung der Mosaischen Gerichtsbarkeit', ZAW, N.F., xxxii, 1961, pp. 169 ff.

appointed royal officials to the fortified cities who were responsible to the king for the administration of justice in the districts under their control, and who could rely on the support of the troops under their command to enforce their authority. How many שׂרים were appointed for each city, and whether they were drawn from the local community, cannot be ascertained.

This deduction is confirmed by Exod. 18:13 ff., which is clearly to be understood as an aetiological account intended to justify a system for the administration of justice at some specific point in Israel's history.[28] By its reference to the levy and use of the שׂרים (Exod. 18:21, 25), this must be Jehoshaphat's reorganization of justice on a military footing.[29]

Finally, it should be noted that those provisions in Deuteronomy which mention the elders as administering justice (19:12; 21:2 ff., 19 f.; 22:15 ff.; 25:7 ff.), while still current law at the time Deuteronomy was promulgated, must ante-date Jehoshaphat's reform.[30] The law of Deuteronomy is meant to be read on the understanding that the local administration of justice was in the hands of professional judges (16:18).[31]

While it might appear at first sight that in Deut. 1:9 ff. the military and executive officers (verses 13 ff.) are intended to be differentiated from the judiciary (verses 16 f.), it would in fact seem that these latter verses are to be interpreted as a hortatory expansion, for the שׂרים of verse 15 were specifically appointed to help carry the burden of the administration of justice (verse 12), and like the judges of Deut. 16:18 had the שׂטרים at their disposal. These also seem to have exercised both military and judicial responsibilities. In fulfilling the latter they acted as officers of the court in charge of all aspects of its administration. Thus their duties would not have been confined to recording the

---

[28] The identity of the author of this account, and the motive for its creation, will be discussed on p. 179.

[29] Knierim, op. cit., pp. 146 ff. No distinction between sacral and civil law is intended here, but merely between lesser and greater cases, the latter coming to Moses (i.e. the king) for decision. Giving judgement on appeal was probably always regarded as consultation of Yahweh (Exod. 18:19), since this might result in the promulgation of new law.

[30] Deut. 22:13–19 should be understood as an ancient provision ante-dating Jehoshaphat's reform to which verses 20 ff. have been attached by the Deuteronomist following his recognition of a woman's criminal liability (see below, pp. 115 f.).

[31] It would seem that Ruth 4 cannot be used in the discussion of the administration of justice in Israel, for the story of Ruth appears to have been consciously set in ancient Israel's past when earlier law (Ruth 4:7), and probably its administration, was no longer perfectly understood. Certainly there is no other evidence for limiting the court to ten members, or for its *ad hoc* selection.

result of any criminal or civil action, but they would also have been charged with communicating or enforcing it either as police or court bailiffs.[32]

That the שרים were still the administrators of justice in Israel after Josiah's reform is confirmed by Jer. 26:10 ff. This records that the prophet was tried before the שרים of Judah, who were evidently gathered at Jerusalem to celebrate a feast.[33] Ezekiel probably envisages a similar system of justice when he refers to the נשיאי ישראל (45:9).

However, the term 'elder' continued in use after Jehoshaphat's reform, and presumably designated the same class of people as before, namely houseowners (cf. Isa. 3:14; Ezra 10:8, 14).

The right of appeal to a higher authority was recognized from the time of the amphictyony, which appointed the so-called minor-judge not only to make known in the covenant festival the covenant stipulations, but also to see to their enforcement and interpretation by acting as an itinerant appellate judge.[34] It is in this capacity that Samuel travelled the country on a clearly defined circuit to dispense justice (1 Sam. 7:15 ff.). Very little is known about these persons, nor can one be entirely certain who should be so designated, as there would appear to have been a blurring of the characteristics of judge and charismatic leader in the tradition.[35] But it seems clear from the two lists in Judg. 10:1 ff. and 12:7 ff. that these minor-judges were not appointed on a dynastic principle, and could be chosen from any tribe.[36] Further, their appointment was for life. Exod. 20:18 ff. should probably be understood as an aetiological account to explain the origin of their office.[37] Their chief judicial function would have been to determine when a crime had been committed, and in consequence the covenant relationship infringed. The casuistic provisions differentiating between the crime of murder and the tort of assault found in the Book of the Covenant (Exod. 21:18 ff.) probably reflect their decisions. Thus the

[32] S. R. Driver, *Deuteronomy*[3], ICC, 1902, pp. 17, 200; van der Ploeg, 'Les šoṭerim d'Israël', *OTS*, x, 1954, pp. 185 ff.; de Vaux, *Ancient Israel*, p. 155.

[33] The fact that the elders from the country did not address the court until the verdict had been pronounced (verse 17) may indicate that they had no right to do so, since they did not reside within its jurisdiction.

[34] Cf. Noth, *History*, pp. 101 ff.; Alt, *Essays*, pp. 102 f.; Clements, *Prophecy and Covenant*, SBT[1], xliii, 1965, pp. 72 ff.

[35] Cf. D. A. McKenzie, 'The Judge of Israel', *VT*, xvii, 1967, pp. 118–21.

[36] H. W. Hertzberg, 'Die kleinen Richter', *TLZ*, lxxix, 1954, cols. 285–90.

[37] H.-J. Kraus, *Worship in Israel*, E.T., Oxford, 1966, pp. 108 f.; Newman, 'The Prophetic Call of Samuel', *Israel's Prophetic Heritage, Essays in Honor of James Muilenburg* (Eds. B. W. Anderson and W. Harrelson), London, 1962, pp. 87 f.

contentions that the minor-judges were solely concerned either with the casuistic law or with the apodictic law must be rejected.

The supreme judicial authority of the minor-judge was inherited by the monarch, one of whose functions was to secure the maintenance of justice throughout his kingdom. Thus appeal could be made to the king, who, if he did not hear appeals personally, was to delegate his authority (2 Sam. 15:2 ff.). Solomon built a special porch from which he could dispense justice (1 Kgs. 7:7). But the right of appeal must not be confused with the application for pardon. The former involved a dispute concerning a fact or a point of law, the latter the overriding of the facts or the law, often for reasons which the court did not have to take into account in reaching its verdict. Thus the petition of the widowed mother for the acquittal of her son who should have suffered execution for the murder of his brother (2 Sam. 14:4 ff.) is not an appeal within the organized machinery of the courts, but an application for the exercise of the royal prerogative of mercy on the grounds that the execution of the murderer would involve the extinction of his family. As Yahweh's representative, the king can grant him pardon in Yahweh's name (2 Sam. 14:11), though he takes the precaution of securing a self-curse from the woman and protection for himself and his house should Yahweh disapprove of his action (2 Sam. 14:9).

Further, while there would have been no difficulty in the defeated party to a civil action appealing to the minor-judge or king against the decision of the local judiciary, normally in the case of a criminal action, this was impossible; for if the local judiciary decided that the accused was guilty of a crime, he would have been executed forthwith. It was only when the local judiciary were themselves uncertain whether a given action constituted a crime or a tort that they would have referred the matter to the higher authority. Thus even when an appeal court was constituted at Jerusalem (Deut. 17:8 ff.), it was only envisaged that the local judiciary themselves should refer cases to it which they found too difficult to decide, and not that the accused himself might make use of it.[38] The appointment of state judges by Jehoshaphat would, however, have greatly reduced any risk of local prejudice, and consequent abuse of the law, though this was apparently shortlived, at any rate in Jerusalem (Isa. 1:21 ff.).

Both Deut. 17:8 ff. and 2 Chr. 19:8 ff. refer to the setting up of an appeal court in Jerusalem, which was no longer to be presided over by the king himself. Although the historicity of 2 Chr. 19:5 has been

[38] von Rad, *Deuteronomy*, E.T., London, 1966, p. 118.

here maintained, one must not therefore automatically assume that the Chronicler must also be accurate in assigning the establishment of this appeal court to Jehoshaphat, but seek supporting evidence.

From the detailed discussion of Israel's crimes it will be shown that apart from disputed property cases in which an oath was required (Exod. 22:7 ff.), the priests appear to have exercised no judicial role in early Israel.[39] However, in Deuteronomy they are three times mentioned as exercising such authority (17:8 ff.; 19:17; 21:5) in the last two of which they have clearly been inserted into older enactments, which already reflect Jehoshaphat's reform by their mention of judges. But the fact that in recording Jehoshaphat's reform the Chronicler makes no attempt to introduce the priests into the *local* administration of justice, conclusively indicates that they were first given judicial authority at a time when the priesthood was centralized at Jerusalem. Accordingly this must have been an innovation of the Deuteronomist. But there is no indication that thereby he intended to compel the centralization of the judiciary itself, for local lay judges were still envisaged as acting as the court of first instance (Deut. 16:18).[40] For him both priests and laity were to constitute a central appeal court to which the local lay judiciary were to refer all difficult cases. Deut. 19:16 ff. is now intended to constitute an example of such reference.[41] Exod. 18:13 ff. supports this argument, for this aetiological account knows nothing of such an appeal court, but in the figure of Moses imagines the king himself as the supreme judicial authority.[42] Accordingly it would seem that until the Deuteronomic legislation was enacted, the king or his deputy heard all appeals at Jerusalem.

Though it may never have had much effect in pre-exilic Israel, it would seem that this central appeal court was re-established after the institution of the priestly legislation, and is in fact described in 2 Chr.

---

[39] Mendenhall, *BA*, xvii, p. 38; Köhler, *Hebrew Man*, p. 163; J. L'Hour, 'Une législation criminelle dans le Deutéronome', *Bibl.*, xliv, 1963, pp. 18 ff. For a discussion of Exod. 22:7 ff. see below, pp. 135 ff. It will be argued on pp. 118 ff. that Num. 5:11 ff. was an extra-judicial rite for ascertaining the paternity of a child.

[40] Cf. Köhler, op. cit., pp. 170 ff.

[41] In view of Deut. 19:17, Deut. 17:9 should be understood to refer to judges and not a single judge, though this may reflect earlier legislation. Noth, 'Das Amt des "Richters Israels"', *Bertholet-Festschrift* (Eds. W. Baumgartner *et al.*), Tübingen, 1950, pp. 415 ff. would connect 'the judge' to the so-called minor-judge. But perhaps more probably it refers to the king's appointed deputy (2 Sam. 15:2 ff.). Cf. Driver, *Deuteronomy*, p. 208.

[42] This might also be argued for Deut. 1:17, but in Deut. 1:9 ff. there appears to be no aetiological intent, but a repetition of the account in Exod. 18:13 ff. of the institution of the judges prior to the making of the covenant law which they would administer.

19:8 ff.[43] Then the high priest would have acted as president of the court in all specifically Jewish legal matters, having in effect succeeded the king as the guardian of the law, which in the post-exilic period came to be intimately associated with admission to the temple. 'The Governor of the house of Judah' would probably refer to the head of state appointed by or recognized by the Persians. Although the words used to denote the office of Governor are different, the position in 2 Chr. 19:11 would appear to be identical with that in Hag. 1:1, 14; 2:2, 21.[44] The Levites act as שטרים to this Court.

Conviction on a criminal charge could only be secured on the evidence of at least two witnesses (Deut. 17:6; 19:15; Num. 35:30). It is, however, probable that originally the evidence of a single witness would have been sufficient. Deut. 19:16 ff., which is in effect merely an expansion of the ninth commandment, seems to envisage such a situation, and verse 15 has all the marks of a later insertion in the light of which verses 16 ff. should now be understood.[45] Since the case of Naboth implies that at this time in the northern kingdom two witnesses were necessary to secure a conviction (1 Kgs. 21:10, 13), it has been held that this reform was carried out during the period of the united monarchy by Solomon.[46] But the details of Naboth's trial have probably been made to conform to later legislation.[47] Since the provision prohibiting conviction on the evidence of a single witness seems to be emphasized by the Deuteronomist, this would indicate that it is new legislation, which is confirmed by the fact that the priestly legislator found it necessary to repeat the enactment (Num. 35:30), thus showing that it was not part of the ancient judicial procedure of Israel which would have been automatically adhered to.

The prescribed penalty for breach of the criminal law during the pre-exilic period was death, for only in this way could the community propitiate Yahweh, and thus secure the maintenance of the covenant relationship.

This was inflicted by communal stoning.[48] Though stoning is

[43] Cf. Ezra 8:29.

[44] The term used in 2 Chr. 19:11 is נגיד, whereas that used in Hag. 1:1, 14; 2:2, 21 is פחה. A further term to denote the same official appears in Ezra 1:8, namely נשיא (cf. Ezra 5:14).

[45] J. Morgenstern, 'The Book of the Covenant—Part II', *HUCA*, vii, 1930, pp. 75, 211.

[46] M. Sulzberger, *The Ancient Hebrew Law of Homicide*, Philadelphia, 1915, pp. 70 f. He also suggests on pp. 87 f. that the two or three witnesses of Deut. 19:15 means two witnesses other than the accuser, who in Num. 35:30 is disqualified as a witness.

[47] Good, *Stanford Law Review*, xix, p. 973. For a discussion of this case, see below, pp. 43 ff.

[48] Cf. Exod. 8:22. Stones often constituted the murder weapon (Exod. 21:18; Num. 35:17).

C

frequently referred to in Deuteronomy (13:10; 17:5; 21:21; 22:21, 24), it is not mentioned in the Book of the Covenant, knowledge of the method of execution being presupposed. But that stoning was the prescribed method of execution is confirmed not only from the case of Naboth (1 Kgs. 21:8 ff.), but also by the fact that the ox which gored a man to death, and which is treated as if it were a human murderer, is stoned to death (Exod. 21:28 ff.). It was because the whole community was responsible for the execution of the criminal that stoning was chosen as the means of effecting this, for all members of the covenant community could thereby actually take part in it, and so both individually and corporately propitiate Yahweh. This is a much more natural explanation than the view that stoning was selected to prevent burial in the family tomb.[49] The fact that the body could be exposed after execution, and was then to be buried, shows that there was no intention of burying the criminal by the act of stoning itself (Deut. 21:22 f.), though subsequently a cairn of stones might be erected over the victim (Josh. 8:29).[50] Nor can one accept the contention that stoning was chosen to prevent defilement, the executioners never coming into direct physical contact with the executed.[51] Indeed in one instance in the priestly legislation itself the witnesses were specifically ordered to lay their hands on the criminal's head prior to his execution (Lev. 24:14). Similarly the procedure outlined in Deut. 21:22 f. would involve handling of the corpse. Stoning was selected simply because of its practicality in putting into effect the purpose of execution under Israel's criminal law.

Though in fact two different verbs are used for the judicial penalty of stoning, סקל, which is not used in the priestly legislation, and רגם, which appears both there and in earlier material, there would seem to be no difference in their meaning.

At first the whole community would have been responsible for a miscarriage of justice, but Deut. 17:7, by enacting that the witnesses were to begin the stoning, places the responsibility for the community's act upon them. Since the community reached its verdict on their evidence, it made them specifically liable for a wrongful execution. In this way the law sought to deter not only the false witness, who was in any event liable as a criminal under the ninth commandment, but the careless or irresponsible witness. Similarly Deut. 13:10 f. pro-

[49] Pedersen, *Israel*, i–ii, p. 428; Köhler, *Hebrew Man*, pp. 112 f.
[50] Cf. Josh. 7:15, 25 f.
[51] Morgenstern, op. cit., pp. 146, 196 f.

vides that in the case of enticement to commit apostasy, the person who was enticed should begin the stoning.[52] Once the witnesses had begun the stoning, all the adult male members of the community joined in. Thus Deut. 21:21 and 22:21 with their reference to men emphasize that in spite of the fact that Deuteronomy made women equal members of the covenant community with men, women still took no part in the execution.

The criminal was executed outside his city not because of any symbolic thought of expulsion from the community, but because this was the only practical place for execution by communal stoning, both as regards space and materials. With the exception of Judg. 9:5, there is no indication that any prescribed place for execution was set aside. In this passage the MT reads that Abimelech put to death seventy of his brothers עַל־אֶבֶן אַחַת ('upon one stone'), which might be thought to refer to an official place of execution. But it is possible that this should be understood as indicating that the brothers were put to death at one fell swoop.

It appears that hanging was not a method of execution in Israel, though after execution the criminal's corpse might be thus exposed. Deut. 21:22 f. enacted that the body had to be taken down at nightfall and buried, for its continual exposure amounted to a 'repudiation of God' (קִלְלַת אֱלֹהִים),[53] which would defile the land.

While the bodies of enemies killed in battle would have been exhibited for publicity purposes,[54] this is unlikely in the case of a criminal, since the whole town would have joined in the execution, itself a sufficient deterrent to the potential criminal. The practice referred to in Deut. 21:22 f. may in fact be connected to a custom whereby in circumstances where the land or people were already suffering, and that suffering was attributable to breach of the criminal law, the corpse of the criminal who was held responsible for the suffering was exposed until this stopped, thus signifying that Yahweh had been propitiated.[55] There is some indication of this in the account

[52] At first sight Deut. 13:6 ff. seems to assume that one witness would have been sufficient to secure a conviction. But the purpose of this legislation is to encourage relatives to prosecute other relatives, and one must presuppose that corroboratory evidence would have been required. Like other Deuteronomic law, this provision regards a woman as subject to criminal liability.

[53] For this translation, cf. H. C. Brichto, *The Problem of 'Curse' in the Hebrew Bible*, *JBL* Monograph Series, xiii, Philadelphia, 1963, pp. 191 ff. The phrase קלל אלהים is discussed below, on pp. 41 f.

[54] Josh. 8:29; 10:26 f. (which both reflect Deut. 21:22 f.); 1 Sam. 31:10; 2 Sam. 21:12. Cf. 2 Sam. 4:12.

[55] Normally the execution of the criminal would have taken place soon after the commission of the crime with the intent of *averting* any disaster which Yahweh might inflict.

of the execution of the seven sons of Saul by the Gibeonites, when the bodies of those who were executed were exhibited until the drought ceased (2 Sam. 21:1 ff.). This explains their execution in the first days of the barley harvest, which had failed for the third time, and Rizpah's watch over their bodies until the rains fell. Num. 25:4 f. may also indicate the public exposure of the bodies of the executed in order to assuage Yahweh's anger. The Deuteronomist evidently considered such a practice not only unseemly, but positively injurious, preventing the very thing that it was supposed to achieve, the welfare of the land. Rather than any concern for the corpse, this Deuteronomic enactment probably represents part of the anti-Canaanite legislation.[56]

But neither in 2 Sam. 21:1 ff. or Num. 25:4 is it certain that in the first place death was actually caused by hanging, or that secondly, if this was not the case, the corpses were in fact hung after execution. The verb used is the Hiph'îl of יקע, which in Gen. 32:26 describes the dislocation of Jacob's thigh, and in Jer. 6:8 and Ezek. 23:17 f. indicates alienation. This verb has caused considerable difficulties in the Versions, often the same Version translating it by a different word in 2 Sam. 21:1 ff. from that in Num. 25:4.[57] It has been held that execution by casting the victim off a cliff is referred to, 2 Chr. 25:12 being cited in support.[58] However, not only is יקע not used there, but the account describes the execution of prisoners of war, and has nothing to do with propitiating Yahweh. Further, in 2 Sam. 21:9 בהר ('on the hill') could hardly indicate a rock.[59] All that can be said with certainty is that the account in 2 Sam. 21:1 ff. indicates that the bodies were exposed.[60] Perhaps their limbs were dislocated by hanging or they

---

[56] Cf. H. Cazelles, 'David's Monarchy and the Gibeonites Claim', *PEQ*, lxxxvii, 1955, pp. 165–75. But the execution of the sons of Saul should not be understood as nothing more than a Canaanite fertility rite. Its purpose was to restore the covenant relationship between the Gibeonites and Israel, which had been severed by Saul's action (Fensham, 'The Treaty between Israel and the Gibeonites', *BA*, xxvii, 1964, pp. 96–100). This is further discussed on pp. 84 f. below. There would seem to be no evidence to support Kapelrud's contention ('King and Fertility: A Discussion of 2 Sam. 21:1–14', *Mowinckel-Festschrift*, Oslo, 1955, pp. 118 ff., 'König David und die Söhne des Saul', *ZAW*, N.F., xxvi, 1955, pp. 204 f.) that the execution was a royal sacrifice comparable to those in 2 Kgs. 16:3; 21:6, the victims having a special sanctity by virtue of their royal blood (cf. H. Bardtke, review of *Mowinckel-Festschrift*, *TLZ*, lxxxiii, 1958, col. 106).

[57] S. R. Driver, *Notes on the Hebrew Text and Topography of the Books of Samuel*[2], Oxford, 1913, p. 351.

[58] Robertson Smith, *The Religion of the Semites*, p. 419; *Peake's Commentary on the Bible*[2] (Eds. M. Black and Rowley), London, 1962, pp. 265b.

[59] Driver, op. cit., p. 351.

[60] K-B, p. 398 renders the Hiph'îl of יקע 'expose with legs and arms broken'. But cf. Driver, op. cit., p. 351.

were dismembered.[61] How death itself was inflicted cannot be determined.

It should, however, be noted that although 2 Sam. 21:1 ff. and Num. 25:4 f. concern propitiation of Yahweh, neither account involves a formal judicial process. In both instances breach of the covenant relationship has occurred not through an isolated individual criminal act, but because of the rejection of the covenant concept itself, in the case of the Gibeonites by an unwarranted attack on a fellow covenanting clan (Josh. 9), and in Num. 25:1 ff. by an open rebellion of a considerable number of Israelites, who allied themselves to a foreign god (Hos. 9:10; Ps. 106:28).

Thus although 2 Sam. 21:1 ff. may illuminate the reason for the hanging mentioned in Deut. 21:22 f., it cannot be held to show that hanging itself was a method of execution in Israel.[62]

On the other hand Gen. 40:22; 41:13 indicate that hanging was practised in Egypt in the time of Joseph, and appears to have caused death itself. In this passage the phrase נשא את־ראש ('lift up the head') occurs (Gen. 40:13, 19 f.). If this is interpreted as indicating pardon, then Gen. 40:19 must be understood to contain a play on words.[63] But even in verse 20 this is an unsatisfactory interpretation for the baker was not pardoned. The phrase could refer to release from prison,[64] but Jer. 52:31 seems to indicate that while release from prison might be the consequence of the procedure of 'lifting up the head', it is not to be equated with it.[65] It would seem that the most acceptable suggestion is that the phrase means 'to take up a case', both Gen. 40 and Jer. 52 indicating that particular royal events, in the former Pharaoh's birthday and in the latter Evil-Merodach's accession to the throne, led to the re-examination of prison sentences.[66] It would thus seem preferable to delete the first מעליך in Gen. 40:19, for which there is some manuscript support, the word having been

---

[61] Cazelles, *PEQ*, lxxxvii, pp. 168 f. parallels the execution of the sons of Saul with the dismemberment of Mot in the Ras Shamra material.

[62] It is not proposed to discuss the book of Esther, for in the first place this is late, and in the second it is not set in Israel.

[63] von Rad, *Genesis*[2], E.T., London, 1963, p. 367.

[64] J. Skinner, *Genesis*, ICC, 1910, pp. 462 f.

[65] Following Jer. 52:31, ויוצא אתו ('and he brought him out') should probably be inserted in 2 Kgs. 25:27 for which there is Versional support (C. F. Burney, *Notes on the Hebrew Text of the Books of Kings*, Oxford, 1903, p. 370).

[66] Sulzberger, *The Am Ha-aretz: The Ancient Hebrew Parliament*, Philadelphia, 1909, pp. 56 ff. Cf. Speiser, 'Census and Ritual Expiation in Mari and Israel', *BASOR*, cxlix, 1958, p. 21; J. J. Rabinowitz, 'Neo-Babylonian Legal Documents and Jewish Law', *JJP*, xiii, 1961, p. 147.

mistakenly interpolated from the end of the verse.[67] There is no indication of a similar practice by Israelite kings. Imprisonment itself was not a penalty of the pre-exilic criminal law, detention only being resorted to for political purposes (1 Kgs. 22:27; Jer. 37:15 ff.), for the convicted criminal had to be executed forthwith to propitiate Yahweh.[68]

When the history of Israel's criminal law is investigated, it will be recognized that with the destruction of Jerusalem by the Babylonians the Mosaic covenant concept came to an end, and was replaced by the priestly legislation.[69] This provided that Israel's relationship with Yahweh should no longer be conditional on obedience to the stipulations of the Decalogue, but should exist independently of any obligation on Israel's part, being guaranteed by the cult with its Day of Atonement. The priestly legislation was therefore designed to act as the guardian of the proper ordering and purity of the cult, through which the divine blessing was secured, and from which the offender must be excluded (Ezek. 20:35 ff.).

One result of this new approach was that there was no longer any need to execute the criminal to propitiate Yahweh. The cult itself achieved this. Thus in the post-exilic period, save in the case of murder,[70] the death penalty was abandoned. But just as adherence to the covenant stipulations of the Sinai Decalogue had determined membership of the covenant community, so the priestly legislators used their law to define the post-exilic community of Israel by resorting to the penalty of excommunication from the cult, such excommunication being irrevocable. The criminal who was excommunicated was thus in the same position as the criminal under the pre-exilic law, for neither could secure their own atonement or restoration to the community.

The punishment of excommunication is expressed by the Niph'al of כרת ('cut off') with the individual to be punished as subject, and usually the community as the indirect object. The only offences specifically mentioned as being punished in this way[71] are either breaches of rites designed to distinguish Israel from the heathen

---

[67] Skinner, op. cit., p. 463.

[68] Imprisonment for debt was unknown, for the debtor sold himself into slavery. While Ezra 7:26 indicates that imprisonment was introduced in post-exilic Israel, as the discussion below indicates, this could not have been for criminal offences, which required execution in the case of murder, and in all other cases excommunication.

[69] See below, pp. 183 ff. By the priestly legislation is meant both the Holiness Code (Lev. 17–26) and the remaining priestly legal material here termed the Priestly Code.

[70] See below, pp. 95 f.

[71] Cf. Gen. 17:14; Exod. 12:15, 19; 30:33, 38; 31:14; Lev. 7:20, 21, 25, 27; 17:4, 9, 14; 18:29; 19:8; 20:17, 18; 22:3; 23:29; Num. 9:13; 15:30, 31; 19:13, 20.

nations[72] or cases of gross misconduct within the cult. It would seem that while breach of any of the priestly legislation would involve temporary suspension from the cult until the appropriate guilt offering had been rendered, it was only serious offences which resulted in excommunication. Thus an uncircumcised man (Gen. 17:14), a sabbath breaker (Exod. 31:14), or an adulterer (Lev. 18:20, 29) could never be members of post-exilic Israel. It was the person who acted with a 'high hand', that is deliberately repudiated Yahweh, who was to be cut off from the community, an illustration of which is supplied by the case of breach of the sabbath law (Num. 15:32 ff.).[73] Probably breach of any of the pre-exilic criminal laws, other than murder, would have led to excommunication. But the priestly legislation recognized that intention determined responsibility, and those who broke the law inadvertently were given the means whereby they might make atonement, and so be received back into the cult community (Lev. 4:1 ff.; Num. 15:27 ff.).

Whether initially excommunication involved physical exile as well as exclusion from the worshipping life of the community cannot now be determined with certainty. The phrase used to describe the excommunication indicates separation from 'the people',[74] but this need imply no more than that the criminal was no longer considered a member of the Israelite community, and so could not take part in the cult, thus suffering social and religious ostracism. But Ezra 7:26; 10:8 seem to indicate that physical exile[75] involving forfeiture of property[76] later became normal practice.

[72] The strict sexual laws are intended to distinguish Israel from the licentiousness of Canaan. Egypt is probably only mentioned in Lev. 18:3 because of Israel's position at Sinai (Noth, *Leviticus*, E.T., London, 1965, p. 134).

[73] G. B. Gray, *Numbers*, ICC, 1903, p. 182. See below, pp. 72 f.

[74] There would seem to be no need to distinguish between the singular and plural use of עַם ('people') (Zimmerli, 'Die Eigenart der prophetischen Rede des Ezechiel', *ZAW*, N.F., xxv, 1954, pp. 17 f.). In Exod. 12:15, 19; Num. 19:13 'Israel' is used, and it would seem that in all cases it is to excommunication from the post-exilic community that reference is being made. Perhaps the phrase מִלְּפָנַי ('from before me') in Lev. 22:3 indicates expulsion from the cult, before physical exile became a possibility.

[75] Neh. 13:28 may have been an instance of physical exile being enforced (Morgenstern, 'The Book of the Covenant—Part III', *HUCA*, viii, 1931, pp. 55 f.).

[76] This may be referred to in the case of Zelophehad's daughters who apparently indicate that their father's property was not forfeit to the state through any treasonable act on his part (Num. 27:3). Cf. J. Weingreen, 'The Case of the Daughters of Zelophchad', *VT*, xvi, 1966, pp. 521 f. who argues that realty was confiscated for treason and cites the case of Naboth (1 Kgs. 21) in support. But he fails to make any distinction between the pre- and post-exilic periods. Whereas in the post-exilic period confiscation of property would have been exacted on anyone who was excommunicated into exile, in the pre-exilic period there is no suggestion that the property of a criminal was so appropriated save for breach of the first commandment (see below, pp. 44 f.).

There was, however, a transition stage between the substitution of excommunication for execution when the only punishment upon which reliance could be placed was direct divine intervention. The stages of development from the pre-exilic position to that following the introduction of the Priestly Code can be discerned in the Holiness Code itself, which sets out as punishments death, divine intervention, and excommunication, some crimes having more than one such penalty prescribed.[77]

In the first place Lev. 20 enacts that death shall be exacted for sacrificing to Molech,[78] repudiating one's parents,[79] adultery, unnatural sexual offences, and acting as a medium or wizard. These enactments reflect a very early stage in the development of the Holiness Code when only execution could be contemplated as the proper penalty for crime. They are therefore to be dated to the period immediately preceding the exile, being for the most part a reflection or development of certain current thought already apparent in the expansion of the criminal law in Deuteronomy. Thus it will be recognized that Deut. 18:10 f. was the first provision to make criminal necromancy and other occult practices, including the sacrifice to Molech,[80] and that it was Deut. 22:22 which first made the married woman herself liable to execution for adultery.[81] Further Deut. 23:1 is to be understood as the earliest provision dealing with an unnatural sexual offence, further examples of which are set out in Lev. 20:12 ff.[82]

The second stage of this development was the abandonment of execution for reliance on direct divine intervention. This is expressed by the Hiph'îl of כרת ('cut off') with Yahweh as subject, which is found in Lev. 17:10; 20:3, 5 f. and Ezek. 14:8, but never in the Priestly Code itself. The law on sacrificing to Molech provides an example of this development. Thus in the earliest stage of the Holiness Code, that is in the last years of the pre-exilic period when this practice was revived following Josiah's death (Jer. 7:31; 19:5; 32:35), execution by stoning was prescribed (Lev. 20:2). But in contrast, when in the exilic situation execution could no longer have been exacted, and yet the polemic against this practice continued (Ezek. 16:21; 23:37), Lev. 20:3 was added.

Two other post-exilic phrases were used to indicate direct divine

---

[77] For suggested dates both for the Holiness Code and the introduction of the remainder of the priestly legislation, see below, pp. 185 ff.

[78] For the interpretation of sacrifice to Molech, see below, pp. 128 ff.

[79] For this interpretation, see the discussion of the fifth commandment, on pp. 80 ff. below.

[80] See below, pp. 57 f.   [81] See below, pp. 110 f.   [82] See below, pp. 122 ff.

activity, namely נשא חטא and נשא עון ('bore sin', 'guilt') found in Ezekiel and both the Holiness and Priestly Codes.[83] Literally these phrases conceive the offender's guilt as a disease sapping his vitality, for which there is no remedy (Ezek. 33:10).[84] Thus they can occur without any further details (Lev. 5:1; 7:18; 17:16; 20:19; 22:16). But they can also be followed by a description of the particular type of divine action envisaged. This may be sudden or premature death (Exod. 28:43; Lev. 22:9; Num. 18:22, 32), but it need not be. Thus the Holiness Code prescribes that a couple who have committed incest shall be punished by childlessness (Lev. 20:20 f.). Further the summary (Num. 5:29 ff.) of the ancient rite prescribed for a case of suspected adultery (Num. 5:11 ff.), which summary is quite probably to be attributed to the priestly writer himself, concludes with the phrase תשא את־עונה (verse 31), thereby directly referring to the divine punishment outlined in verse 27.[85] These phrases could even be used to introduce particular human punishments (Lev. 5:17 f.; 24:15 ff.), thus coming to mean 'pay the penalty (for his guilt)', which penalty is then specified.

With the introduction of the remainder of the priestly legislation, the third stage was reached. Now excommunication from the community replaced the necessity to rely on divine intervention to punish the criminal. This can be recognized both from the absence in the Priestly Code of the use of כרת in the Hiph'îl with Yahweh as subject, and in the insertion of the excommunication formula, itself an adaptation of the 'cutting off' phrase used to indicate divine activity, in provisions which already contained the phrases נשא חטא or נשא עון (Lev. 19:7 f.; 20:17; Num. 9:13; 15:30 f.).[86] Since the Holiness Code was incorporated into the priestly legislation, it occasions no surprise that the excommunication formula has been introduced into it. Thus it will be argued that Lev. 20:17 f. is the final stage in the development of Lev. 20:10 ff.[87] Similarly Lev. 18, by the insertion of verse 29, not only provided excommunication for those sexual offences which had once been punishable by death (Lev. 20:10 ff.), but also for those for whose punishment reliance on divine activity had been placed (Lev. 20:19 ff.).[88] Further, in Exod. 31:14 f., which may

---

[83] Outside these works, נשא חטא is found once in Isa. 53:12.

[84] Pedersen, *Israel*, i–ii, pp. 432 ff.; Zimmerli, *ZAW*, N.F., xxv, p. 12.

[85] See below, pp. 118 ff.

[86] Morgenstern, *HUCA*, viii, pp. 38 ff. He also considers Exod. 12:15, 19; Num. 19:13, 20; where the excommunication formula occurs, and deduces that this is a later addition. Similarly Gen. 17 is also to be considered late.

[87] See below, pp. 127 f.   [88] See below, p. 128.

originally have been part of the Holiness Code,[89] excommunication
replaced the old pre-exilic provision of death for breach of the sabbath
commandment. Finally, Lev. 17:14 is to be regarded as an addition to
the previous enactment of Lev. 17:11, and Lev. 23:29 as a later
insertion into the law of the Day of Atonement.

There are therefore no grounds for maintaining that the excommunication formula was synonymous with those expressions denoting
reliance on divine activity, or that all four expressions indicate divine
action resulting in the premature death of the offender.[90] This may be
the Talmudic understanding of these expressions, but it is not to be
found in the Old Testament.[91]

(iii) *Liability*

As has been recognized, the covenant was deemed to have been
entered into both with each individual Israelite and with Israel as a
people. Thus on its breach, both individual and communal liability
arose, a man being liable not only for his own acts, but also, by reason
of his membership of the covenant community, for the acts of others.
Further, the same criminal act could result in two different sources of
punishment, human or divine. Thus Yahweh could directly punish
the individual or the community for breach of the covenant stipulations, and the community itself was under a duty to execute the
criminal in order that it might propitiate Yahweh, and so avert or
bring to an end divine punishment. In discussing liability these two
sources of punishment need to be kept distinct.

It is not proposed here to consider human punishment in detail, but
to state general principles. A full discussion of the passages involved
will follow at various points during the examination of the individual
commandments.

Save for breach of the first commandment, no one other than the
actual criminal was executed under Israel's criminal law. Thus no
other members of the criminal's family were punished with him, nor,
in spite of Exod. 21:23, 31, which will be discussed in connection with

---

[89] L. E. Elliott-Binns, 'Some Problems of the Holiness Code', *ZAW*, N.F., xxvi,
1955, p. 27.

[90] Cf. M. Tsevat, 'Studies in the Book of Samuel', *HUCA*, xxxii, 1961, pp. 195 ff.
Death is regarded as premature rather than immediate because in the two cases of
immediate death in the Pentateuch (Lev. 10:1 ff.; Num. 16:1 ff.) these expressions
are not used (cf. Morgenstern, ibid., viii, p. 38). It would, however, seem that the
timing of death by divine action was entirely a matter for Yahweh, but that there is no
reason to assume that it could not have been immediate (Exod. 28:43; Lev. 22:9;
Num. 18:22, 32; Cf. 2 Sam. 6:6 f.).

[91] Zimmerli, *ZAW*, N.F., xxv, p. 19.

the sixth commandment,[92] was anyone executed vicariously. This is in sharp contrast to the position under the Code of Hammurabi,[93] the Middle Assyrian Laws[94] and the Hittite Laws.[95] When the first commandment is examined, it will be held that since breach of that commandment involved a total repudiation of Yahweh for some other deity, it therefore necessitated the extermination of the apostate family.[96] Further, it will be argued that the legislation contained in Deut. 24:16 abolished this necessity, and brought the punishment of this crime into line with that of other criminal offences.[97] Of other cases often cited in this connection, neither Achan and his family (Josh. 7),[98] nor the seven sons of Saul (2 Sam. 21)[99] were executed on a criminal charge, and the slaughter at Nob recorded in 1 Sam. 22 represents a political massacre.

In contrast, divine punishment was in no way restricted. It could fall not only on the individual personally, or on members of his family, but also on the community as a whole, with the consequence that those who had not committed the crime could suffer for it. But one must be careful to distinguish between communal punishment proper, and the punishment of an individual through persons over whom he exercised control. Thus where the king had been guilty of an offence against Yahweh, divine punishment of his subjects might in fact be an example of the individual punishment of the king himself (2 Sam. 24), just as a father might be individually punished by Yahweh through the death of his son (2 Sam. 12:14). The term 'ruler punishment' has been coined to distinguish this punishment from communal liability.[100]

The formula prescribing punishment to the third and fourth generation (Exod. 20:5; 34:7; Num. 14:18; Deut. 5:9; cf. Jer. 32:18) describes the absolute nature of Yahweh's judgement on the community resulting from breach of the covenant law. The phrase is intended to include all living members of each family, for a fifth generation was not contemplated.[101] It is simply a concise way of referring to the whole family, and thus indicates total annihilation.[102]

---

[92] See below, pp. 88 ff.
[93] Cf. §§ 116, 210, 230.
[94] Cf. Tablet A, §§ 10, 32, 50, 55.
[95] Cf. §§ 1–4, 44.
[96] See below, pp. 40 ff.
[97] See below, p. 46.
[98] See below, p. 40.
[99] See below, pp. 84 f.
[100] Daube, *Studies in Biblical Law*, Cambridge, 1947, pp. 160 ff.; J. R. Porter, 'The Legal Aspects of the Concept of "Corporate Personality" in the Old Testament', *VT*, xv, 1965, pp. 373 f.
[101] Köhler, *Hebrew Man*, p. 62.
[102] S. Segert, 'Bis in das dritte und vierte Glied', *CV*, i, 1958, pp. 37 ff. has argued that the phrase 'to the third or fourth generation' may be derived from the bedouin practice of limiting blood vengeance to the fourth generation. But it will be argued on pp. 83 ff. that blood vengeance was not practised in Israel.

Even though the Deuteronomist absolutely prohibited the execution of anyone other than the criminal himself (Deut. 24:16), this did not alter his understanding of the nature of divine judgement (Deut. 5:9). Thus these two Deuteronomic enactments should not be connected in any way, for while the latter expresses the nature of divine punishment, the former is a judicial measure governing human punishment.[103]

The explanation of this contradiction between human and divine punishment, with the apparent implication that the former was of a higher moral standard than the latter, lies in the covenant concept itself. This ensured that the relationship between Yahweh and Israel was that between suzerain and vassal.[104] Thus, as in the Hittite suzerainty treaties, any breach of the covenant stipulations severed the covenant itself, and Yahweh was free to punish indiscriminately not only the individual criminal and his family, but also the community, whether local or national. It was in order to avoid such punishment that the community forthwith executed the criminal. But since Israel also regarded the covenant as a personal undertaking between the individual himself and Yahweh, other than in the case of the first commandment, it was only the individual criminal who was executed, for it was he alone who had broken the covenant, and thereby brought into operation the self-imprecation he was deemed to have made on entering into it. The case of the unknown murderer (Deut. 21:1 ff.) illustrates both the liability of the community for any crime committed in its midst, and the fact that no one other than the actual criminal could be executed to propitiate Yahweh.

How much the morality of divine communal liability was questioned in pre-exilic Israel is uncertain. One instance of this is Abraham's prayer for Sodom, though this does not in fact argue against the propriety of judging the community as a whole, for Sodom is still treated as a corporate entity (Gen. 18:22 ff.). Instead Abraham raises the possibility of communal salvation through the righteousness of a few. But the place of this account in the evolution of Israel's thought is uncertain. David's prayer in 2 Sam. 24:17 would seem to be a later reflection on the morality of divine punishment.[105]

[103] P. J. Verdam, ' "On ne fera point mourir les enfants pour les pères" en droit biblique', *RIDA*[2], iii, 1949, pp. 406 ff.; M. Greenberg, 'Some Postulates of Biblical Criminal Law', *Yehezkel Kaufmann Jubilee Volume* (Ed. M. Haran), Jerusalem, 1960, pp. 21 ff.
[104] M. Weiss, 'Some Problems of the Biblical "Doctrine of Retribution" ', *Tarbiz*, xxxi, 1961/2, pp. 236 ff. (English summary, p. II).
[105] Hertzberg, *I and II Samuel*, E.T., London, 1964, p. 413. Cf. Num. 16:22.

While Jeremiah clearly understood that divine punishment would involve the punishment of the whole community (11:22 f.; 13:14; 14:16; 16:1 ff.; 18:21; 32:18 f.), he none the less looked forward to a time when the principles of human punishment (Deut. 24:16) would be applied in the divine sphere (31:29 f.). However, this could not occur under the Mosaic covenant with its insistence on both communal and individual liability, which explains why Jeremiah had to link this prophecy with that of the new covenant (31:31 ff.).[106] It was Ezekiel who in the exilic situation, following on the final breach of the Mosaic covenant concept, brought Jeremiah's eschatological prophecy to fulfilment (3:16 ff.; 14:12 ff.; 18:1 ff.; 33:1 ff.). By abandoning the principle of communal liability for a strict doctrine of individual liability, he showed that the fate of the exiles was in their own hands. Although judgement had rightly fallen on Jerusalem and Judah, it was Yahweh's will that men should live and not die.

The result of the post-exilic rejection of communal liability in the sphere of divine punishment was that misfortune had now to be directly related to the sin of the individual afflicted. This led eventually to the problem of Job. Further, Ezekiel's application of this strict juridical view to individual liability led him to reject the possibility of vicarious salvation. Thus Ezek. 14:12 ff. directly contradicts Jer. 5:1. But the question of vicarious salvation was again taken up in Isa. 53:11 and Job 42:8.

[106] H. G. May, 'Individual Responsibility and Retribution', *HUCA*, xxxii, 1961, pp. 114 f.

PART II

THE DECALOGUE

CHAPTER THREE

THE PROHIBITION OF OTHER DEITIES

(Exod. 20:3; Deut. 5:7)

Reference has earlier been made to the historical prologue and to the fact that Exod. 20:2 fulfilled this function in the Sinai pericope.[1] The agreement to obey the stipulations that follow results from certain historical events which explain the covenantees' indebtedness. Thus Exod. 20:2 is not to be understood as the first commandment, but the *raison d'être* for the covenant itself, and therefore is to be treated as a single sentence. Though to include verse 3 with verse 2 may be grammatically possible,[2] to do so ignores both the form of the Decalogue, and the fact that it is all ten commandments, and not the first alone, which depend on this opening proclamation—a proclamation which it has been affirmed should be rendered with LXX, 'I am Yahweh your God'.[3] Here one may recognize the self-presentation of Yahweh made to Moses at Sinai, and repeated whenever the covenant was renewed in the cult (cf. Ps. 50; 81).

There is therefore no justification for reading Exod. 20:2 as the first commandment as in Jewish tradition.[4] It is neither drafted as such, nor must its inclusion be determined by a decision to exclude the prohibition of images. The Decalogue begins with Exod. 20:3 whether the commandment concerning images is original or not.

But a recent exposition has read Exod. 20:3 as part of the historical prologue, which it describes as the opening epiphany proclaiming the

---

[1] See above, p. 4.

[2] Meek, 'Lapses of Old Testament Translators', *JAOS*, lviii, 1938, pp. 126 f.

[3] Zimmerli, 'Ich bin Jahwe', *Geschichte und Alten Testament, Alt-Festschrift*, Tübingen, 1953, pp. 179 ff.

[4] Cf. J. M. P. Smith, *The Origin and History of Hebrew Law*, Chicago, 1931, p. 6.

victory of Yahweh over all other gods. These are now subject to Yahweh, and Israel is free to worship him alone. It is then argued that the Decalogue begins with Exod. 20:4, the prohibition of images, in the same manner as the list of curses in Deut. 27:15 ff.[5]

This view cannot be substantiated. In the first place, as will be argued later, the content of Deut. 27:15 ff. indicates that it is to be associated with the priestly legislation, and has nothing to do with the Decalogue.[6] Secondly, the covenant at Sinai is not concerned with Yahweh's triumph over other gods, but with the establishment of a new community which will accept Yahweh as their sole god. Finally, there is nothing in Exod. 20:3 which prevents it being regarded as an imperative, the third person form of the verb being necessitated by the absence of a Hebrew transitive verb 'to have'.

The expression עַל־פָּנַי literally means 'before me'. But there have been those who have sought to give it a stronger force than this. Thus relying on Deut. 21:16 it has been held that it means 'in preference to', in the sense of the exclusion of the one who was not preferred at the expense of the other,[7] though this view has been modified in favour of 'to the disadvantage of'.[8] Further it has been contended from Gen. 16:12; 25:18 that עַל־פָּנַי indicates defiance,[9] and the expression has accordingly been rendered 'in defiance of me', 'in opposition to me', 'in contradiction to me'.[10] However, these suggestions must be rejected for the use of פָּנִים ('face') indicates the divine presence,[11] and thus עַל־פָּנַי must be understood to refer to the possibility of other gods being placed in Yahweh's sight, that is in his shrine where he manifests himself.[12] Yahweh alone was to be acknowledged in the cult of the covenant community (cf. Ps. 81:10). While initially the commandment would have referred to the presence of other gods before the ark at Kadesh, with the spread of Yahwism, the scope of this commandment would have been extended to cover any shrine at which Yahweh was acknowledged, and therefore would have meant that those who adopted Yahwism would have had to renounce their gods (Josh. 24). Thus Israel was to acknowledge no other gods in her

[5] Reventlow, *Gebot und Predigt*, pp. 26 ff.
[6] See below, pp. 187 f.
[7] BDB, p. 818b; Albright, *From the Stone Age to Christianity*, p. 331.
[8] Meek, *Hebrew Origins*, p. 209.
[9] BDB, p. 818b; K-B, p. 767b.
[10] Köhler, 'Der Dekalog', *TR*, N.F., i, 1929, p. 174; W. Keszler, 'Die literarische, historische und theologische Problematik des Dekalogs', *VT*, vii, 1957, p. 9; Reventlow, op. cit., p. 27.
[11] Beyerlin, *Origins and History*, pp. 103 ff.
[12] Knierim, 'Das erste Gebot', *ZAW*, N.F., xxxvi, 1965, pp. 23 ff.

cult, and as worship outside the cult was not envisaged, this meant that for her there could be no contact with any other deity.[13]

The first commandment therefore established the exclusive covenant relationship between Yahweh and Israel by transferring the concept of political suzerainty to the religious sphere. Thereby it effectively ensured the covenant community's independence of all political powers, for political suzerainty would result in the adoption of the suzerain's deities alongside those of the vassal.[14] Thus to argue that there was no need for this commandment until foreign cults were encountered in Canaan[15] misses the creative nature of the commandment which constituted the basic declaration of the covenant relationship.[16] Further to introduce the question of monotheism at this point is to confuse the issue, for the commandment is not concerned with repudiating the *existence* of other gods, but with establishing Israel's exclusive allegiance to Yahweh. There is no reflection in the term 'other gods', nor is there anything derogatory in the use of אלהים to describe them.[17] The other gods are not denied, but Israel is directed to ignore them.

One consequence of the commandment was that although Yahweh was continually spoken of and pictured in human terms, both physical and emotional, sexual ideas were forestalled because by the commandment itself it was impossible for Yahweh to have a female consort.[18] Further, the shrines could not follow the common practice of being used for the worship of a number of different deities (2 Kgs. 23:4, 11 f.).

Variations of this commandment are contained in both the so-called ritual Decalogue (Exod. 34:14a) and the Book of the Covenant (Exod. 22:19). Thus in contrast to the creative nature of the original commandment, the reference to the worship of 'another god' in Exod. 34:14a presupposes that there already existed a definite relationship with Yahweh.[19] Exod. 34:14a must therefore be later than Exod. 20:3.[20]

---

[13] Noth, *Exodus*, p. 162.

[14] It would, however, seem that alliances which involved no form of political domination would not have been prohibited (cf. Solomon's treaty with the king of Tyre), but only those that would result in the presence of foreign deities in the Yahweh cult (cf. Ahaz's treaty with Assyria). Such a distinction is not made by Mendenhall, *BA*, xvii, p. 64.

[15] Knierim, op. cit., pp. 27 ff.   [16] Schreiner, *Die zehn Gebote*, pp. 70 ff.

[17] Cf. the term אלילם ('worthless gods', 'idols') used in Lev. 19:4; 26:1 (BDB, p. 47).

[18] Cf. the community at Elephantine (A. Cowley, *Aramaic Papyri of the Fifth Century B.C.*, Oxford, 1923, pp. xviii ff.; ANET, p. 491; DOTT, pp. 257 f.).

[19] Noth, *Exodus*, p. 263.   [20] See below, pp. 168 ff.

D

On the other hand, Exod. 22:19 not only specifically refers to sacrifice to a deity other than Yahweh, but prescribes that those who are found guilty of this crime are not merely to be executed, but put to the ban. This is not to be thought of as excommunication from the community,[21] a penalty which Israel did not practise until after the exile, but the extermination of a particular class of persons. It was usually inflicted as a result of military operations, and could be of varying severity.[22] The classical Old Testament example is the case of Achan who was condemned for appropriating to himself objects already under the ban (Josh. 7:24 ff.). Although only he had actually committed the offence, his whole family, together with their animate and inanimate property were deemed to be contaminated by the taboo attaching to the stolen property, and had to be destroyed. The infliction of the ban in this case was, however, not for breach of the criminal law, but represented an extension of the area of the military ban, to which Jericho was already subject.[23]

In view of the fact that Exod. 22:19 records the only instance of the infliction of the ban being ordered for breach of the criminal law, it might be argued that יחרם ('he shall be put to the ban') should be regarded as an error for אחרים ('other') which has clearly been omitted from the text,[24] and that the usual execution formula מות יומת ('he shall be put to death') should be inserted.[25]

But if there was no crime for which persons other than the actual criminal could be executed, then Deut. 24:16 would be inexplicable, for it clearly relates to the infliction of human and not divine punishment. Further, even if the application of Deut. 24:16 has been inserted into the account of 2 Kgs. 14:6, it none the less indicates that prior to Deuteronomy it was the normal procedure to execute both the criminal and his sons for regicide. There is also the case of Naboth, whose sons were executed for their father's crime (2 Kgs. 9:26). Can then these executions be understood as the infliction of the ban referred to in Exod. 22:19, the practice of which Deut. 24:16 made illegal?

Naboth and his sons were, however, not executed under Exod.

---

[21] Cf. Noth, op. cit., p. 186.

[22] There were three categories of military ban:

i Total destruction of all persons and property (Deut. 20:16 ff.; 1 Sam. 15:3);

ii Total destruction of all persons, but not property (Deut. 2:34 f.; 3:6 f.);

iii Destruction of all males only (Deut. 20:10 ff., though the term חרם is not used here).

[23] Porter, *VT*, xv, pp. 376 ff.

[24] This occurs in both the Samaritan text and LXXᴬ. The omission may have necessitated verse 19b which is missing in the Samaritan text.

[25] Alt, *Essays*, p. 112; Noth, *Exodus*, p. 186.

22:19, but for breach of the law contained in Exod. 22:27, the precise meaning of which must first be determined.

Commentators have generally understood Exod. 22:27 to refer to blasphemy, for which they hold execution was prescribed in Lev. 24:10 ff.[26] But in an age in which, as far as one is aware, there were no atheists, a law against blasphemy would appear to have been meaningless, since to curse the god whom one acknowledged, whether this was Yahweh or not, could only invite automatic divine action. Consequently blasphemy could only be contemplated as an act of suicide (Job 2:9). It might, however, be argued that since any crime could result in divine intervention not only against the community, but also against the individual (2 Sam. 12:14), there was therefore no reason to exclude blasphemy from Israel's criminal law. But the difference lies in the fact that Israel's crimes are only crimes because they are included in the covenant stipulations, and not, as in the case of blasphemy, because they represent a common religious belief.[27]

Apart from Exod. 22:27 קלל is only found with God as object in Lev. 24:10 ff. and probably Isa. 8:21, to which must be added 1 Sam. 3:11 ff., where, as with the LXX, אלהים ('god') must be read for להם ('for themselves') in verse 13, this being designated a *tiqqūn sopherim*.[28] In addition ברך is used euphemistically for קלל in 1 Kgs. 21:10, 13 and Job 1:5, 11; 2:5, 9.

A recent examination of קלל in the Pi'ēl has shown that there is nothing inherent in its use which indicates that it is to be confined to spoken action, and rendered 'curse'. Instead it appears to have a very wide meaning, whose basic idea is 'repudiate', 'spurn', 'renounce'. Where there is a verbal content then this expresses disparagement.[29]

There is no need to repeat the detailed arguments put forward to substantiate this view. An examination of 1 Sam. 3:11 ff. alone confirms that קלל need not be confined to spoken action, for Eli's sons are condemned for their disgraceful conduct in the abuse of their office by their attitude to the sacrificial offerings (1 Sam. 2:12 ff.), and their sexual immorality with sanctuary personnel (1 Sam. 2:22).[30]

---

[26] Burney, *Kings*, p. 247; J. A. Montgomery and H. S. Gehman, *The Books of Kings*, ICC, 1951, p. 331; Noth, *Exodus*, p. 187. On the other hand J. Gray, *I and II Kings*, London, 1964, pp. 391 f. seems to understand Naboth to have been guilty of slandering the king, which by virtue of the father-son relationship between Yahweh and the king, involved Yahweh as well.

[27] S. H. Blank, 'The Curse, Blasphemy, the Spell and the Oath', *HUCA*, xxiii. 1, 1950/1, p. 83; Brichto, *The Problem of 'Curse'*, pp. 147, 164 f.

[28] Driver, *Samuel*, p. 44. [29] Brichto, op. cit., pp. 118 ff.

[30] It does not seem necessary here to isolate which of these two offences might constitute the repudiation referred to in 1 Sam. 3:13, but cf. ibid., pp. 149 ff.

It would therefore seem that when קלל ('repudiate') is applied to
God, it must signify total rejection of Yahweh. Consequently it would
include any breach of the covenant stipulations of the Sinai Decalogue, that is the criminal law, though not of the civil law, since this
did not involve any direct recourse to Yahweh. This interpretation is
supported by the parallel Akkadian expression, which has been
rendered 'to commit an offence against his god/the gods'.[31] קלל
אלהים may accordingly be rendered 'repudiate God'.[32]

The same study has also subjected the verb ארר to a detailed investigation, and drawn the conclusion that it cannot automatically be
rendered 'curse', but has the meaning 'anathematize', 'ban', 'place
under a spell'.[33] This is also confirmed from the cognate Akkadian
word.[34]

Apart from Exod. 22:27, the term נשיא is exclusively confined to
the exilic and post-exilic material,[35] and it must therefore be questioned whether the meaning which can be deduced for it there can be
used to determine the nature of the office described in Exod. 22:27b.
Relying on later material, it has been suggested that the term described
the leaders of the twelve tribes ('spokesmen') gathered at the central
amphictyonic shrine.[36] But it must be considered doubtful whether
the phrase 'נשיא of your people' could refer to tribal leaders, for it
would seem that by using עם ('people') the legislator intended to
indicate a single overall ruler.[37] The identity of this person depends

---

[31] Ibid., pp. 177 ff.

[32] Lev. 24:10 ff. is discussed on pp. 55 f. below. It would, however, seem that in the
case of Job 1:11; 2:5, 9, the particular form of repudiation envisaged was blasphemy,
since Satan's earlier activity resulted in Job's formal blessing of Yahweh (1:21), and
Job's wife seems to be advising him to commit suicide. This may also be the significance of על־פניך ('to your face') in 1:11; 2:5. If this is so, then the passage has a
very high dramatic content, for Satan argues that Job will not just commit any crime,
but will take a course of action of the possibility of which not even the criminal law
itself had to take cognizance. Brichto argues (p. 170) that it is the euphemistic use of
ברך which has led to the misunderstanding of קלל through the former always being
understood in the sense of utterance, and never concrete action, in which utterance
may or may not be present.

[33] Ibid., pp. 77 ff. Cf. Speiser, 'An Angelic "Curse": Exodus 14:20', *JAOS*,
lxxx, 1960, pp. 198–200.   [34] Brichto, op. cit., pp. 115 ff.

[35] The LXX rendering of 1 Kgs. 11:34 makes the MT's reference to נשיא very
uncertain. Thus Gray, *Kings*, pp. 270, 275, would read נָשֹׂא אֶשָּׂא לֹו ('I will assuredly
lift up for him (his face)', i.e. 'I will forbear with him').

[36] Noth, *Das System der zwölf Stämme Israels*, BWANT, iv. 1, 1930, pp. 151 ff.,
History, p. 102. Cf. *Exodus*, pp. 187 f.

[37] Porter, *Moses and Monarchy*, Oxford, 1963, p. 18 *contra* Cazelles, *Études sur le
code de l'Alliance*, Paris, 1946, p. 82. For further discussion cf. van der Ploeg, *RB*,
lvii, pp. 47 ff.; Speiser, 'Background and Function of the Biblical Nāśī', *CBQ*, xxv,
1963, pp. 111–17.

on the date which one assigns to the promulgation of the Book of the Covenant. If this preceded the inauguration of the monarchy, then it could only refer to the so-called minor-judge; but if the Book of the Covenant was issued after the monarchy was established, then it would seem that reference is being made to the king. In either event Exod. 22:27 should be rendered 'You shall not repudiate God (i.e. commit a crime) or bring under a ban a ruler of your people'.[38] Deut. 1:37 has been cited as an example of the infliction of such a ban on the leader as a result of the people's apostasy.[39] The same idea would appear to be present in Exod. 32:32,[40] the significance of which will be discussed later.[41]

Further consideration will be given to the identity of the נשיא when the Book of the Covenant is examined.[42] But to whomever the term originally referred, during the monarchy it was undoubtedly applied to the king (1 Kgs. 21:10).

One is now in a position to consider the trial of Naboth, the charge against whom does not identify the actual criminal offence of which he is accused, but merely asserts that a breach of the criminal law has occurred.[43] That this is so is confirmed by the fact that a fast is to be proclaimed (1 Sam. 7:6), thereby indicating that some local disaster has already taken place, which was interpreted as due to the wrath of Yahweh following a serious breach of the covenant law.[44] It is from the general public's recognition of this fact the Jezebel seeks to profit. Acting in the king's name, she summons the local elders to convene a court for the apparent purpose of ascertaining the identity of the criminal, in order that through his execution the covenant relationship might be restored between Yahweh and his people in accordance with the general principle of Israelite criminal law. Though only Naboth himself was charged, the result of his conviction was the execution of both him and his sons (2 Kgs. 9:26), together with the confiscation of his property. Although that conviction was secured on false evidence, one has no right to assume that had the evidence been valid, conviction and subsequent execution, together with the seizure of the vineyard, were not in accordance with Israelite law. It is probable that

---

[38] Brichto, *The Problem of 'Curse'*, pp. 150 ff.
[39] Ibid., pp. 158 f. Cf. Deut. 3:26; 4:21 and note Driver, *Deuteronomy*, pp. 26 f.
[40] Cf. Porter, op. cit., pp. 21 f.   [41] See below, p. 173.
[42] See below, p. 160.   [43] Cf. Brichto, op. cit., pp. 159 ff.
[44] It has been suggested that this may have been the drought of 1 Kgs. 17. Cf. Burney, *Kings*, p. 245; Montgomery and Gehman, *Kings*, p. 331; Gray, *Kings*, p. 391; Brichto, op. cit., pp. 161 f. But perhaps the disaster should be understood as particularly associated with Jezreel.

Naboth's refusal to sell his property was public knowledge, and even if this was not so Jezebel would have been aware that she had to act with care if she was to avoid giving the impression that the vineyard was being seized on a trumped up charge. While she was able to suborn the judges, though she appears to have had to rely on Ahab's seal in order to do so, she would have had to make sure that in the eyes of the people justice was seen to be done, for it was the people as a whole who had to inflict the death penalty. Thus it may be assumed that both the execution and the subsequent confiscation of the vineyard were in accordance with Israelite law, had the offence for which Naboth was convicted been committed. What was this offence?

The only law which prescribes for its breach the execution of other people besides the actual criminal is Exod. 22:19, that is breach of the first commandment by entering into relations with other gods, for this imposed the infliction of the ban, which in its scope is not there defined. It would therefore appear that the case of Naboth is an illustration of this legal ban, which was evidently restricted to the death of the criminal and his lineal male descendants. Its undoubted purpose was to blot out for ever the memory of the criminal, so that it would appear that he had never existed. This could only be achieved by exterminating his name, and therefore of necessity demanded the execution of all lineal male descendents (cf. 2 Sam. 14:7). But neither women, who in any event prior to the Deuteronomic reform were not subject to the criminal law, nor collateral male relatives were included under the ban. The latter would only pass on their own name. But since the criminal and his family were deemed never to have existed, there could be no question of any collateral male relative inheriting his realty (Num. 27:9 ff.).[45] The land was treated as if it had never belonged to an Israelite, and therefore was forfeit to the state.[46] In no other case in pre-exilic Israel is there any suggestion that the property of the criminal was to be appropriated. David's attitude to Mephibosheth seems entirely arbitrary (2 Sam. 16:4; 19:29). Therefore Naboth's sons were not executed in order to prevent their succession to their father's property, but because they were subject

[45] Where there was no son, the nearest male relative inherited, thus ensuring the retention of the property within the family (Pedersen, *Israel*, i–ii, pp. 89 ff.; de Vaux, *Ancient Israel*, pp. 53 ff.).

[46] F. I. Andersen, 'The Socio-judicial Background of the Naboth Incident', *JBL*, lxxxv, 1966, pp. 46 ff. has argued from the Alalakh material that Naboth was executed for failing to carry through the agreed sale of his property to Ahab to whom the vineyard was in consequence forfeited. But this study will show that Israel's criminal law nowhere considers property more important than the life of an individual member of the covenant community.

to the ban, which ban allowed Ahab to seize the vineyard 'legally'. The irony of the case is that in order to achieve her purpose the foreign queen had to rely on the covenant law, which she did not acknowledge, in order to rid herself of a stubborn opponent. The fact that the execution appears to have taken place in the vineyard itself (2 Kgs. 9:25 f. Cf. 1 Kgs. 21:19),[47] which one must assume was outside the city, may be held to indicate that this location was specially selected in order to eradicate certain pollution which the land was deemed to have contracted, and so allow Ahab to take possession and enjoy it. Thus it may be conjectured that the witnesses indicated that Naboth's refusal to part with the vineyard was not due to filial piety (1 Kgs. 21:3),[48] but to the fact that he was secretly carrying out on that very land practices which involved the recognition of other gods.

The only other crime for which infliction of the ban is recorded is regicide, where in 2 Kgs. 14:6 it is stated that Amaziah did not follow the normal practice, but only put to death the actual murderers of his father. Had this been a simple case of murder, only the criminal himself could have been executed.

There is no legal sanction concerning regicide. But even before the Davidic covenant was established, the person of the king as Yahweh's anointed was peculiarly sacrosanct, which explains David's attitude to Saul.[49] However, under the Davidic covenant the king acquired a position quite different from that of the charismatic leader, for this covenant ensured that succession to the Judaean throne should remain with the Davidic dynasty, the king being designated Yahweh's adopted son (Ps. 2:7). So in contrast to the northern kingdom where murder of the king could be undertaken in Yahweh's name,[50] to assassinate the Davidic king was understood as a direct repudiation of Yahweh himself. Thus it would appear that just as under the Mosaic covenant a person who rejected Yahweh for other gods had put himself outside the covenant community, and therefore his name must be blotted out, so under the Davidic covenant a man who was guilty of regicide had severed all allegiance to the Davidic throne, and so to Yahweh, and therefore together with his lineal male descendants must be put to the ban. The first commandment was thus extended to include murder of the Davidic king. But there is no means of knowing

[47] Gray, *Kings*, p. 392.
[48] On the question of the legality of Ahab's offer to purchase Naboth's vineyard, see below, p. 151, n. 11.
[49] 1 Sam. 24:7, 11; 26:9, 11, 23; 2 Sam. 1:14, 16.
[50] 2 Kgs. 9 and cf. 1 Kgs. 15:27 ff., 16:2 ff.

whether treason in general without the actual death of the king would
have also resulted in infliction of the ban.

The fact that 2 Kgs. 14:6 cites the law contained in Deut. 24:16,
probably indicates that the Deuteronomic historian applied it to an
earlier well known instance of unusual clemency. This Deuteronomic
provision, which confirms that the legal ban was restricted to lineal
male descendants, and prohibits its infliction in the future, would have
been quite meaningless had there not been a crime for which persons
other than the actual criminal were executed. It has been suggested
that a distinction should be made between crimes committed against
God and those against men,[51] and that while the latter only demanded
the execution of the actual criminal, the former involved the exaction
of the ban. This cannot be accepted. Rather the distinction is between
total rejection of the covenant concept—in the case of the Mosaic
covenant by entering into relations with other deities, and in that of
the Davidic covenant by regicide—and all other crimes. Only for the
former would the ban have been exacted.

Other Deuteronomic provisions confirm that the ban was no longer
to be inflicted for breach of the first commandment (Deut. 13:2 ff.,
7 ff.; 17:2 ff.). Similarly Lev. 20:1 ff. indicates that only the individual
was liable for what is there deemed to be a breach of Exod. 22:19.

Finally, returning to the case of Naboth, can one discover the
Deuteronomic historian's motive in concealing the identity of the
crime under which Naboth was convicted and executed? In fact it
would appear that this was due to his desire to make the narrative
conform to the Deuteronomic legislation. Knowing that prior to that
legislation, breach of the first commandment demanded exaction of the
ban, and yet having before him Deut. 24:16, which he regarded as
sufficiently important to work into his historical narrative (2 Kgs.
14:6), he chose to avoid any ambiguity with which he might be faced
by avoiding the mention not only of the specific crime which Naboth
was alleged to have committed, but also of the execution of his sons.
It is only because of a chance remark in 2 Kgs. 9:26 that one knows
that Naboth was executed for a crime which demanded exaction of the
ban. It has already been suggested that the mention of the two witnesses is to be understood as a conscious attempt by the Deuteronomic
historian to conform to the Deuteronomic legislation (Deut. 17:6 f.;
19:15).[52] Further, since the abolition of the ban would have meant
that a criminal's land could no longer have been confiscated it would

[51] Verdam, *RIDA*², iii, pp. 393 ff.; Greenberg, *Yehezkel Kaufmann Jubilee Volume*,
pp. 20 ff.   [52] See above, p. 23.

seem that the Deuteronomic historian intended Ahab's action in taking possession of the vineyard to be understood as an illegal seizure, for according to the narrative, Ahab is merely informed that Naboth is dead, which could have indicated death by natural causes, and not that he and his sons had been executed under the ban (cf. 1 Kgs. 21:19).

There is thus no reason to reject the reference to the ban in Exod. 22:19, for it is this provision which explains both the trial of Naboth and Deut. 24:16. But it must be remembered that here the discussion concerns human and not divine punishment. It was to be left to those in the exilic situation to abandon communal liability in the latter sphere as well.

CHAPTER FOUR

THE PROHIBITION OF IMAGES

(Exod. 20:4 ff.; Deut. 5:8 ff.)

The original commandment given at Sinai, like the other commandments, would have consisted of a short apodictic order, in this case Exod. 20:4a. This prohibited the making of a פסל, which originally denoted an image hewn from wood or stone (1 Kgs. 5:32; Exod. 34:1, 4; Deut. 10:1, 3), materials which would have been readily available for the covenant clans gathered at Kadesh. While this graven image is most frequently contrasted with the molten image (מסכה) (Deut. 27:15; Judg. 17:3 f.; 18:14; Nahum 1:14; 2 Chr. 34:3 f.), it could itself be overlaid with gold or silver (Deut. 7:25; Isa. 30:22; Hab. 2:19). But in fact as far as the commandment was concerned the distinction between graven and molten images was of very little importance for the latter were also prohibited (Exod. 20:23; 34:17). However the reference to metals in these variations of the original Sinai commandment *prima facie* indicate that they are later.[1] Eventually פסל came to have the general meaning of 'idol' (Jer. 10:14).[2]

The contention that Exod. 20:3 was part of the introductory epiphany has been rejected, and it has been read as the first commandment.[3] Consequently the פסל of Exod. 20:4a must be of Yahweh, for relations with any other deity had already been forbidden.[4] Thus the Sinai Decalogue, having ensured that only those who acknowledged Yahweh alone could be members of the covenant people, went on to enact that the cult should be imageless. It would indeed have been meaningless to state in a code concerned to establish the exclusive covenant relationship between Yahweh and Israel, that the latter should not make any heathen images. It was with representations of Yahweh himself that the legislation was concerned.

The פסל would have been of a human form (Deut. 4:16; Isa.

---

[1] See below, pp. 168 ff.   [2] Cf. Isa. 40:19; 44:10.   [3] See above, pp. 38 f.
[4] Stamm, *TR*, N.F., xxvii, pp. 284 f.; Stamm and Andrew, *The Ten Commandments*, pp. 83 f.

44:13; Hab. 2:18 f.; Ps. 115:4 ff.) for from earliest times Israel visualized Yahweh in this way.[5] This is why 'the face' of Yahweh is so frequently alluded to, though there is no suggestion of an idol before whom men might appear in the various expressions involving the use of this concept.[6] Israel was forced to use analogy in speaking of Yahweh, and being conscious of man's direct personal relationship with him,[7] chose the human form to describe him.

The reason for the original commandment does not lie in the realization that Yahweh the invisible could not be visibly portrayed, for other religions knew perfectly well that their god was not confined to its image, but transcended it.[8] But these religions none the less saw in their images a means whereby they could gain control of the divine. The god would enter the image thereby enabling it to become an instrument of power to be used for man's advantage. Thus while Yahweh, like other deities, remained invisible, he forbade men to have a tangible object in which they could hold that he was automatically present. Like the Hittite kings in their relations with their vassals, Yahweh was a free agent and could never be contained by men for their own purposes, nor confined to a particular place. He entered into a direct personal relationship with men by virtue of his covenant, and there was consequently no need for an image of him. It is to this living relationship that the Old Testament bears witness.

Thus the second commandment ensured the sovereignty of Yahweh, who would manifest himself in history when and where he willed, and who remained outside men's control.[9] It is true that the ark and the temple both seem to assure Israel of the divine presence. Yet Yahweh is not to be thought of as controlled by either ark or temple. It was only if Israel obeyed the covenant law that Yahweh guaranteed his presence. This was the essence of the Mosaic covenant. It was because Yahweh could not be tied to ark or temple that faith in him could survive the exile, and the cult be restored.

Whether or not the Old Testament provides evidence that there

---

[5] von Rad, *Old Testament Theology*, i, E.T., Edinburgh, 1962, p. 219 cites Exod. 15:3; 1 Kgs. 22:19; Isa. 30:27; Ezek. 1:26.

[6] Cf. the use of בקש ('seek'), ראה ('see') and חלה ('make sweet') with פנים ('face'). Cf. E. Jacob, *Theology of the Old Testament*, E.T., London, 1958, pp. 77 ff.

[7] It would seem that this is what one is to understand by the concept of man made in the image of God (R. Davidson, *The Old Testament*, London, 1964, pp. 194 ff.).

[8] von Rad, *Theology*, i, pp. 212 ff.

[9] Zimmerli, 'Das zweite Gebot', *Bertholet-Festschrift*, pp. 558 ff.; Eichrodt, 'The Law and the Gospel', *Interpr.*, xi, 1957, pp. 29 f., *Theology*, i, p. 215; Stamm, *TR*, N.F., xxvii, pp. 285 ff.; Stamm and Andrew, *The Ten Commandments*, p. 86; Noth, *Exodus*, pp. 162 f.

were images of Yahweh, the fact that the commandment may subsequently have been broken is no argument against its existence.[10] There can, however, be no doubt that the official cult remained imageless for neither at Kadesh, Shechem, Shiloh nor in the temple was any image of Yahweh erected. Archaeology itself further supports the Old Testament picture. Although this is an argument from silence, it is none the less remarkable that in excavations to date no male human figures have been found at Israelite sites. Many female figurines have however been discovered. But even if these were modelled on Canaanite figures of female deities of fertility, it appears they were used in Israel as charms for child bearing, or inducing pregnancy by sympathetic magic, or even for ensuring milk for the child, and not as objects of worship.[11]

But one must be careful not to confuse cult objects with images of the deity. Thus the *teraphim* and *'ephod* are not to be understood as idols, but legitimate cultic apparatus used in divination,[12] and it is only due to later polemical writing that Jeroboam's bulls (1 Kgs. 12:28 f.) are portrayed as gods.[13] Indeed it is even probable that Micah's פסל was a later polemical addition to an ancient story concerning the original legitimate Danite sanctuary (Judg. 17 f.).[14] Cult objects only came to be condemned when they were confused with the worship of Yahweh himself.

Undoubtedly without such a commandment the official cult would have attempted to make images of Yahweh, for, unlike blasphemy, the making of images of one's god was a normal action. No people would have 'naturally' observed this remarkable phenomenon of worshipping an imageless god.[15] Thus the second commandment made of the clans

---

[10] Rowley, *BJRL*, xxxiv, pp. 105 f.

[11] Albright, *From the Stone Age to Christianity*, pp. 237 f.; *Archaeology and the Religion of Israel*[3], Baltimore, 1955, p. 115; J. Gray, *Archaeology and the Old Testament World*, London, 1962, p. 176.

[12] See below, pp. 60 ff.   [13] See below, pp. 170 ff.   [14] See below, p. 172, n 28.

[15] Thus support cannot be given to H. Th. Obbink's contention ('Jahwebilder', *ZAW*, N.F., vi, 1929, pp. 264 ff.) that since, as he alleges, images of Yahweh did not exist, there was no need to prohibit them, and therefore the commandment concerned heathen cult material. While the commandment came to be expanded and reinterpreted to include such material, its original purpose was to establish the cult of the imageless Yahweh. Reventlow, *Gebot und Predigt*, pp. 29 ff. reaches the same conclusion as Obbink, though he argues that since there *were* images of Yahweh in the cult, such images were legitimate. There would certainly seem to be no evidence for this as far as the official cult was concerned, and perhaps none at all. Nor can the contention of J. Dus, 'Das zweite Gebot', *CV*, iv, 1961, pp. 37 ff. that the second commandment represents a later insertion into the Decalogue to mark the triumph of the ark or throne image over the bull or pedestal image be accepted.

which gathered at Sinai a unique people, for alone among the communities with whom she came into contact, Israel was prohibited any image of her god. It is this creative aspect of the commandment which has not always received sufficient attention, for the Sinai Decalogue was not given to an already existing community, but brought that community into being, and secured its continuance.

At sometime in the pre-exilic period the original short apodictic commandment was considerably expanded and reinterpreted. In Deut. 5:8 the expansion is achieved by means of a clause in apposition to פסל, thus explaining that the image in question is no longer to be limited to an image of Yahweh in human form, but includes an image of anything from the realm of nature, whether found in the sky, on earth, or in the sea. In Exod. 20:4 the copula is used, but this has been explained as a *waw* explicative to be translated by 'namely', as in Lev. 18:7.[16] Accordingly there would appear to be no difference between the two versions.

But the plural suffixes in the injunction לא־תשתחוה להם ולא תעבדם ('you shall not bow down to them and serve them') in Exod. 20:5; Deut. 5:9 cannot refer to the singular פסל of the original commandment.[17] Further the phrase 'bow down and serve' is used neither of Yahweh nor of idols. It is therefore evident that direct reference is being made to the 'other gods' mentioned in the first commandment.[18] This is confirmed by the use of the term אל קנא ('jealous god'), an expression which is only applied to Yahweh when his claims over Israel are threatened by other deities.[19] Thus whoever expanded the second commandment understood the first two commandments as one, and reinterpreted the prohibited images as images of heathen deities. The identification of this author, together with a consideration of the similar legislation in the so-called ritual Decalogue (Exod. 34:17), and what appears to be a preface to the Book of the Covenant (Exod. 20:23), will be the subject of later investigation.[20]

The expansion concludes with the hortatory passage Exod. 20:5 f. It has earlier been recognized that the reference to punishment to the third and fourth generations indicates the absolute nature of

---

[16] Meek, *JAOS*, lviii, p. 124.

[17] Reventlow's argument (op. cit., p. 31) that the plural suffixes refer directly to the expanded verse 4 cannot be maintained (Knierim, *ZAW*, N.F., xxxvi, pp. 26 f.). Knierim argues (p. 27) that it is the phrase על־פני ('before me') which provides the necessary connection between verses 3 and 5.

[18] Zimmerli, *Bertholet-Festschrift*, pp. 550 ff.

[19] Obbink, op. cit., pp. 265 ff.; Knierim, op. cit., p. 33.

[20] See below, pp. 168 ff.

divine judgement which would result from breach of the commandment.[21] Clearly this constitutes a solemn warning. On the other hand,
if Yahweh's sole sovereignty was acknowledged, his love would know
no bounds.

Finally, it should be noted that the scope of the commandment is
taken a stage further in the exegetical passage Deut. 4:15 ff. Thus in
verse 16 images in human form are attacked, that is the פסל of the
original commandment, and in verse 17 f. the expansion of the original
commandment is referred to with the listing of animals, birds, rep-
tiles and fishes. But in verse 19 a further situation is envisaged,
namely the worship of astral powers, which only became a danger to
Yahwism after foreign conquest, and not through the indigenous
Canaanite cults.[22] Although the Deuteronomic historian polemically
attributes such practices to the northern kingdom (2 Kgs. 17:16),
they are in fact to be associated with the last years of the monarchy in
Judah (2 Kgs. 21:3, 5; 23:4 f., 12; Zeph. 1:5; Jer. 7:18; 8:2; 19:13;
44:17; Ezek. 8:16).

[21] See above, p. 33.

[22] Perhaps astral worship was first introduced into Judah by Ahaz, though his roof
building (2 Kgs. 20:11; 23:12; Isa. 38:8) is nowhere specifically connected with it.
Cf. S. Iwry, 'The Qumrân Isaiah and the End of the Dial of Ahaz', *BASOR*, cxlvii,
1957, pp. 30 ff.

CHAPTER FIVE

THE PROHIBITION OF THE IMPROPER
USE OF THE DIVINE NAME

(Exod. 20:7; Deut. 5:11)

The first two commandments of the Sinai Decalogue ensured that Israel should only worship the imageless Yahweh. But in order that she might know her god, and be able to invoke him, Yahweh was forced to reveal his name, which self-disclosure forms the opening declaration of the historical prologue (Exod. 20:2). By disclosing his name, Yahweh in part surrendered himself to Israel in giving her the means whereby she might ever have access to him. Thus knowledge of the divine name gave Israel considerable power. It was in effect her 'image',[1] for it had almost tangible properties. Consequently Exod. 20:7 was concerned to protect the use of the divine name, and prevent its invocation for improper purposes.

שׁוא refers to that which has no substance, is unreal or groundless. The LXX translates by ἐπὶ ματαίῳ ('for an empty', 'useless', 'worthless purpose'). Owing to the inherent vagueness in the term itself, the commandment has been widely interpreted. It would, however, seem that while שׁוא can mean quite generally any worthless purpose, in view of the precise nature of the other commandments, a particular situation was envisaged.

As has already been indicated, this commandment could not have referred to blasphemy, for to curse Yahweh would have amounted to suicide. Self-interest made such legislation unnecessary.[2] Similarly it does not refer to false oaths, for every oath contained an implicit self-curse which it was universally believed would result in direct divine action should that oath prove false.[3] To have summoned the support

---

[1] von Rad, *Theology*, i, p. 183.   [2] See above, p. 41.

[3] Brichto, *The Problem of 'Curse'*, pp. 61 f. Thus the commandment cannot be interpreted as prohibiting the use of an oath in Yahweh's name as a false act of defence to clear oneself from a rightful criminal charge (Köhler, *TR*, N.F., i, p. 180; Nielsen, *The Ten Commandments*, pp. 100 f.). In any event, evidence did not have to be given under oath (see below, pp. 143 f.).

of the law to make false oaths illegal would in effect have amounted to a repudiation of the efficacy of the oath itself.

It has been suggested that the commandment was directed against syncretism of nature gods with Yahweh.[4] But by its opening commandments, the Decalogue excluded any possibility of relations with other deities or identification with their images. While it is true that in Jer. 18:15; Ps. 31:7 and Jonah 2:9, שוא is specifically applied to idols, it will be shown that even as late as Lev. 24:10 ff. these were not the concern of the commandment.

It would in fact appear that the commandment was designed to prevent the use of the divine name for magical purposes.[5] Just as an Israelite was forbidden an image through which he might literally get Yahweh into his hands, so he was forbidden use of the divine name for exercising power over another. By the covenant itself, based on the Hittite suzerainty treaty form, Yahweh was to be ensured his absolute freedom, and on no account placed in the control of man. While knowledge of the divine name made the cult possible, it might also lead unscrupulous people to use it privately to effect curses, spells and other magical practices. Since invocation of any deity other than Yahweh was already forbidden, the third commandment thus ensured the total prohibition of all such practices, for appeal would have been made to divine forces to effect them. Both primitive religion and black magic were based on a proper invocation of the divine name.[6]

Thus the commandment sought to ensure that Yahweh should never be manipulated by the individual for his own ends. Though Yahweh had been obliged to disclose his name in order that Israel could enter into the covenant relationship, no infringement of his sovereignty was to be tolerated by its improper use. The consequence of the commandment was that it ensured for each individual Israelite complete freedom from the world of magical influence, the importance of which can hardly be exaggerated.

The most common instrument for exercising power over another was the אלה ('curse').[7] This was a deadly weapon which could destroy all those who came within its sphere.[8] Quite apart from private use,

---

[4] W. E. Staples, 'The Third Commandment', *JBL*, lviii, 1939, pp. 325–9.

[5] Mowinckel, *Psalmenstudien*, i, Kristiania, 1921, pp. 50 ff.; Eichrodt, *Interpr.*, xi, p. 30; Andrew, 'Using God', *ET*, lxxiv, 1962/3, pp. 305 f.; von Rad, *Deuteronomy*, p. 57; Schreiner, *Die zehn Gebote*, pp. 82 f.

[6] J. W. Wevers, 'A Study in the Form Criticism of Individual Complaint Psalms', *VT*, vi, 1956, pp. 82 f., 89; S. Goldman, *The Ten Commandments*, Chicago, 1956, p. 157.

[7] Cf. Brichto, op. cit., pp. 22 ff., who argues that the verb אלה does not mean to swear an oath, but to curse in the sense of imprecate. For a discussion of his understanding of this commandment, see pp. 146 f. below.   [8] Pedersen, *Israel*, i–ii, pp. 437 ff.

it could be encountered in various ways. Thus every oath (שְׁבוּעָה) carried an implicit אלה, which if that oath was broken or false, would automatically come into effect. Similarly breach of a covenant would bring into effect the curses contained within it. It was in order to avoid such action that Israel executed her criminals (cf. 2 Chr. 34:24; Isa. 24:6; Jer. 23:10; Dan. 9:11).

But the third commandment utterly prohibited the private use of an אלה, which crime is referred to in Hos. 4:2, though examination of that passage will be deferred until the ninth commandment is discussed.[9] Thus in Job 31:29 f., Job argues that even though he rejoiced at the downfall of the man who hated him, he was not guilty of having sought his life by means of an אלה. Only in two instances in connection with adultery (Num. 5:11 ff.)[10] and theft (Lev. 5:1; Judg. 17:2; Prov. 29:24)[11] does one find an אלה being legitimately pronounced, and in both cases it is specifically associated with the cult, being under the supervision of the priests. Its use would therefore appear to have been restricted to Yahweh's accredited agents, his cult officials.[12]

Lev. 24:10 ff. contains an example of breach of the third commandment.[13] The interpretation of this passage has been confused by the translation of וַיִּקֹּב in verse 11 by 'curse', with the understanding of blaspheme, from the verb קבב, when in fact verse 16 would *prima facie* indicate that it is derived from the root נקב ('pierce', 'prick off', 'designate').[14] But even here translators have insisted on understanding נקב as referring to blasphemy, with the result that on the strength of this verse alone a second root has been postulated for נקב with the meaning 'curse'.[15] There is, however, no necessity for this, for if one derives וַיִקֹב in verse 11 from נקב giving it its usual meaning, one discovers that the offence which has been committed is the improper ejaculation of the divine name in a fight, presumably in a curse formula, with the evident aim of gaining control over the adversary through magical force. It is for this reason that verse 11 adds וַיְקַלֵּל ('and he repudiated'),[16] thereby indicating that *prima facie* a crime had been committed, Yahweh being the implied object of the verb.

---

[9] See below, pp. 145 ff.   [10] See below, pp. 118 ff.   [11] See below, pp. 138 ff.

[12] This would explain the background to 1 Sam. 14:24 ff. Saul finds himself trapped by his own אלה, because he has appropriated to himself powers which belonged to the religious head of the community, the minor-judge Samuel. For other instances of similar tension between Saul and Samuel, cf. 1 Sam. 13:8 ff.; 15:17 ff.

[13] The *excursus* on the *lex talionis* (Lev. 24:17–21) is a late insertion. See below, pp. 96 ff. On the question whether Ps. 24:4 also refers to the third commandment, see below, p. 187.

[14] Brichto, op. cit., pp. 143 ff.   [15] BDB, p. 666b.

[16] This rendering was discussed on pp. 41 f. above.

E

The issue in Lev. 24:10 ff. is, therefore, not whether action which could be termed criminal has occurred, but whether the court has the necessary jurisdiction to convict the alleged criminal. There is no doubt that had the arrested man been a full Israelite he would have been liable, for, as verse 11 indicates, the third commandment had been broken. But since the man had a foreign father, he himself was a foreigner in spite of his Israelite mother,[17] which renders his liability under Israel's criminal law doubtful. This explains the emphasis on the arrested man's parentage. The purpose of Lev. 24:10 ff. is to make it clear that the גֵּר ('resident alien') was to be held liable in exactly the same manner as an Israelite himself.[18]

The close relationship in form of Lev. 24:10 ff. with Num. 15:32 ff. indicates that it is itself a later insertion into the Holiness Code. The fact that both passages picture actual stoning of the criminal, when it has been argued that, save in the case of murder, the post-exilic penalty of the criminal law was excommunication, is no bar to this interpretation, for since the crime is purported to have been committed in Israel's desert period, no other punishment could have been prescribed.

In contrast to the first two commandments, Exod. 20:7, like the expanded fourth and fifth commandments, refers to Yahweh in the third person. Even when the first five commandments have been reduced to their original short apodictic form (Exod. 20:3, 4a, 7a, 9–10a, 12a) the third commandment still speaks of Yahweh in the third person. But this is to be attributed to the expansion of the commandment by the hortatory passage Exod. 20:7b, through which an original שְׁמִי ('my name') has been altered to שֵׁם־יְהוָה אֱלֹהֶיךָ ('the name of Yahweh your God'). Reference might however be made to the expansion of the second commandment where in Exod. 20:5 the first person form is still used. But the reason for its retention there is that the author took the first two commandments as one, and was therefore conditioned by עַל־פָּנַי in Exod. 20:3.[19] But in Exod. 20:7, 10, and 12 he abandoned the first person form, the third person being far more suitable for his hortatory purpose.[20]

As with all crimes before the Deuteronomic reform, the third

---

[17] Noth, *Leviticus*, p. 179.
[18] Cf. above, p. 17.
[19] See above, p. 51, n. 17.
[20] Cf. Nielsen, *The Ten Commandments*, pp. 128 ff. On p. 88 he raises the possibility that a copyist might have understood the *yodh* of שמי as an abbreviation for Yahweh (cf. Judg. 19:18). For the suggested author of these hortatory passages, see below, pp. 178 f.

commandment only applied to men, for women were not members of the covenant community, and were therefore free from criminal liability. This would explain the additional criminal law enactment of Exod. 22:17, which provides for the apparently summary execution of the מכשפה ('sorceress'), though the significance of the feminine gender has eluded the Versions.

The root meaning of כשף would appear to be 'cut', as the cognate Assyrian and Arabic words indicate. But the precise magical act envisaged is uncertain. Mic. 5:11 indicates that the כשפים can be of a concrete nature,[21] and it has been suggested that they should be understood as shredded herbs, which the מכשפה used in her magic brew.[22] But it has been pointed out that there is no direct evidence of this, and reference has instead been made to the practice of carving figures of persons whom one wished to place under a spell by means of sympathetic magic.[23] It would, however, seem probable that the term מכשפה should not be restricted to those who used tangible objects to perform their skill, but understood to include anybody who resorted to magical practices for the purpose of exercising power over another.[24] This would then include the use of the אלה ('curse').

While the use of the masculine מכשף in Deut. 18:10, confirms that this practice need not be confined to women, Exod. 22:17 indicates that when the Book of the Covenant was compiled such a practice by men was already considered illegal. This was achieved by the Decalogue itself, for the first commandment ensured that only Yahweh could be invoked, and the third commandment prohibited the use of his name for magical purposes. But since a woman was not subject to criminal legislation, she was free to invoke what powers she liked including Yahweh in order to render effective her potion, spell or curse. Exod. 22:17 is therefore a deliberate attempt to stem a loophole in the existing criminal legislation by preventing members of the covenant community, that is men, from resorting to sorcerers, who of necessity must be women, in order to effect a practice which had it been carried out by men would have been a crime. Thus in this one instance the Book of the Covenant brought women within the scope of the criminal law, and made them liable for execution.

Deut. 18:10 ff. rendered illegal every type of occult practice. In addition to sorcery, this included what is presumably the ritual to

---

[21] Cf. MAL A 47 (ANET, p. 184).
[22] Robertson Smith, 'On the Forms of Divination and Magic Enumerated in Deut. xviii. 10, 11', *JPhil*, xiv, 1886, pp. 124 ff.; Driver, *Deuteronomy*, p. 225.
[23] AL, p. 488.   [24] Ibid., pp. 118 f.

Molech [25] and all forms of divination, whether from cultic or natural objects, or through communion with the dead.[26] Although no penalty is prescribed, since sorcerers are included in the list, it may be assumed that all these practices were declared criminal, and resulted in the execution of the offender. While with the possible exception of necromancy, divination had until the Deuteronomic reform been a legitimate part of the cult (Isa. 3:2; Mic. 3:7), for the Deuteronomist, the prophet was to take the place of the diviner associated by him with heathen religions.[27] The reason for the Deuteronomic prohibition of all forms of divination lies in the fact that the Deuteronomist understood such practices as an infringement of Yahweh's essential freedom from man's control guaranteed by the covenant relationship itself. Men were only to be informed of what lay in the future as and when Yahweh himself decided through the activity of his own mediums, the prophets.

It was as a result of Deut. 18:10 ff. that the formerly legitimate cult objects of divination, the *teraphim* and *'ephod*, were condemned as idolatrous. This would seem to be the purpose of the Deuteronomist's use of קסם, which is the general term for 'divine', and is found in conjunction with the *teraphim* in 1 Sam. 15:23; Ezek. 21:26 and Zech. 10:2. Thus it is specifically recorded that in addition to the necromancers, Josiah also put away the *teraphim* (2 Kgs. 23:24). For the Deuteronomic historian the *'ephod* became an object of worship (Judg. 8:27).[28]

But while it seems certain that divination from cultic and natural phenomena was first prohibited by Deut. 18:10 ff., one must be more hesitant concerning divination through necromancy, for 1 Sam. 28:3 records that Saul expelled the necromancers from the land.[29] However, it is possible that Saul's expulsion of the necromancers was a unilateral act which did not become part of the criminal law until

---

[25] See below, pp. 128 f.

[26] The terms used in this legislation are discussed by Robertson Smith, *JPhil*, xiii, 1885, pp. 273 ff., xiv, 1886, pp. 113 ff.; Driver, *Deuteronomy*, pp. 221 ff.

[27] von Rad, *Deuteronomy*, pp. 122 ff.

[28] Both *teraphim* and *'ephod* are discussed in the *excursus* to this chapter.

[29] On the meaning of the term אוב, cf. H. Schmidt, 'אוב', *Marti-Festschrift*, BZAW, xli, 1925, pp. 253–61; M. Vieyra, 'Les noms du "mundus" en hittite et en assyrien et la pythonisse d'Endor', *RHA*, xix, 1961, pp. 47–55; H. A. Hoffner, 'Second Millennium Antecedents to the Hebrew *'ÔB*', *JBL*, lxxxvi, 1967, pp. 385–401. For the possibility that אוב is to be connected with the special use of אב ('father') as the possessor of hidden information not accessible to ordinary people, cf. my essay 'The Ecstatics' Father', *Words and Meanings, Essays presented to D. Winton Thomas* (Eds. P. R. Ackroyd and B. Lindars), Cambridge, 1968, p. 194, n. 1.

prohibited by Deuteronomy along with other forms of divination. Is there any evidence of this in the Old Testament itself?

In the first place the emphasis on necromancy in the Holiness Code would seem to indicate that its prohibition was a matter of recent legislation which still had to be stressed (Lev. 19:31; 20:6, 27). Further while the Code refers to other forms of divination first prohibited by Deut. 18:10 (Lev. 19:26), together with the ritual to Molech (Lev. 18:21; 20:2 ff.), it makes no mention of sorcery. This would seem to indicate that in contrast to divination in general, including necromancy, and the ritual to Molech, the priestly legislators felt no necessity to repeat legislation concerning sorcery, even though this practice reappeared in the last years of the Davidic monarchy (Jer. 27:9; cf. Deut. 18:10 f.), since it alone had always been forbidden to men by virtue of the Decalogue, and to women by Ex. 22:17.[30]

Secondly, though both the northern kingdom (2 Kgs. 17:17) and Manasseh (2 Kgs. 21:6; 2 Chr. 33:6) were charged with the practice of necromancy by the Deuteronomic historian, apart from 1 Sam. 28 there is no record of its actual condemnation in the historical works until Josiah's reform (2 Kgs. 23:24). Though the text of Isa. 8:19 f. is so obscure that little can definitely be deduced from it, while necromancy is there frowned upon, there is nothing to suggest that it was actually illegal.

Thirdly, even though the woman clearly fears for her life (1 Sam. 28:9), the fact that Saul did not put the necromancers to death, but merely expelled them from the land (1 Sam. 28:3), indicates that he was aware that their action could not be considered a breach of the criminal law. They were treated as undesirables rather than criminals.

Accordingly, it seems probable that Saul's expulsion of the necromancers was an act of excessive zeal, which was not subsequently enforced as part of Israel's criminal law.[31] Since necromancy was a form of divination which in no way involved the exercise of magical powers over another, there would appear to have been no reason to prohibit it.[32]

As has been indicated, the Holiness Code emphasizes the prohibition of divination (Lev. 19:26, 31; 20:6, 27). The fact that in Lev. 20:27 the death penalty is demanded for the necromancer shows that

---

[30] Ezek. 13:17 ff. is another exilic passage dealing with divination. Cf. W. H. Brownlee, 'Exorcising the Souls from Ezekiel 13:17–23', *JBL*, lxix, 1950, pp. 367–73.

[31] If this judgement is correct, then his action against necromancy is an important element in the evaluation of Saul himself.

[32] The popularity of necromancy would seem to be evidenced by the fact that the whereabouts of a medium was common knowledge even to Saul's court (1 Sam. 28:7).

this is an early enactment, and its position after the concluding clause of verse 26 would indicate that once it belonged elsewhere. Perhaps it should be placed before Lev. 20:6, which states that Yahweh himself will take action against those who consult necromancers, direct divine action being the only punishment which could be relied upon in the exilic situation. If this is so then it forms a very good parallel to the legislation concerning Molech in Lev. 20:2 ff.[33]

Excursus

(i) The teraphim

Though the etymology of the word *teraphim* remains uncertain,[34] one need have no hesitation in asserting that they were used in the cult as instruments of divination (Judg. 17:5; 18:14, 17; 1 Sam. 15:23; Ezek. 21:26; Hos. 3:4; Zech. 10:2). In addition there were household *teraphim* (Gen. 31; 1 Sam. 19:13, 16).[35] Much recent discussion has centred on the identification of the *teraphim*, which can be alternatively described as אלהים ('gods') (Gen. 31:30, 32), with the Nuzu etymological equivalent of אלהים, the *ilāni*, which the Nuzu texts indicate were also to be found both in the sanctuary and the household.[36] Thus it will be argued that whereas in Exod. 21:6

---

[33] See above, p. 30.

[34] C. J. Labuschagne, '*Teraphim*—A New Proposal for its Etymology', *VT*, xvi, 1966, pp. 115–17 argues that *teraphim* is derived from the root פתר ('interpret') found in the Old Testament only in Gen. 40 f., the form *teraphim* being due to metathesis.

[35] It has generally been assumed from Nuzu material that Rachel's purpose in stealing her father's *teraphim* was to ensure Jacob's position as Laban's heir and head of the family. But this view has recently been questioned by Greenberg, 'Another Look at Rachel's Theft of the Teraphim', *JBL*, lxxxi, 1962, pp. 239–48, who relying on a note in Josephus, suggests that it was the custom of those travelling abroad to take their household gods with them. On the other hand, M. H. Segal, 'The Pentateuch', *The Pentateuch and Other Biblical Studies*, Jerusalem, 1967, p. 140, argues that Rachel took the *teraphim* to prevent Laban from consulting them to obtain information concerning Jacob's flight. Although there is no recorded instance in the Old Testament of household *teraphim* being used for obtaining oracles, this may however reflect their original purpose. It has been argued that in Gen. 31 a tradition that Rachel brought the cult of the mother goddess to Israel, represented by female figurines, has been combined with the story of the theft of Laban's *teraphim* (W. C. Graham and May, *Culture and Conscience*, Chicago, 1936, pp. 93 f.; M. Burrows, *What Mean These Stones?*, New York, 1941, pp. 259 f.; Ackroyd, 'The Teraphim', *ET*, lxii, 1950/1, pp. 379 f.).

[36] Cf. C. J. Gadd, 'Tablets from Kirkuk', *RA*, xxiii, 1926, p. 127; S. Smith, 'What were the Teraphim?', *JTS*, xxxiii, 1931/2, pp. 33 ff.; Gordon, 'Parallèles Nouziens aux lois et coutumes de l'ancien Testament', *RB*, xliv, 1935, pp. 35 f., 'אלהים in Its Reputed Meaning of Rulers, Judges', *JBL*, liv, 1935, pp. 139 ff., 'Biblical Customs and the Nuzu Tablets', *BA*, iii, 1940, pp. 5 ff.; J. W. Jack, 'Recent Biblical Archaeology', *ET*, xlviii, 1936/7, p. 549; J. N. Schofield, 'Some Archaeological Sites and the Old Testament', *ET*, lxvi, 1954/5, pp. 317 f.; A. E. Draffkorn, 'Ilāni/Elohim', *JBL* lxxvi, 1957, pp. 216 ff.

אלהים refers to the household *teraphim*,[37] in Exod. 22:7 ff. it indicates sanctuary *teraphim*.[38]

In identifying the nature of the *teraphim* the crucial text has been 1 Sam. 19:13, 16,[39] where it used to be supposed that an object the shape and size of a man was inserted in David's bed. However, this would conflict with Gen. 31, which clearly denotes something small. Consequently it was argued that the *teraphim* were small figurines which were placed by or facing the bed to warn visitors that sickness was present.[40] This led to a derivation from רפא ('heal') being postulated, the *teraphim* being 'those who bring health'.[41] But there is no other evidence that the *teraphim* are to be connected with sickness. Further it is by no means certain that *teraphim* is to be understood as a genuine plural, for it has been argued that like *Urim* and *Thummim* its present form is due to mimation.[42]

The suggestion which seems to have most merit is that the *teraphim* was a mask worn when giving oracles, Exod. 34:29 ff. being an aetiological account showing that Moses himself had worn the *teraphim*. Because this was later condemned, the word *teraphim* was changed to מסוה ('covering', 'veil'), which only occurs in this passage.[43] Since it may be assumed that the household and sanctuary *teraphim* had the same identity, this would indicate that Michal used the *teraphim* and the goat's hair as a disguise for David's face. In the case of household *teraphim*, the mask may have been that of an ancestor.[44]

It has already been argued that there is no indication that the *teraphim* were regarded as illegitimate until Josiah's reform (2 Kgs. 23:24).[45] But consequent upon the general ban on divination (Deut. 18:10 ff.), the oracular instruments of divination were themselves

---

[37] See below, pp. 74 f.   [38] See below, pp. 136 f.

[39] Albright, *Archaeology and the Religion of Israel*, p. 207 rejects the rendering *teraphim* and substitutes 'old rags' from the Canaanite *trp* ('wear out'). He is followed by Gray, *Kings*, p. 677. On the question whether the *teraphim* are mentioned in Ugaritic literature, see Albright, 'Are the Ephod and the Teraphim Mentioned in Ugaritic Literature?', *BASOR*, lxxxiii, 1941, pp. 39–42, 'Anath and the Dragon', ibid., lxxxiv, 1941, p. 15.

[40] W. E. Barnes, 'Teraphim', *JTS*, xxx, 1928/9, pp. 177–9.

[41] Smith, *JTS*, xxxiii, p. 36.

[42] A. Jirku, 'Die Gesichtsmaske des Mose', *ZDPV*, lxvii, 1944/5, p. 45, 'Die Mimation in den Nordzemitischen Sprachen und einige Bezeichnungen der Altisraelitischen Mantik', *Bibl.*, xxxiv, 1953, pp. 78–80.

[43] H. Gressmann, *Mose und seine Zeit*, Göttingen, 1913, pp. 246 ff.; *Die Anfänge Israels*, Göttingen, 1914, pp. 76 f.; Jirku, *ZDPV*, lxvii, pp. 43 ff.

[44] Brinker, *The Influence of Sanctuaries in Early Israel*, pp. 63 f.

[45] Thus the LXX in rendering Hos. 3:4 uses δῆλοι, which in Deut. 33:8 is used to render *Thummin*, thereby indicating that a legitimate means of divination was being described.

declared idolatrous (cf. 1 Sam. 15:23). Naturally under the banning of *teraphim* within the sanctuaries, *teraphim* within the house would also have been banned. Thus in contrast to Exod. 21:6, they are omitted from the domestic rite in Deut. 15:17. The mention of *teraphim* in Zech. 10:2 could indicate that they reappeared in the post-exilic period.[46]

(ii) *The 'ephod*

While the term *'ephod* is applied to a garment (1 Sam. 2:18; 2 Sam. 6:14), and particularly to the high priest's vestments,[47] there are a number of occasions where it is used of a solid portable object (Judg. 8:24 ff.; 17:5; 18:14 ff.; 1 Sam. 21:10; 23:6; 30:7; Hos. 3:4), which is undoubtedly to be connected with obtaining oracles (1 Sam. 23:6 ff.; 30:7 ff.). Thus in Judg. 17:5; 18:14 ff.; Hos. 3:4 the *'ephod* is found alongside the *teraphim*, both being legitimate cultic objects.

An attempt to resolve the difficulty of this double use has been made on the basis of the different readings in the MT and LXX of 1 Sam. 14:18, namely that whenever a solid object is referred to אָרוֹן ('ark') should be read for *'ephod* (אֵפוֹד).[48] But such a suggestion must be rejected for, since 1 Sam. 7:1 indicates that at the time of 1 Sam. 14:18 the ark was at Kiriath-Jearim, and was only moved from there by David (2 Sam. 6), it would be necessary to maintain that there was more than one ark, of which the Old Testament supplies no evidence. Hence in 1 Sam. 14:18, הגישה האפוד ('bring the *'ephod* here') must be read with the LXX as in 1 Sam. 23:9; 30:7, for Ahijah was carrying the *'ephod* that day (1 Sam. 14:3). נשא is always to be rendered by 'bear' in connection with the *'ephod* (1 Sam. 2:28; 22:18, where the LXX rightly omits בד ('linen')).[49] Only in 1 Sam. 2:18 and 2 Sam. 6:14 is a garment referred to in the pre-exilic period, and there a different verb is used, namely חגר ('gird').[50] Indeed in 1 Kgs. 2:26, *'ephod* should probably be read for 'ark', as the allusion appears to be to 1 Sam. 23:6, 9.[51] The *'ephod*, not the ark, was the means whereby oracles were obtained.

[46] On the use of the *teraphim* by the King of Babylon (Ezek. 21:26), see Smith, *JTS*, xxxiii, pp. 35 f.

[47] On the question whether the *'ephod* is mentioned in Ugaritic literature, see Albright, *BASOR*, lxxxiii, pp. 39 ff.

[48] W. R. Arnold, *Ephod and Ark*, HTS, iii, 1917, pp. 10 ff.   [49] Driver, *Samuel*, p. 182.

[50] It would seem that the linen *'ephod* does not denote a cultic garment, but a small loin cloth which one would expect a child to wear (1 Sam. 2:18), but which was unsuitable for an adult (2 Sam. 6:14).

[51] Burney, *Kings*, p. 22; Montgomery and Gehman, *Kings*, p. 100; Gray, *Kings*, p. 106.

But since the same word is used to describe two different objects, it is reasonable to suppose that there must be an inner connection between these two uses. This can be ascertained from the use of אפדה in Isa. 30:22, which indicates that the basic meaning of 'ephod is 'covering'. In the one case this is an actual garment, while in the other it appears to be an empty case, like a stiffened garment, which could be used in obtaining an oracle by means of inserting one's hand (1 Sam. 14:19). Probably the Urim or Thummim was drawn out (cf. 1 Sam. 14:41 f.).[52] Exod. 28:30 pictures these as being attached to the high priest's 'ephod, though the passage no longer envisages their practical use.[53] In contrast to the teraphim, it therefore seems unlikely that the 'ephod was worn. Indeed, when the oracle was consulted, it was probably thought that Yahweh was present within it.

With the general ban on divination (Deut. 18:10 ff.) the 'ephod was declared idolatrous (Judg. 8:27). After the exile the term is only applied to the vestment worn by the high priest.

[52] de Vaux, Ancient Israel, pp. 351 f. connects Prov. 16:33 with this consultation of the 'ephod.
[53] Ibid., p. 353; Noth, Exodus, p. 222.

CHAPTER SIX

THE INJUNCTION TO OBSERVE THE SABBATH[1]

(Exod. 20:8–11; Deut. 5:12–15)

(i) *The Pre-Exilic Legislation*

Both the so-called ritual Decalogue (Exod. 34:21a) and the Book of the Covenant (Exod. 23:12a) understand the commandment as an injunction to work for six days, but to desist on the seventh. But in both cases the verb תשבת could have been rendered 'You shall keep sabbath'. However, in view of the injunction to work on six days, it is clear that, in contrast, the seventh day must involve some cessation of labour. Almost identical words appear in the Decalogue (Exod. 20:9–10a; Deut. 5:13–14a), where the technical noun שבת ('sabbath') is used. It might be thought that the original commandment merely consisted of Exod. 20:8, there being no reference to work. But it has been recognized that the infinitive absolute זכור is not to be rendered as an imperative 'remember', but given gerundive force and translated 'remembering'.[2] Further, the use of זכור together with the definite article before 'sabbath' implies that reference is being made to an already existing institution of which there is no knowledge earlier than the Decalogue. Exod. 20:8 is therefore to be treated as a later introductory insertion. Since Exod. 20:9–10a; 23:12a and 34:21a can all be reduced to 'Six days you shall work,[3] but the seventh day sabbath', it would seem that this was the original commandment, being a short apodictic sentence comparable with the other commands of the Sinai Decalogue.[4]

---

[1] For recent surveys of the sabbath problem, cf. Meek, 'The Sabbath in the Old Testament', *JBL*, xxxiii, 1914, pp. 201–12; E. G. Kraeling, 'The Present State of the Sabbath Question', *AJSL*, xlix, 1932/3, pp. 218–28; G. J. Botterweck, 'Der Sabbat im Alten Testamente', *TQ*, cxxxiv, 1953, pp. 134–47, 448–57; de Vaux, *Ancient Israel*, pp. 475 ff.; Stamm, *TR*, N.F., xxvii, pp. 290 ff.; Stamm and Andrew, *The Ten Commandments*, pp. 90 ff.

[2] J. D. W. Watts, 'Infinitive Absolute as Imperative and the Interpretation of Exodus 20⁸', *ZAW*, N.F., xxxiii, 1962, p. 144.

[3] There would seem to be no material significance in the use of תעשה מעשיך instead of תעבד in Exod. 23:12. But see below, p. 69.

[4] Watts, op. cit., pp. 144 f.

Etymologically the origin of the sabbath has most commonly been sought from the Akkadian word *shabattu/shapattu*, which denoted the fifteenth day of the month, that is the division of the month, which was the day of the full moon. This was a propitious day on which the king sought to appease the gods, but there is no evidence that it was a day of cessation of work. In contrast the sabbath is consistently regarded as a weekly event, is celebrated regularly without reference to the moon or any lunar calendar, and initially was not a day of worship, but of rest from routine work. Nor can the Babylonian practice of regarding the seventh, fourteenth, nineteenth, twenty-first and twenty-eighth days as evil days resulting in some cessation of work as unprofitable provide the origin of the sabbath, for they are nowhere termed *shapattu*. Further the sabbath was a day of joy (Hos. 2:11).

The connection of the sabbath with the new moon (2 Kgs. 4:23; Isa. 1:13; 66:23; Hos. 2:13; Amos 8:5) proves nothing save that both were feast days.[5] The reason that they are placed together is that they alone constantly recurred throughout the year, whereas the other festivals were only celebrated once. Those who would connect the sabbath to a phase of the moon have to explain the abandonment of this connection and the introduction of the smooth seven day week. For this change the Old Testament supplies no evidence, but consistently regards the sabbath as celebrated every seven days.[6]

It has been held that שבת is to be connected with שבע ('seven'), and to be derived from an Akkadian dual form, possibly via שבתון.[7] The Akkadian form is, however, hypothetical, and שבתון would itself appear to be derived from שבת by the priestly writer.[8]

The old Testament understands the sabbath as a derivative of the verb שבת meaning 'cease', 'desist'. Since the noun שבת must have an

---

[5] It has been argued from Ps. 81:4 that as חדש ('new moon') appears to be contrasted with כסה ('full moon') then the latter must have been celebrated in Israel and in fact refers to the sabbath (Meek, *JBL*, xxxiii, p. 205). But the Psalm has generally been interpreted as referring to the feast of Tabernacles which began on the day of the full moon, 15th Tishri (Lev. 23:34), whereas the mention of the new moon refers to the beginning of the civil year on the 1st Tishri on which the horn was blown (Lev. 23:24) (E. J. Kissane, *The Book of the Psalms*, ii, Dublin, p. 54; de Vaux, *Ancient Israel*, p. 477). However, N. H. Snaith, *The Jewish New Year Festival: Its Origins and Development*, London, 1947, pp. 96 ff. argues that both words refer to the same day, חדש meaning 'full moon' in the pre-exilic period.

[6] Cf. J. Meinhold, 'Zur Sabbathfrage', *ZAW*, N.F., vii, 1930, pp. 121–38; Budde, 'Antwort auf Johannes Meinholds "Zur Sabbathfrage"', ibid., pp. 138–45; W. W. Cannon, 'The Weekly Sabbath', ibid., viii, 1931, pp. 325–7; Snaith, op. cit., pp. 111 ff.; de Vaux, op. cit., pp. 476 ff.; Stamm, *TR*, N.F., xxvii, pp. 290 ff.

[7] R. North, 'The Derivation of the Sabbath', *Bibl.*, xxxvi, 1955, pp. 195 ff.

[8] de Vaux, op. cit., p. 475.

active meaning, it has accordingly been suggested, and this would seem to be the most acceptable explanation of its meaning, that it is to be understood as the day which stops, that is divides or marks a limit.[9] This explains how it can be etymologically connected to the Akkadian *shabattu/shapattu* as the 'divider', and yet have no other resemblance to Babylonian practice.

Since it appears that the Sinai Decalogue itself instituted the sabbath as a distinct practice of the covenant people, there can be no objection to the positive formation of the fourth commandment, for whereas in the earlier commandments it was sufficient to prohibit a certain area of activity, in the case of the sabbath that area had first to be defined, namely the seventh day on which there must be a cessation of work. Thus to create the sabbath, the Sinai Decalogue had also to create the smooth seven day week. To have legislated 'You shall not do any work on the sabbath day', would therefore have been meaningless unless the sabbath was either already known as the regular seventh day, or was some other specific day. Of either of these contingencies there is no indication, nor of any other origin of the smooth seven day week. It is true that Exod. 16:4 f., 29 ff., which has been attributed to J and is therefore the oldest reference to the sabbath in the Old Testament,[10] records the existence of the sabbath prior to the giving of the Decalogue at Sinai. But the present position of this account which itself presupposes that the sabbath commandment had already been given, for otherwise Yahweh could not be said to 'test' Israel, is due to the P arrangement. The commandment cannot be excised from the Sinai Decalogue simply because of the lack of the negative.

The position of the commandment in the first half of the Decalogue indicates that it particularly concerns Israel's relations with Yahweh. It might be thought that the sabbath was designed to be a day of worship, but there is no evidence that in ancient Israel it ever had any cultic connection.[11] It was this lack of association with the sanctuaries or temple that enabled it to become so important for the exiles.

But why then was the sabbath created? By the first three commandments the Sinai Decalogue had established the exclusive covenant relationship with Yahweh, and ensured that he could not be manipu-

---

[9] Ibid., pp. 475 ff. Cf. S. Langdon, *Babylonian Menologies and the Semitic Calendar*, Schweich Lectures 1933, London, 1935, pp. 90 ff. It thus formed a natural day on which to change the guard (2 Kgs. 11:5 ff.).

[10] Noth, *Exodus*, pp. 132, 135 f. These verses confirm that the connection of the noun שבת with the verb שבת is older than P.

[11] Noth, *History*, p. 297, *Exodus*, p. 164; von Rad, *Theology*, i, p. 16. But cf. M. Jastrow, 'The Original Character of the Hebrew Sabbath', *AJT*, ii, 1898, pp. 318 ff.

lated by man for his own advantage. The fourth commandment was intended to drive home to Israel her special position, namely that she existed solely through the free act of Yahweh, upon whom she was utterly dependent. What could be more effective in achieving this than a unique law on work and leisure, which only the covenant clans would possess by virtue of the covenant itself? But the choice of a 'stopping' day to fulfil this function can only be understood in relation to the clans' slavery in Egypt where there would have been no break in daily routine work. It was in direct contrast to this that the Decalogue provided for Israel a day of rest, which was not intended to be a day of total inactivity, but of release from the drudgery of man's daily occupational work. Thus the sabbath indicated Israel's national freedom from subjugation in Egypt, which became known as the בית עבדים ('the house of slavery').[12] It was as free men who could regulate their own worl 'ng life that those who gathered at Sinai voluntarily entered into the covenant relationship thereby binding themselves as vassals not to a temporal power, but to Yahweh. Exodus and covenant cannot be divorced. There is therefore no suggestion of a *restitutio in integrum* ('a return to an original state'),[13] but instead the sabbath constitutes an exceptional and unique break in man's normal condition of endless toil. Consequently it was a day of joy. It is surprising that the benefits arising from such a regular ordering of labour have received such little attention.[14] Only an advanced social programme could so regulate its affairs. It was, however, only male occupational work which was prohibited, for the Decalogue was only addressed to adult male Israelites, though it would have been understood that women and children were forbidden to undertake their tasks for them. But as can be deduced from the priestly legislation, the commandment did not extend to the domestic sphere.[15]

The reason for the choice of the *seventh* and not some other day cannot be established with certainty. The most probable explanation is that this number had already acquired a sacred and symbolic character throughout the ancient Near East, which is evidenced from

---

[12] The plural noun עבדים should most probably be understood in a singular abstract sense (cf. G. R. Driver, 'Problems in the Hebrew Text of Proverbs', *Bibl.*, xxxii, 1951, p. 196).

[13] As argued by Noth, *Exodus*, pp. 189 f. On p. 75 it is argued that there is no direct connection between the sabbath provision in Exod. 23:12 and that on the fallowing of the land in Exod. 23:10 f. They are placed together in Exod. 23 because both are part of the provisions which set out an Israelite's positive duties to Yahweh. See below, p. 159.

[14] Cf. B. Jacob, 'The Decalogue', *JQR*, N.S., xiv, 1923/4, pp. 161 ff.

[15] See below, pp. 71 f.

the use elsewhere of seven day periods, though not of a regular seven day week.[16]

Reference has already been made to the appearance of the sabbath commandment in the so-called ritual Decalogue (Exod. 34:21) and the Book of the Covenant (Exod. 23:12). By specifically mentioning ploughing and harvesting, Exod. 34:21 seeks to emphasize that even in the busiest times of the year, the sabbath was to be kept.[17]

Exod. 23:12 enacts that the commandment should apply to working animals, slaves (for the son of a female slave must include all slaves by implication), and the resident alien (גר). This expansion reflects the current social conditions at the time the Book of the Covenant was issued, for neither slaves nor the גר would have been present at Kadesh. The reason for this enactment was not a love of working animals or persons who had not got the status of free Israelite citizens, and therefore were not subject to criminal liability, but to ensure that there should be no loophole in the existing criminal law. Thus just as the original commandment prevented the male Israelite from engaging in his regular occupational work on the sabbath, and by implication his family, so the expansion ensured that animals and persons whom he might command or ask might not do his work for him. Thus where an Israelite was engaged in agriculture, all agricultural work whether undertaken personally by the Israelite himself, or by his slaves or animals must cease. In addition, those who had taken up residence in Israel were not to be exploited. But the legislation only ensured for the animals and servants rest from helping their master in his occupational work. This is the significance of נוח, which indicates rest from the weariness and trouble of daily toil, rather than cessation of work, inactivity.[18] That neither animals nor servants were entitled to this on the sabbath is confirmed from 2 Kgs. 4:22 ff., which indicates the annoyance of the husband that one of his beasts and a servant must be released from aiding him in his weekday work for his wife's sudden journey. Normally this would have been undertaken on the sabbath.

It would seem from the same hortatory style that the present form of Exod. 20:8–10 is also the work of the author who expanded the second and third commandments. His purpose in inserting the introduction (Exod. 20:8) was to stress that though the sabbath was not a day of worship, it had been created by Yahweh, and not the state,

---

[16] Snaith, *Jewish New Year Festival*, pp. 115 f.; de Vaux, *Ancient Israel*, p. 187.

[17] Cf. Meinhold, *ZAW*, N.F., vii, pp. 131 f.; Budde, ibid., p. 143; Noth, *Exodus*, p. 264.

[18] G. R. Berry, 'The Hebrew Word נּוּחַ', *JBL*, l, 1931, p. 209.

whose maintenance in part depended on its observance.[19] It was therefore not a secular holiday to be enjoyed in licentious behaviour more fitting to the cult of Baal (cf. Hos. 2:11), but a day to be treated with reverence as befitted its origin as the sign of the covenant relationship with Yahweh, Israel's God (Exod. 20:10). Thus the emphasis of the introductory phrase falls on לקדשׁו ('to keep it holy'), השׁבת being a *casus pendens*.[20]

Those who are to obey the sabbath commandment are now set out in broad classes. In effect this is only a fuller version of Exod. 23:12. Wives are omitted to avoid any ambiguity that the law applied to domestic activity as well. The reason the author felt it necessary to make the commandment as explicitly comprehensive as Exod. 23:12 will be adduced later.[21] It is probably this aim that also explains the addition of ועשׁית כל־מלאכתך ('and do all your work'), since Exod. 23:12 reads תעשׂה מעשׂיך. By this phrase the author was able to stress that it was every type of occupational work which was to cease on the sabbath including commercial undertakings. It was to the merchant class in particular that the sabbath became such an unnecessary incumbrance, for it deprived them of the opportunity of trading on a day on which their fellow citizens were on holiday (Amos 8:5).

The Deuteronomic version of the sabbath commandment not only supplies a reason for its observance, but also strengthens the introduction by both substituting שׁמור ('being careful') for the more neutral זכור ('remembering'), and adding the phrase כאשׁר צוך יהוה אלהיך ('as the Lord your God commanded you'). The ox and the ass are included in the list of those who are to have rest. The reason for the commandment now specifically connects it both with Israel's origin as slaves in Egypt, and with her deliverance through Yahweh's intervention. But it has already been recognized that the sabbath cannot be understood except in relation to Israel's slavery in Egypt. In that respect the explanation was only enunciating what had always been understood.

But as a recent study has indicated[22] both the introduction of the exodus at this point, and the use of catch phrases from the beginning and end of the Decalogue, are designed to raise the sabbath commandment to a place of central importance. Just as the exodus had been used in Exod. 20 to stress the principal commandment, the

---

[19] Consequently there seems no reason for denying Jer. 17:19 ff. to the prophet, though the precise situation against which he spoke cannot be known (Barnes, 'Prophecy and the Sabbath', *JTS*, xxix, 1927/8, pp. 386–90).
[20] Meek, *JAOS*, lviii, p. 123.   [21] See below, p. 179.
[22] N. J. Lohfink, 'Zur Dekalogfassung von Dt 5', *BZ*, N.F., ix, 1965, pp. 17–32.

first commandment, so now it is again used for the same purpose in the Deuteronomic version. The sabbath commandment has become *the* commandment of the Decalogue. This emphasis is not to be attributed to the author of the original book of Deuteronomy, for this collection of laws shows a total lack of interest in the sabbath. Since its preoccupation was with the central sanctuary, it was only concerned with days of worship. Rather this heightening of the commandment must reflect the exilic situation, when with the temple destroyed, and the land occupied, Israel was to be encouraged to keep the distinctive 'covenant' day. Since in all probability the Decalogue did not form part of the original introduction to the Deuteronomic laws, it would seem that this Deuteronomic version of the sabbath commandment was the work of the author of the Deuteronomic historical work, Deuteronomy—2 Kings.[23]

Even though the Deuteronomist made women equal members of the covenant community with men, and therefore understood the Decalogue to have been addressed to both sexes, his laws indicate that there was no attempt to extend the scope of the commandment to include domestic activity. This was to be the task of the priestly legislator.

(ii) *The Post-Exilic Legislation*

Following the fall of Jerusalem with the destruction of the temple, the exile in Babylon involved a return to what were in effect the conditions of Sinai, namely the isolation of Israel among foreign people. Hence the absence of idols and sabbath observance, to which was now added the rite of circumcision, became for the exiles the visible distinguishing marks of true Israelites, and separated them from their conquerors. Through hallowing these practices, the former covenant community could remain bound together, and hope of restoration kept alive. This accounts for the stress of the sabbath in Ezekiel (20:12 ff.; 22:8, 26; 23:38).

When the priestly legislation as a whole is considered it will be shown that, in contrast to the Deuteronomic school, for the priestly legislator the Mosaic covenant was seen to have been irrevocably broken by the events of 586 B.C.[24] He made no attempt to return to this concept, but instead understood Israel's relation with Yahweh solely as a matter of divine grace through which Yahweh had elected Israel as his chosen people. The God-man relationship was to be maintained not by obedience to a code of laws, but through the cult.

[23] See below, p. 181.   [24] See below, pp. 183 ff.

Both circumcision and sabbath were used by the priestly writer to establish this doctrine of election by which the Mosaic covenant concept was replaced. Thus, while he connected circumcision to the election of Abraham (Gen. 17), he made the sabbath the climax of his creation narrative by imposing it on what was formerly an eight day creation scheme (Gen. 1–2:4a; Exod. 20:11).[25] To emphasize that the sabbath was the culmination of creation itself, inconsistently he noted that it was on the seventh day that Yahweh completed his work.[26] Thus for P, the sabbath, once a sign of the Mosaic covenant (and still so in the D-work), now became a sign that in the very creation of the world Yahweh had designated Israel his elect people, for they alone were the people of the sabbath (Exod. 31:12 ff.).

The reference to קדשׁ ('set apart', 'keep holy') in Exod. 20:8 and 11 has been held to indicate that both verses must belong to the same expansion.[27] But in fact Exod. 20:11 is intended to explain the reason why the sabbath was *already* regarded as holy. This accounts for the fact that Exod. 20:11 forms a better unity with Exod. 20:8 ff. than the Deuteronomic explanation, which would never have been inserted had the sabbath been earlier connected with creation. The P explanation is to be attributed to the distinctive priestly theology of election.[28]

In order to make the sabbath known to man for the first time, P utilized the J tradition that the giving of *manna* conformed with the sabbath commandment (Exod. 16:4 f., 29 ff.). But it has already been noted that it cannot be assumed from Exod. 16 that the sabbath was practised by Israel prior to the disclosure of the Sinai legislation, for Exod. 16:4 f. (J) itself presupposes the existence of that legislation. The position of Exod. 16 is due to P's desire to begin his account of the wilderness period by stressing sabbath observance.[29] Neh. 9:14 records that the sabbath was unknown to the patriarchs.

Whereas in pre-exilic Israel only male occupational work was prohibited, under the priestly legislation sabbath observance, to which

---

[25] W. H. Schmidt, *Die Schöpfungsgeschichte der Priesterschrift*, WMANT, xvii, 1964, pp. 69 ff., 156 f. It has been suggested that the idea of Yahweh resting was inherent in the original creation account, but referred not to rest from work, but from the conflict with chaos (Jastrow, *AJT*, ii, pp. 343 ff.; Berry, *JBL*, l, pp. 207 ff.).

[26] The Versions dogmatically correct this to the sixth day. The statement that Yahweh completed his work of creation on the sabbath of creation was regarded as a contradiction of the sabbath commandment itself (Schmidt, op. cit., p. 156).

[27] Nielsen, *The Ten Commandments*, pp. 39 ff.

[28] 4 QDeut[n] adds the priestly reference to creation after Deut. 5:15 (F. M. Cross, *Scrolls from the Wilderness of the Dead Sea* (Catalogue), Norwich, 1965, pp. 31 f.).

[29] Noth, *Exodus*, pp. 131 ff.

F

both men and women were subject,[30] was extended to the domestic field. Thus Exod. 35:3 prohibits domestic fires, and Num. 15:32 ff., which is intended to be a new criminal law precedent being deliberately set in the Mosaic period,[31] condemns to death the man who gathers firewood on the sabbath. Exod. 16:23 also implies that cooking is not to be undertaken on this day.[32] But there is no indication that the sabbath thereby became a day of total inactivity: it was still only routine daily work, whether performed by man or woman, which was prohibited.

These passages, together with the reference to Kaiwan in Amos 5:26, have, however, given rise to the Kenite theory of the origin of the sabbath.[33] It is argued that the prohibition of fire would have amounted to a general prohibition of all work for this tribe of smiths, and that Kaiwan is to be identified with Saturn, the dark planet, hostile to fire. Israel is alleged to have taken over this prohibition, and since her work was not limited to acting as smiths, to have extended it to a prohibition of all labour. But it would seem that however one is to interpret Amos 5:26,[34] this observation in the eighth century can tell one nothing about the worship of the Kenites five hundred years earlier. Exod. 35:3 refers to domestic and not industrial fires, both Exod. 35:3 and Num. 15:32 ff., like Exod. 16:23, being the work of the priestly legislator. Further, there is no evidence that the Kenites worshipped Saturn, nor that they knew of a seven day week.

Only in P is the penalty for breach of the commandment specified (Exod. 31:14 f.; 35:2), but as part of the criminal law, this would from the first have been death by communal stoning. However, as has already been recognized, the priestly legislation substituted excommunication for execution.[35] Thus Exod. 31:14 f., which probably

---

[30] Since the wife was already understood to be subject to the commandment through the Deuteronomist's inclusion of women in the covenant community, the priestly legislator did not attempt to extend the list in Exod. 20:10 to include her.

[31] Weingreen, 'The Case of the Woodgatherer (Numbers xv. 32-6)', VT, xvi, 1966, pp. 361 ff. But there would seem no need to interpret this as a case of intent to commit a crime, which receives the same penalty as the crime itself. The gathering of the firewood is itself judged a breach of the commandment, the point at issue being whether or not this extends to the domestic sphere. Cf. my short note 'The Case of the Woodgatherer Reconsidered', VT, xix, 1969, pp. 125-8.

[32] Botterweck, TQ, cxxxiv, p. 143; Peake's Commentary, p. 239a.

[33] B. D. Eerdmans, 'Der Sabbath', Marti-Festschrift, BZAW, xli, 1925, pp. 79-83; Budde, 'The Sabbath and the Week', JTS, xxx, 1928/9, pp. 10 ff. Cf. Meinhold, ZAW, N.F., vii, pp. 134 ff.; Budde, ibid., pp. 144 f.

[34] Cf. the recent study of Gevirtz, 'A New Look at an Old Crux: Amos 5:26', JBL, lxxxvii, 1968, pp. 267-76.

[35] See above, pp. 28 ff.

belonged to the Holiness Code,[36] contains both the old penalty of death and the new one of excommunication. Further, the sabbath law precedent of Num. 15:32 ff. must be understood as an illustration of what constitutes 'sin with a high hand' (Num. 15:30), for which excommunication was prescribed.[37] Execution is only mentioned in the precedent itself because it is set in the Mosaic period.[38]

It would seem that as a result of the exile the sabbath became associated with worship, for whereas prior to the exile it had no connection with the cult, in both Lev. 23:3 and Num. 28:9 f. it now heads priestly regulations on the feasts. Denied the temple and its cult, the exiles must have used the sabbath as a day on which to congregate for communal lamentation, reading of the law and instruction, and hearing the prophets. It would seem that gradually this became a matter of regular occurrence, and it is probable that from these gatherings the synagogue developed.[39]

Sabbath observance continued to be enforced in the post-exilic period (Neh. 10:32; 13:15 ff.) until in the time of the Maccabees it even included refusal to practice self-defence (1 Macc. 2:34 ff.).

Excursus

The Sabbatical Year

The only possible references to the sabbatical year in the Book of the Covenant are to the release of male Hebrew slaves in the seventh year (Exod. 21:2 ff.), and the release of the land every seventh year (Exod. 23:10 f.).

Exod. 21:2 ff. enacts that a Hebrew male slave shall serve a term of six years, and 'in the seventh year' must be released, but makes no reference to a universal year of release.[40] Female slaves are not given their freedom (Exod. 21:7).[41] But the legislation offers no explanation as to why it only applies to male slaves, why these must be Hebrews, why the term should be six years, and precisely when in the seventh year the slave should be released. The reason for this is to be found in Deut. 31:10 f. which describes the seventh year as a year of release,

---

[36] Elliott-Binns, *ZAW*, N.F., xxvi, p. 27.
[37] Gray, *Numbers*, p. 182.   [38] Cf. the discussion of Lev. 24:10 ff. on p. 56.
[39] There is, however, no evidence of such a building until the third century (Bright, *A History of Israel*, London, 1960, pp. 422 f.).
[40] Morgenstern, *HUCA*, vii, p. 40.
[41] Exod. 21:8 ff. contains special regulations should the former slave girl be given in marriage.

and provides for a festival at which the law was to be recited. Although this enactment now appears in the book of Deuteronomy, it would appear to reflect very ancient practice, and to refer to a covenant renewal festival originally held at the central amphictyonic shrine.[42] Since a Hebrew male slave would have lost his status as a member of the covenant community, if he was to be able to take part in the covenant ceremony, then there must have been some provision which compulsorily ensured his release. This was the measure which lies behind Exod. 21:2, which evidently provided for the release of Hebrew male slaves at the end of every seventh year in order that they might be able to take part in the covenant renewal festival. The freeing of female slaves was not contemplated because women had no part in the covenant relationship.

But with the destruction of the amphictyonic central shrine at Shiloh, the seven year covenant festival evidently ceased to be celebrated, and it would seem that with the institution of the monarchy the recitation of the Decalogue was transferred to the annual royal festival at Jerusalem (Pss. 50; 81). Even with the inauguration of the northern kingdom, Jeroboam made no attempt to return to the seven year covenant festival, but instituted a rival annual autumnal festival to that in Jerusalem. Thus the necessity for a fixed year of release of Hebrew male slaves lapsed, and instead the legislation merely enacted that this should be after a period of six years service, no matter when this might terminate, but did not specify an exact date. Sometime in the seventh year would satisfy the law. Thus Exod. 21:2 secularizes what was once a compulsory religious obligation. Obviously this provision has a very important significance for the dating of the Book of the Covenant.[43]

It would therefore appear that before the abandonment of the seven year covenant festival permanent slavery of a fellow male Hebrew could not have occured.[44] It thus follows that the ceremony for making slavery permanent (Exod. 21:5 f.) has been specifically devised to meet a new situation. The expression 'to אלהים' in Exod. 21:6 does not indicate that this ceremony took place in the sanctuary, for no oath was required (cf. Exod. 22:7 ff.), but refers to the master's household gods or *teraphim*. It has already been argued that *teraphim* and אלהים can be interchangeable terms (Gen. 31), and are to be equated

[42] Cf. Alt, *Essays*, pp. 126 ff. and above, pp. 7 f.

[43] See below, pp. 159 f.

[44] Cf. CH, 117–19 (ANET, pp. 170 f.). Section 117, in contrast to Section 118, provides that free citizens cannot become permanent slaves (Meek, 'A New Interpretation of the Code of Hammurabi, § 117–119', *JNES*, vii, 1948, pp. 180–3).

with the *ilāni* of the Nuzu texts.[45] These texts similarly show the existence of both sanctuary and household *ilāni*, the former being concerned with communal law, the latter with family law, which in Israel was never a matter for the courts.[46] Thus the expressions 'to אלהים' and 'to the door or doorpost' refer to the same procedure, the latter possibly being a later insertion to explain the former.[47] The ceremony signified that the slave was now part of his master's permanent property, and, together with the household gods before whom it was performed, would comprise part of the inheritance of his estate. Thus there was no religious content to this procedure.[48]

Exod. 23:10 f. enacts that the land should be left fallow every seven years, but gives no direct indication whether or not this year was to be observed simultaneously throughout Israel. The fact that this provision is placed alongside the sabbath commandment might suggest that like the sabbath it was of universal application. However, since the social reason for this enactment seems to envisage the permanent sustenance of the poor and wild beasts,[49] one must conclude that there was always land lying fallow.[50] Further, no attempt has been made to connect this provision with the sabbath commandment, nor is the verb שבת ('cease', 'desist') used. Had there been a point of contact, it would certainly have been drawn out as in Lev. 25:1 ff.

But the social reason given for this enactment cannot have been its original purpose. Nor can this be found in the idea of protecting the fertility of the ground, thereby ensuring staple production. The use of a seven year period, and the specific reference to 'release' (שמט) undoubtedly connect it to the ancient year of release associated with the seven year covenant festival at the central amphictyonic shrine (Deut. 31:10 f.). While it is possible that this provision merely sought to facilitate the release of slaves who would otherwise have been engaged in agriculture, it is perhaps more probable that it was a deliberate attempt to recall Israel to her origins by re-enacting the

<hr/>

[45] See above, pp. 60 f. Cf. Gordon, *JBL*, liv, pp. 139 ff. and Draffkorn, ibid., lxxvi, pp. 216 ff. with Fensham, 'New Light on Exodus 21⁶ and 22⁷ from the Laws of Eshnunna', ibid., lxxviii, 1959, pp. 160 f. and O. Loretz, 'Ex. 21, 6; 22, 8 und angebliche Nuzi-Parallelen', *Bibl.*, xli, 1960, pp. 167 ff. LE 37 is discussed on p. 137, n. 42 in the chapter on theft.

[46] Cf. the discussion on divorce on p. 111, n. 7.

[47] Morgenstern, *HUCA*, vii, pp. 38 ff.; Noth, *Exodus*, p. 178. But cf. M. David, 'The Manumission of Slaves under Zedekiah', *OTS*, v, 1948, pp. 66 f.

[48] *Contra* Falk, 'Ex. xxi. 6', *VT*, ix, 1959, pp. 86–8.

[49] The poor would have been those without land. Slaves and domestic animals would have been cared for by their owners.

[50] Cf. Morgenstern, op. cit., p. 40.

conditions of the exodus in which Yahweh himself fed his people, and which culminated in the arrival at Sinai and the making of the covenant. But whichever is the case, it would again appear that the law has been secularized, and what was once a universal year of fallowing has become a method of crop rotation, whereby once in every seven years land should be left uncultivated.

An examination of Deut. 15 seems to indicate that the Deuteronomist deliberately sought to restore the connection of the release of slaves with the ancient seven year covenant festival. Although the legislation about this festival now appears in the framework to the laws (Deut. 31:10 f.), the use there of the second person singular indicates that this enactment once formed part of the Deuteronomic legislation itself (Deut. 12–26), and has been subsequently used to form the conclusion to the book as it now appears.[51]

In the first place the Deuteronomist specifically extended the legislation contained in Exod. 21:2 ff. to include the release of a Hebrew female slave (Deut. 15:12 ff.), in accordance with his view that women were to be regarded as equal members of the covenant community with men.

Secondly, the addition of Deut. 15:1 ff. clearly shows that he sought to reconstitute a fixed year of release, which would occur at the end of every seven years. That Deut. 15:1 ff. is in fact an extension of the law of the release of slaves can be recognized by the stress that it is only the debts of fellow members of the covenant community which are to be released, and not those of foreigners. The reason for this extension was that debt was the chief cause of slavery in Israel (2 Kgs. 4:1 f.; Isa. 50:1; Neh. 5:5).[52] Thus the Deuteronomic extension provided that even if the creditor withheld enslaving the debtor prior to the year of release, he was to be given no opportunity for doing so afterwards.

That Deut. 15:12 ff. is to be understood in the light of Deut. 15:1 ff. is confirmed from Jer. 34:14, where it is expressly stated that it is only at the end of seven years that the Hebrew slave is to be set

---

[51] On the use of the second singular and plural persons in the book of Deuteronomy, cf. G. Minette de Tillesse, 'Sections "tu" et sections "vous" dans le Deutéronome', *VT*, xii, 1962, pp. 29–88, and see further below, pp. 181 f. G. Widengren, 'King and Covenant', *JSS*, ii, 1957, pp. 12 ff. argues that this commandment is to be understood as addressed to the ruler in Israel.

[52] See above, pp. 16 f. Elsewhere in the ancient Near East debt leading to slavery usually resulted from the exorbitant rates of interest charged on loans, but in Israel it was forbidden to charge interest to fellow members of the covenant community (Exod. 22:24; Deut. 23:20 f.; Lev. 25:35 ff.), but not foreigners (Deut. 23:21). Cf. Neh. 5:7.

free, and not, as in Exod. 21:2, during the seventh year of his enslavement.[53]

Thus the Deuteronomist recovered the old basis of the law of the release of slaves, namely that all Hebrews should be able to take part in the seven year covenant festival, which for him included women as well as men. But permanent slavery was not abolished, and the slave could still surrender his or her right to freedom (Deut. 15:16 ff.). In addition the Deuteronomist introduced certain humanitarian reforms to the legislation contained in Exod. 21:2 ff. This had actively discouraged the release of slaves, for if they were married after their enslavement, their wives and children remained their respective masters' property (Exod. 21:4), and in any event no financial provision was made for them on their release. Provided a slave felt well treated, there was no point in exchanging security without freedom for freedom without security. To counteract this, the Deuteronomist enacted that the released slave should be provided with certain provisions with which he could start a new life (Deut. 15:13 f.). In addition, his failure to refer to the slave's wife and children (cf. Exod. 21:5 with Deut. 15:16), indicates that he intended to repeal Exod. 21:4.

Naturally in Deut. 15:17 no reference is made to the household gods, *teraphim*, whether sanctuary or household, having become illegal in the Deuteronomic reform (2 Kgs. 23:24).

However, the Deuteronomist makes no mention of any regulation for letting the land lie fallow, whether or not in a universal year. It would therefore seem that even Exod. 23:10 f. had lapsed, Deut. 24:19 ff. perhaps being intended as a substitute law providing harvest for the poor. Thus it would seem that the release of debts in Deut. 15:1 ff. is not to be associated with a fixed fallow year, and explained as necessary legislation to prevent the landowner, who in such a year would have been deprived of his normal source of income, from enforcing payment of debts owed to him. Further, it is due to this false connection with Exod. 23:10 f. that Deut. 15:1 ff. is held to imply mere suspension of debts, rather than total remission, both the landowner and the creditor being held to surrender their rights for one year. The intention of the legislator in Deut. 15:1 ff. is clear. Like the

---

[53] The LXX's substitution of six years is an attempt to smooth over this discrepancy. It would appear that the release of slaves in Zedekiah's reign was an exceptional act caused by a political emergency rather than a desire to observe the Deuteronomic law. Indeed, verses 13b f. seem to have been subsequently inserted into the narrative (*Peake's Commentary*, p. 557b). Jeremiah complains that a particular covenant (verse 15) has been broken (verse 18), which will result in the implementation of the covenant oath. But cf. David, *OTS*, v, pp. 74 f.

slaves themselves, the debts which cause slavery shall be remitted entirely. Deut. 15:7 ff. would have been unnecessary if in the eighth year the creditor could have enslaved the debtor for a loan made in the sixth year. Such a loan is in fact to be regarded as a gift.

As part of the emphasis on sabbath observance, the priestly legislator created the sabbatical year by reinstituting Exod. 23:10 f. as a fixed universal year of fallowing throughout Israel (Lev. 25:1 ff.), and specifically connecting it to the sabbath concept by creating the term שנת שבתון ('the sabbatical year'). שבתון itself is only found in P, and therefore must be regarded as a derivative of שבת. The social reason for this practice was abandoned, the provision being no longer applicable for the regular sustenance of the poor and wild beasts. Perhaps Lev. 19:9 f.; 23:22, like Deut. 24:19 ff., were intended as substitute measures. The produce of the sabbatical year was to be common property (Lev. 25:6 f.).

That the priestly legislator was able to turn the seventh year into a new institution was due to his rejection of the Mosaic covenant concept in favour of the doctrine of election. This resulted in the abolition of the year of release specifically connected with the seven year covenant festival, and left both the release of debts and slaves without a motive.

The release of debts appears to have been attached to the sabbatical year, for Neh. 10:32, which apparently refers to the post-exilic sabbatical year provision of foregoing the crops, in addition notes that debts will not be exacted. There is, however, no indication that slaves were also released in the sabbatical year. Since there was no covenant festival for which their liberty from the status of slavery was required in order that they might take part in it such a provision was unnecessary. Nor is there any indication that Exod. 21:2 ff. was enforced, that is that the term of slavery was limited to six years, no matter when that should terminate. Instead, the priestly legislator instituted the Jubilee year, apparently in the fiftieth year (Lev. 25:10), itself based on the sabbatical year principle, in which both land and slaves were to be released (Lev. 25:8 ff.). Lev. 25:39 ff. cannot be harmonized with the earlier legislation on release of slaves, and indicates that this was repealed.[54] But though there is evidence of the sabbatical year in Neh. 10:32, and 1 Macc. 6:49, 53, there is no indication that the

[54] Driver, *Deuteronomy*, p. 185. It would seem that Exod. 21:2 ff.; Deut. 15:12 ff.; and Lev. 25:39 ff. make no distinction between those who enter into their slavery voluntarily, and those who are seized as defaulting debtors (cf. Mendelsohn, *Slavery*, pp. 18 f., 89 ff.). Neh. 5:1 ff. recounts a special act of general release, but tells one nothing about the law, save that interest should not have been exacted.

Jubilee year was ever celebrated, and it would seem probable that the legislation inaugurating it was in fact an idealistic conception, which was never put into practice.[55]

To sum up, the sabbatical year, unlike the sabbath itself, was the creation of the priestly legislator, though it would seem that a similar institution was practised in connection with the seven year covenant festival at the central amphictyonic shrine, for which all Hebrew male slaves had to be released, and which was preceded by a universal year of fallowing.

[55] de Vaux, *Ancient Israel*, pp. 175 ff.

CHAPTER SEVEN

THE INJUNCTION TO HONOUR ONE'S PARENTS

(Exod. 20:12; Deut. 5:16)

Like the sabbath commandment, the fifth commandment is also in a positive form which there appears to be no very good reason to reject. Since it has been shown that the original fourth commandment had of necessity to be in a positive form, there is no reason at all why other commandments should not also have been framed in the same way. But care must be taken in the rendering of כבד by 'honour'. This not only implies acknowledgement of someone, but also submission to his authority (1 Sam. 15:30; Ps. 86:9). This explains why the negative form of the commandment uses the Pi'ēl of the verb קלל, which does not simply mean 'curse', but carries the wider meaning of 'repudiate'.[1] Thus Exod. 21:17 is not to be restricted to verbal repudiation, but is to be understood quite generally.

Both the Book of the Covenant and Deuteronomy provide examples of the sort of action which would constitute breach of this commandment. Exod. 21:15 enacts that anyone who strikes either parent is to be executed. Now when the sixth commandment is discussed, it will be shown that assault was only a tort for which a civil action for damages would be brought by the injured party. Death had to occur before the tort could become the crime of murder.[2] But the person who infringes Exod. 21:15 is not executed for assault, but for breach of the fifth commandment. The act of striking a parent is understood as incontrovertible proof of repudiation of parental authority. This is made clear by Exod. 21:17, which in the LXX precedes the MT's enactment on manstealing (Exod. 21:16).

In Deut. 21:18 ff. parents of a 'stubborn and rebellious' son, who, in spite of chastisement, continually repudiates their authority, bring their son before the elders and prosecute him for breach of the fifth commandment. The particular facts of the case are that he is a 'glutton

---

[1] See above, pp. 41 f. Cf. Brichto, *The Problem of 'Curse'*, pp. 132 ff.
[2] See below, pp. 86 ff.

and a drunkard' (Prov. 23:19 ff.; 28:7), but this is only an example of the kind of evidence which might be adduced to secure conviction.[3] The commandment has commonly been given a social explanation, for it undoubtedly ensured that parents need never fear old age, and the possibility of expulsion from the home leading to enforced suicide.[4] Further, children would see to the burial of their parents, for this was a duty of a kinsman (Amos 6:10). But the results of the commandment must not be confused with its original purpose. While it ensured a unity and authority among the Hebrew family, which is in sharp contrast to the situation encountered among the Arabs renowned for their individualism and the ineffectuality of parental authority,[5] this was not the reason for its enactment. Rather, like the other first five commandments, its concern was with relations with Yahweh, for its aim was to secure that sons would automatically maintain the faith of their parents.[6] Once a man entered into the covenant relationship, then his children would be born into that relationship, and were to have no opportunity of repudiating it. One could never contract out of Yahwism. To do so amounted to a breach of the criminal law, to which one was automatically subject, and so led to execution.

But, as the two precedents in Exod. 21:15 and Deut. 21:18 ff. indicate, it was the social results of the commandment which came to be stressed, rather than its original purpose of maintaining the ancestral religion. This was due to the establishment of Yahwism as state religion under David. Since the constitution of the state itself was founded on Yahweh's election of both David and of Mount Zion, Yahwism was ensured as the religion of future generations. Thus the emphasis of the commandment was altered to secure filial obedience in general, and was extended from the more serious acts of disobedience (Exod. 21:15)[7] to include any conduct which parents thought improper (Deut. 21:18 ff.).[8]

It was, of course, a corollary to this commandment that parents were prohibited from taking the law into their own hands. By making parental repudiation a criminal offence, it became subject to the procedure of the criminal law court, and was therefore the concern of the

---

[3] Driver, *Deuteronomy*, pp. 247 f.
[4] Stamm and Andrew, *The Ten Commandments*, pp. 95 f.
[5] Robertson Smith, *Kinship and Marriage*, p. 68.
[6] R. H. Kennett, *Deuteronomy and the Decalogue*, Cambridge, 1920, pp. 66 f.
[7] This is further evidence for assessing the date of the Book of the Covenant (see below, p. 160).
[8] Cf. Mal 1:6; 3:17 where the relationship between father and son can be likened to that between master and servant.

community rather than the individual parents. These acted as chief witnesses, but it was for the court to decide whether the accused was guilty, and capital punishment should be exacted. Thus while the commandment had a social value in respect of parents in their old age, it also acted as a protection to the children.[9]

Since women were not members of the covenant community, it may seem surprising that the mother was given equal status with the father. But it has earlier been recognized that initially marriage would have been with another member of the clan, and so with a daughter of a member of the covenant community.[10] Both parents took part in the instruction of their son (Prov. 1:8; 6:20).

That originally sons only were addressed by the commandment follows from the fact that daughters could not enter into the covenant relationship. Further, these sons are not minors, but represent the younger adult members of society capable of committing any of the crimes set out in the Sinai Decalogue.

The present form of the commandment is due to the fact that it has attracted the same sort of hortatory addition which has been encountered earlier, and which is itself expanded in the Deuteronomic version.[11] Alternative forms of both its positive and negative formulations are found elsewhere in the Old Testament. Thus in Lev. 19:3 ירא meaning 'revere' is used, while in contrast to Ezek. 22:7 and Lev. 20:9, Deut. 27:16 relies on קלה meaning 'despise'. Since both these words are concerned with the acknowledgement of authority, their use adds nothing to this discussion.

CH 195[12] provides that a son who assaults his father shall have his hand cut off, the punishment being made to fit the crime. Thus in Babylon such an assault was not as severely punished as in Israel (Exod. 21:15). This is due to the fact that in Israel such action was interpreted as a crime, and therefore demanded the exaction of the death penalty in order to propitiate Yahweh. It is Israel's fully developed concept of crime based on the covenant relationship with Yahweh that differentiates her laws from those of other ancient Near Eastern countries.[13]

---

[9] Gen. 38:24 is discussed on p. 129.   [10] See above, p. 15.

[11] Lohfink, BZ, N.F., ix, pp. 30 f. argues that the phrase ולמען ייטב לך ('and that it may go well with you'), like the explanation to the fourth commandment, reflects the exilic situation.   [12] ANET, p. 175.

[13] CH 192–3 should not be compared with the fifth commandment for these sections do not concern the repudiation of natural parents, but the wrongful breach of an adoptive tie. It is possible that the purpose of this adoption was to ensure that the adopted son would be responsible for the funerary rites of his foster-parent (Brichto, The Problem of 'Curse', p. 133)

CHAPTER EIGHT

THE PROHIBITION OF MURDER

(Exod. 20:13; Deut. 5:17)

(i) *The Crime of Murder*

The verb selected to describe the crime prohibited by the sixth commandment[1] is רצח ('kill'), which is either used absolutely, or with a person as object, but never of an animal. Indeed, in spite of a recent attempt to extend the commandment to any killing,[2] the Book of the Covenant conclusively shows that to cause the death of an animal was a tort, for which damages were prescribed (Exod. 21:33 ff.). Thus there can be no doubt that man is the unexpressed object of the commandment. Further, the verb should not be given an intensive meaning and understood to denote a violent act, for its predominant use is in the Qal rather than the Pi'ēl. It simply means 'kill' and does not denote the method adopted. The significance of רצח is not that it defines a particular illegal act, but that in distinction from other words for killing, it indicates where the killing takes place, namely within the covenant community.[3] While it can therefore be used as a parallel to הרג (Ps. 94:6) and קטל (Job 24:14) where those verbs are used of Israelites, it can never be used to describe death in war, for even if this was civil war between members of the covenant community, the declaration of war would sever the covenant relationship. Further since רצח merely denotes a killing within the community it is not to be confined to the crime of murder, but also includes unpremeditated killing,[4] and may even describe an authorized killing within the community (Cf. Num. 35:27, 30).[5] However, normally the מות יומת formula was used to denote the execution of a criminal.

While it has generally been accepted that the blood feud was practised in Israel, in fact the covenant itself made the exercise of such a

---

[1] On the question of the original order of the sixth and seventh commandments, see below, p. 120.

[2] H. S. Nahmani, *Human Rights in the Old Testament*, Tel Aviv, 1964, pp. 40 ff.

[3] Stamm, 'Sprachliche Erwägungen zum Gebot "Du sollst nicht töten" ', *TZ*, i, 1945, pp. 81–90, *TR*, N.F., xxvii, pp. 296 f.; Stamm and Andrew, *The Ten Commandments*, pp. 98 f.   [4] See below, pp. 99 ff.   [5] See below, p. 109.

custom impossible, for a blood feud could only arise between members of different kin-groups.[6] Although it is not denied that tribal identity persisted throughout the amphictyony and beyond, by entering into the covenant relationship, whether at Sinai or subsequently, the tribes effectively bound themselves into one kin-group, the people of Yahweh. On the other hand, whereas it was usual for a kin-group itself to determine punishment for murder within its midst, often expelling the guilty person from the clan,[7] in Israel, the covenanting clans had no choice over what punishment was to be inflicted. Since murder was prohibited by the Sinai Decalogue, on the observance of which the whole covenant relationship depended, the covenant community was under an absolute duty to execute the murderer in order to propitiate Yahweh. Consequently from the inception of the covenant itself, murder constituted a crime, and was therefore of no concern to the family or clan of the deceased, who could neither engage in a private act of vengeance,[8] nor come to some financial agreement whereby the murderer might save his life. The family would play no part in the criminal proceedings, save perhaps to act as witnesses, nor could they recover damages in respect of the death of their relative. Their duty as fellow members of the covenant community was to ensure that the murderer was convicted and executed. Anyone who took the law into his own hands would himself be guilty of murder. Thus Exod. 21:12 gives no indication that murder was treated in a different manner from other crimes mentioned in the Book of the Covenant.[9]

Of course, if there was a breach of the covenant relationship between clans, they ceased to belong to the same kin-group, and a blood feud might arise. This constitutes the background to 2 Sam. 21:1 ff. As a result of Joshua's covenant with the Gibeonites (Josh. 9), the latter had become part of the covenant community of Israel, bound both to Yahweh and to the other Israelite tribes (2 Sam. 21:2).[10] But Saul's action against them severed the covenant relationship, which at the time of the famine had not been healed (2 Sam. 21:3). It was this flagrant breach of the covenant relationship by an unwarranted attack on a fellow covenanting clan which was held to be the cause of the drought, for the fertility of the land was intimately associated with

---

[6] Robertson Smith, *Kinship and Marriage*, pp. 25 ff.; de Vaux, *Ancient Israel*, p. 11. Cf. Gen. 4:24.

[7] Cf. Gen. 4:12.

[8] For a discussion of the identity and role of the גאל הדם see below, pp. 102 ff.

[9] Thus Reventlow's contention (*Gebot und Predigt*, pp. 72 ff.) that רצח refers to a killing which sets in motion blood revenge and its retaliation must be rejected.

[10] Cf. Fensham, *BA*, xxvii, pp. 96–100.

maintenance of the covenant relationship.[11] In order to effect their reconciliation and re-entry into the covenant relationship the Gibeonites demanded the execution of the seven sons of Saul as an act of blood vengeance.[12]

But once the covenant relationship had been restored, there could be no subsequent exercise of the blood feud. Thus while Abner was justified in killing Asahel in battle (2 Sam. 2:23), since war had severed the covenant relationship, Joab by slaying Abner after he had been reconciled to David (2 Sam. 3:27), was guilty of murder (1 Kgs. 2:5), for which, along with the murder of Amasa (2 Sam. 20:10), he was subsequently executed (1 Kgs. 2:32).[13]

Once it is recognized that the blood feud did not operate in Israel, then the major difficulty in interpreting 2 Sam. 14:4 ff. is removed, namely that blood vengeance was not exercised in a kin-group.[14] Thus the brother's death was not being sought as an exceptional act of blood vengeance, but in accordance with Israel's criminal law. Regardless of his relationship to the deceased, the murderer had to be executed to propitiate Yahweh. It was to effect this execution that the whole community (משפחה) sought his life.[15]

Thus the Decalogue was also concerned with crimes which directly governed relations between men, for having bound the clans into the exclusive covenant community with Yahweh, it had to ensure the protection of members of that community, each of whom was regarded individually as a vassal of Yahweh. Further, the absolute nature of this commandment indicates that it extended this protection not only to adult male Israelites, but to their wives and children as well. The reason for this is that Israel regarded all life as the gift of Yahweh, to whom it belonged (Jer. 38:16). The נפש, that is the life force or vitality of men and animals, was held to have its seat in the blood, which in consequence might in no circumstances be appropriated by man.[16] This can be most clearly recognized from the regulations

---

[11] A parallel situation to that recorded in 2 Sam. 21:1 ff. has been found in the Hittite sources, which record the conclusion of a treaty between the Hittites and the Egyptians, its breach by the Hittites, and subsequent national disaster attributed to divine activity (A. Malamat, 'Doctrines of Causality in Hittite and Biblical Historiography: A Parallel', *VT*, v, 1955, pp. 1–12).   [12] See above, pp. 25 f.

[13] Snaith, 'The Hebrew Root G'L(I)', *ALUOS*, iii, 1961/2, p. 61.

[14] Cf. de Vaux, *Ancient Israel*, p. 12.

[15] The term משפחה refers to the local community responsible for the execution of the criminal. For a discussion of the term, cf. Pedersen, *Israel*, i–ii, pp. 46 ff.; Wolf, 'Terminology of Israel's Tribal Organisation', *JBL*, lxv, 1946, pp. 45–9. For further discussion of this passage, see below, p. 105.

[16] A. R. Johnson, *The Vitality of the Individual in the Thought of Ancient Israel*[2] Cardiff, 1964, pp. 8 f., 69 f.; Noth, *Leviticus*, p. 132.

concerning the eating of meat, where an absolute prohibition was placed on the consumption of blood (Gen. 9:4; Lev. 17:11, 14; Deut. 12:23; cf. 1 Sam. 14:32 ff.). Indeed Deut. 12:20 f. implies that until the centralization of the cult, animals were always killed in the local sanctuary, where their blood was immediately returned to Yahweh. Thus when a man took the life (נפשׁ) of another, he was understood to gain control of his blood (2 Sam. 4:11), which if it was not released by the execution of the murderer, would cry to Yahweh for delivery from its new master (Gen. 4:9 f.).[17] This explains the designation of Yahweh as the 'Seeker' (דרשׁ or בקשׁ) of the blood of the murdered, for this blood had been taken out of his control (Gen. 9:5; 42:22; Ps. 9:13; Ezek. 3:18, 20; 33:6, 8; cf. 2 Chr. 24:22).[18] There was therefore an added reason why the *murderer* had to be executed, which while murder was one of the ten covenant stipulations was partially obscured, but which became of prime importance in the post-exilic period.[19] But where there was a duty to execute someone, or appropriate warning had been given, the victim's blood would not pass into the hands of the killer, but remained on the victim himself (Lev. 20:9, 11 ff., 16, 27; Josh. 2:19; 2 Sam. 1:16; 1 Kgs. 2:37).[20] Similarly where death occurred in battle or through the infliction of the ban, the blood of the defeated would have been understood to have been devoted to Yahweh.[21]

Neither the Code of Hammurabi or the Middle Assyrian Laws have any general provisions on murder, though there need be no doubt that even if the scope of the blood feud was reduced, murder itself was not treated as a crime, but as a matter for the relatives of the deceased.[22] MAL A 10[23] and B 2[24] indicate that in Assyria these relatives were free to determine the murderer's fate, and could accept damages in place of death. HL 1–4,[25] 174[26] do not demand the death of the murderer but the giving of persons to make good the loss in the fighting and working strength of the community caused by the murder.

(ii) *Murder and Assault*

In order to constitute the crime of murder, there must be a death.

---

[17] Cain's answer to Yahweh is singularly ironic, for by his action Cain had taken control of Abel's blood. Cf. Job 16:18.
[18] Daube, *Studies in Biblical Law*, pp. 72, 122 ff. The murderer could therefore be termed a thief (Job 24:14).   [19] See below, pp. 95 f.
[20] K. Koch, 'Der Spruch "sein Blut bleibe auf seine Haupt" und die Israelitische Auffassung vom vergossenen Blut', *VT*, xii, 1962, pp. 396–416.
[21] Cf. Johnson, op. cit., pp. 69 ff.   [22] BL, i, pp. 314 f.; AL, pp. 33 ff.
[23] ANET, p. 181.   [24] ANET, p. 185.
[25] ANET, p. 189.   [26] ANET, p. 195.

Otherwise the criminal law was not infringed, and the injured party would himself bring an action in tort for assault to recover damages. Thus a number of precedents in the Book of the Covenant are concerned to distinguish between murder and assault. Exod. 21:18 f. confirms that even if there is both intent and the requisite blow, this is immaterial as far as the criminal law is concerned, unless the victim dies. If he is saved by the skill of the doctor, the case is one of assault. The purpose of this precedent is to fix a time limit after which the possibility of criminal liability should cease.[27] Thus once the injured man had walked abroad with his staff, which presumably implies without human aid, perhaps signifying that he can now resume his work,[28] his assailant can no longer be charged with murder, even if his victim dies on the next day. Further, damages must now be assessed, which are to amount to the loss which the injured man has suffered through his enforced idleness, and his medical expenses.[29] The possibility of permanent disability is here not envisaged. Since the family of the injured man would receive no damages should the assault become murder, it was in the interests of all parties that he should recover.[30]

The same principle is applied in Exod. 21:20 f. to the case of a master beating his slave. To constitute murder, the death of the slave must occur during the actual beating or on the same day. While the master had every right to chastise his slave, it is presumed that if the slave died in these circumstances, then the rod, which normally caused no harm (Prov. 23:13), must have been used with intent to kill. If the slave died after the day of his beating, then his death is attributed to his own internal weakness, and no charge of murder can be brought against the master. The law presumes that no master would want to deprive himself of his own property.[31]

Though this made no difference to the practical consequences,

[27] Daube, 'Direct and Indirect Causation in Biblical Law', *VT*, xi, 1961, p. 248.

[28] Alt, *Essays*, p. 90 argues that this does not refer to a return to work, but to the return of the injured man to playing his part in the local community, and in particular by taking his seat in the gate.

[29] Fensham, 'Exodus xxi. 18–19 in the Light of the Hittite Law § 10', *VT*, x, 1960, pp. 333–5 emends the text of Exod. 21:19 in order to arrive at a parallel enactment to HL 10 (ANET, p. 189), translating 'But he shall provide someone in his place'. However, שבת is never used in the sense of 'place', and CH 206 (ANET, p. 175) makes no mention of any temporary substitute to do the injured man's work.

[30] CH, 206 ff. (ANET, p. 175) deal with assault and murder consequent upon a fight, and provide that if the accused swears that he did not act intentionally, the death penalty is not exacted. Death in a fight reduces the amount of damages payable in HL 174 (ANET, p. 195) compared with deliberate murder (HL 3) (ANET, p. 189).

[31] Sulzberger, *The Ancient Hebrew Law of Homicide*, pp. 113 f.

G

technically a master could not have been executed for the *crime* of murder, for in contrast to a wife and child, a slave, whether an Israelite or not, was not included in the original scope of the commandment, for slaves would not have been present at Sinai.[32] This accounts for the use of נקם ינקם ('he shall be avenged') in Exod. 21:20 in place of the normal execution formula מות יומת ('he shall be executed'). The master is not being executed for murder as defined by the Sinai Decalogue, but blood vengeance, the private use of which was forbidden in Israel, is being exacted by the community on behalf of someone of whom the community had to take cognizance in the changed social circumstances of life in Canaan.[33] Further, it may be deduced from this enactment that if a foreigner was murdered while in Israel, the community would exercise blood vengeance on his behalf. It should also be noted that this precedent deals with death caused in one specific way, namely by beating, and is designed to protect the master, who otherwise would have been liable to suffer death no matter when a slave whom he had beaten died.[34] Only if the slave dies on the day of the beating is there sufficient evidence to show that the master intended to kill him. But there can be no doubt that if in other circumstances the master deliberately murdered a slave, blood vengeance would also have been exacted. It may be assumed, although other ancient Near Eastern codes are silent on the matter, that elsewhere the slave would not have been protected.

On the other hand a slave could not have brought an action for assault against his master, as the only person who would have suffered loss would have been the master himself, whose property the slave was. However, Exod. 21:26 f. indicates that where permanent injury was inflicted on a slave by his master, the latter must release him, whether male or female. This is in effect a payment of damages, namely the purchase price of the slave, and represents a direct interference by the state with a man's personal property.

In view of the two previous precedents, it would seem that Exod. 21:22 f. should also be understood as distinguishing between murder and assault, for it would appear from the only other occasion on which

---

[32] Since Exod. 21:2 specifically distinguishes a Hebrew slave from other slaves, it would seem that outside Exod. 21:2 no distinction is intended in the Book of the Covenant between an Israelite and a non-Israelite slave. An Israelite slave would have lost his status as a member of the covenant community on entering into slavery.

[33] The Samaritan version fails to grasp the point of this distinction and substitutes the execution formula for this reference to the exercise of blood vengeance. It has been noted above (p. 68) how the sabbath commandment also had to take slaves into account.   [34] Daube, *VT*, xi, pp. 248 f.

אסן is used, namely Jacob's fears as to what will befall Benjamin if
he allows him to go down to Egypt (Gen. 42:4, 38; 44:29), that it
must signify death.[35] Exod. 21:22 f. would then form a parallel precedent to CH 209 f.[36] and MAL A 50,[37] namely a case of assault
causing a miscarriage, but not the death of the mother (Exod. 21:22),
and a case where the mother died, thus constituting murder (Exod.
21:23). Discussion of this precedent is made more difficult by the fact
that the *lex talionis*, as is confirmed by its change of person and total
lack of connection with the case in hand, has replaced the previous
punishment formula in verse 23.[38] Originally in contrast to the literal
retaliation of CH 210, this would have provided for the death of the man
who struck the fatal blow, which was also the position in MAL A 50.[39]

However, the LXX substitutes ἐξεικονισμένον ('fully formed') for
אסן and contrasts the case where the foetus is not fully formed, with
that in which it is, and apparently extends the crime of murder to
include 'death' of a child still unborn. Comparison has been made
with HL 17 f., where hurting a pregnant woman in the fifth
month is distinguished from hurting her in the tenth month.[40] Perhaps the LXX preserves the original meaning of the enactment.[41]

The meaning of the final clause of verse 22 is obscure. It is probably
best to understand it as limiting the right of the husband in respect of
the amount of damages which he might claim. Before payment by
the defendant, his claim must be submitted to assessors appointed
by the court (פללים), who are to determine whether the amount claimed
is reasonable.[42] The reason that in this case court assessors are required is that in contrast to Exod. 21:19 there is no ready criterion
for the calculation of damages. But since the plaintiff had already had
the case decided in his favour, it was unnecessary to burden the court

[35] While BDB, p. 62a renders אסן by 'mischief', 'evil', 'harm', K-B, p. 71a understands it to mean 'deathly accident'. Cf. BL, i, p. 416.
[36] ANET, p. 175.
[37] ANET, pp. 184 f.
[38] Morgenstern, *HUCA*, vii, pp. 68 ff.; Noth, *Exodus*, p. 182.
[39] In contrast to MAL A 53 (ANET, p. 185), in Israelite law there is no mention of
a woman causing her own miscarriage.
[40] ANET, p. 190. Hittite law does not consider the possibility of the woman's death.
[41] Daube, *Studies in Biblical Law*, p. 148.
[42] Morgenstern, op. cit., pp. 67 ff.; E. Neufeld, *Ancient Hebrew Marriage Laws*,
London, 1944, pp. 251 f.; B. Gemser, 'The *Rîb* or Controversy Pattern in Hebrew
Mentality', *Wisdom in Israel and in the Ancient Near East*, Rowley-Festschrift (Eds.
Noth and Winton Thomas), VTS, iii, 1955, p. 124. However, Speiser 'The Stem *PLL*
in Hebrew', *JBL*, lxxxii, 1963, pp. 301–6 argues with the support of the LXX that
פללים is to be understood as an abstract noun. He therefore renders the clause
'according to (the husband's) estimate'. But it seems very doubtful if the Israelite
court would have refrained from examining the amount of the husband's claim.

as a whole with detailed arguments as to their amount. Thus both in
Exod. 21:19 and Exod. 21:22 the purpose of the damages is the same,
namely to restore the injured party as far as possible to the position he
was in before the injury. As a wife was deemed her husband's property,
he naturally received the damages.

Israelite law extended 'murder' to include death caused by animals,
and execution was inflicted by the local community.[43] Thus Exod.
21:28 enacts that an ox which gores a man or a woman to death is
to be stoned. Its flesh is regarded as taboo, and must not be eaten,
for blood guilt rests upon it. The animal, which had appropriated its
victim's blood, was probably regarded as being possessed by an evil
demon, which would have been laid by its execution.[44]

Further, prior to the amending legislation of the Book of the
Covenant, the owner was treated as an accessory before the fact if he
knew that the ox had a propensity to gore, and was to be executed as a
murderer. However, the state legislation of Exod. 21:30 provides that
a man who was under sentence of death as an accessory to a murdering
ox can ransom his life, a practice which in other cases of murder was
strictly forbidden. In effect he is to be treated as a tortfeasor, and must
pay damages to the appropriate relative of the deceased. These would
presumably be assessed in much the same manner as that set out in
Exod. 21:22.[45] The ox alone is regarded as the murderer.

Leaving aside for a moment Exod. 21:31, Exod. 21:32 enacts that
if an ox known by its owner to be dangerous[46] kills a slave, the owner
is in no way criminally liable himself, but must pay damages to the
master. The ox is to be stoned as a murderer. Unlike Exod. 21:30,
here there is no need to make the damages a matter of negotiation, for
they can be fixed at the current purchase price of a slave. The master
is thus restored to the position he was in prior to the slave's death.
Although the criminal law contains no enactment concerning the
liability of a third party for directly causing the death of a slave, in
view of the earlier argument in connection with Exod. 21:20, and the
fact that in Exod. 21:32 the ox is still treated as a murderer, there
need be no doubt that in this case too the state would have exacted
blood vengeance on behalf of the slave.[47]

---

[43] Cf. Prov. 22:13 where רצח is used of the action of a lion. LE, 56 f. (ANET, p.
163) legislates for death caused by a dog.
[44] Morgenstern, op. cit., pp. 87 ff.   [45] Ibid., p. 92.
[46] The whole of this section is dependent on Exod. 21:29 (Noth, *Exodus*, p. 183).
[47] HL, 1–4 (ANET, p. 189) indicate that the only difference between killing a free-
man and a slave is that the compensation for the former is greater. But in neither case is
the death of the murderer demanded.

But where an ox gored another ox to death, there was no question of any criminal liability, for an animal could not be murdered, and accordingly the offending ox did not have to be stoned (Exod. 21: 35 f.).

Exod. 21:31 provides that if an ox known to be dangerous gores a man's son or daughter, the case is to be treated in exactly the same way as if the victim had been an adult. The purpose of such an enactment is to make it clear that literal retaliation was not part of Israel's criminal law.[48] Comparison with CH 116,[49] 210[50] and 230[51] shows that in Babylon for causing the death of another's son or daughter, one's own son or daughter was killed. It is probable that prior to their incorporation into the covenant community, the Canaanite tribes inflicted this form of punishment.[52] But by virtue of the covenant relationship, only the execution of the person who had broken one of the covenant stipulations of the Decalogue could propitiate Yahweh. Thus there is no occasion in Israelite criminal law where someone was punished *instead of* another, though as has been recognized, where the ban was inflicted other lineal male relatives would have been executed *alongside* the criminal.[53]

These enactments on the goring ox constitute another illustration of the way in which the state would intervene against a man's personal property. Naturally in the case of an ox the execution formula is omitted, for technically an animal could not commit the *crime* of murder, since only adult male Israelites were subject to criminal liability. But in contrast to the ox, an abbreviated execution formula is used of its owner (Exod. 21:29). The effect of these provisions, together with that on the murder of a slave (Exod. 21:20), is that whenever a case of murder arose, even though one party was not subject to criminal liability, the state would none the less exact blood vengeance. Thus, although there are no provisions in the Old Testament concerning murder by a woman,[54] child or slave, there can be no doubt that the state would have treated them like the goring ox.

[48] Porter, *VT*, xv, pp. 365 f.   [49] ANET, p. 170.
[50] ANET, p. 175.   [51] ANET, p. 176.
[52] Any knowledge of Babylonian law would have been mediated to the covenant community through Canaan (A. Bentzen, *Introduction to the Old Testament*[4], i, Copenhagen, 1958, pp. 217 f.; Eissfeldt, *Introduction*, pp. 27 ff.).   [53] See above, pp. 40 ff.
[54] In 1 Kgs. 3:19 the possibility that the accidental death of the prostitute's child by the mother lying on it might constitute a case of murder is not considered. This may be due to the fact that the woman was asleep, and therefore could not be held responsible (Daube, 'Error and Accident in the Bible', *RIDA*[2], ii, 1949, p. 195). But there can be little doubt that in spite of the law's silence, a married woman who committed infanticide would have been executed.

LE 53 ff.[55] and CH 250 ff.[56] also govern the goring ox,[57] but while there are apparent similarities, particularly as to whether or not the owner knew that his animal was dangerous, in contrast to the Book of the Covenant, LE and CH do not regard the ox as a murderer.[58] Thus no mention is made of its fate, monetary compensation being paid by its owner, which varies according to the status of the deceased.[59]

(iii) Self-help

Exod. 22:1–2a enacts that a householder would not be liable for a charge of murder if he killed a burglar in the night, but would if he killed him by day. This enactment has obviously been displaced and brought into the section on theft. Originally it must have belonged with those precedents determining whether or not a murder had been committed (Exod. 21:12–32), for its sole concern is the question of the liability of the householder should he kill the intruder. If the latter escaped, whether or not his entry had been at night, the householder could take no physical action against him, though presumably he could bring him before the elders. Perhaps this was an occasion on which whipping was inflicted for conduct likely to cause a breach of the peace (Deut. 25:1 ff.).[60] If the burglar succeeded in stealing anything, it would appear that he would merely have been liable for twofold restitution (Exod. 22:6).

The reason for the distinction between entry by day and entry by night is probably due to the fact that since the householder would normally have been present in his house at night, the intruder must

---

[55] ANET, p. 163.   [56] ANET, p. 176.

[57] A detailed comparison between Babylonian and Israelite law has been made by A. van Selms, 'The Goring Ox in Babylonian and Biblical Law', ArOr, xviii, 1950, pp. 321–30, who, however, rejects the contention that at the time of the Book of the Covenant, criminal and civil law were distinguished, and fails to recognize that it is the state itself which exercises blood vengeance on behalf of a slave both in Exod. 21:20 and 32.

[58] BL, i, p. 444. Cf. David, 'The Codex Hammurabi and Its Relation to the Provisions of Law in Exodus', OTS, vii, 1950, pp. 174 f.

[59] A. Goetze, The Laws of Eshnunna, AASOR, xxxi, 1956, p. 139 notes that the value of a slave had risen by the time of the Code of Hammurabi.

[60] See below, p. 116. There is evidence that uninvited entry into another's house was regarded with the utmost disapproval. This is probably part of ancient customary law (cf. Deut. 24:10 f.). Daube, Studies in Biblical Law, p. 202 notes this element in the account of Laban's pursuit of Jacob (Gen. 31:25 ff.). Further CH 16 (ANET, p. 167) clearly indicates that the police had no power to enter the house of a person known to be harbouring a runaway slave. Comparison may also be made with the Shurpu Tablet II, 47–9 in which entry into another's house is placed alongside approaching a neighbour's wife and the shedding of blood (Mendelsohn, Religions of the Ancient Near East, New York, 1955, p. 213).

have taken this into account, and it was therefore reasonable for the householder to presume that the intruder was intent on murder.[61] Accordingly the householder might defend himself, and even if it was subsequently shown that the intruder was only a burglar, he would incur no liability. No question of unintentional killing arises (Exod. 21:13), for where death occurred in self-defence, no charge would have been brought. However, if the entry was by day, the intruder could not be assumed to be intent on murdering the householder, for he would have expected the latter to be absent from his home at his labour. Therefore, if the householder struck him with such force that he died, he must be assumed to have intended to kill him. A householder would only be absolved from liability if he could be presumed to have acted in the defence of life.

While it is readily apparent that direct reference to this enactment is made in Jer. 2:34, what is not so obvious is that it is also alluded to in Hos. 4:2. When this verse is examined it will be argued that it concerns those crimes which might harm the individual Israelite, and refers to the third, sixth, seventh, eighth and ninth commandments.[62] But because, at any rate as far as Judah was concerned, the tenth commandment had ceased to be applicable,[63] Hosea or a later scribe deliberately substituted for it Exod. 22:1–2a, being another provision concerning one's neighbour's house.[64]

LE 12 f.[65] similarly distinguishes between illegal entry by night and by day. While in the former the intruder is executed, in the latter he is fined. These provisions apply not only to a house, but also a field. Under CH 21[66] the burglar is to be put to death no matter when his breaking and entry occurs. But since under the Code of Hammurabi the penalty for theft would in any event appear to have been death, this occasions no surprise.

(iv) *The Deuteronomic Provisions*

In what must be considered a much earlier piece of legislation than the publication of the Deuteronomic law,[67] Deut. 21:1 ff. enacts that even in the case of murder by a person unknown, propitiation must

---

[61] B. Cohen, 'Self Help in Jewish and Roman Law', *RIDA*³, ii, 1955, p. 111.
[62] See below, pp. 145 ff.   [63] See below, pp. 151 f.
[64] Clearly פרץ can indicate illegal entry into another's house (2 Chr. 24:7).
[65] ANET, p. 162.
[66] ANET, p. 167. Cf. the alternative rendering in BL, ii, p. 21.
[67] The use of the term 'elders' indicates that this enactment preceded Jehoshaphat's reform, which is itself reflected in the insertion of 'judges' in verse 2 (see above, pp. 18 ff.). Verse 5 is a Deuteronomic expansion reflecting the introduction of the priesthood into the administration of justice in Israel (17:8 ff.) (see above, pp. 21 f.).

be made to Yahweh, for a covenant stipulation had undoubtedly been broken. The responsibility for effecting this was placed on the town nearest to which the murdered man's corpse was found. But since only the murderer himself was liable for his act, no other person could be executed as a substitute. The blood of the deceased was in his possession. Instead the elders were to take an unworked and unmated[68] heifer to an uncultivated valley in which water was perennially flowing, and having broken its neck, perform a ritual washing disclaiming any responsibility for the murder. The blood would either be carried away by the water, or sink into the earth, where it would remain undisturbed by cultivation. Then on behalf of all Israel, the elders were to invoke Yahweh's pardon for breach of the covenant relationship, which they were powerless to restore in any other way.

Deuteronomy extends the law of murder to include causing the death of someone by omission rather than commission. Thus Deut. 22:8 enacts that new houses must be built with a parapet surrounding the roof, or if there is an accident, blood guilt will fall upon that house. This must mean that the owner will be held liable for constructive murder.[69]

Outside references to the *lex talionis*,[70] the only specific reference to the infliction of mutilation in Israel's law is contained in Deut. 25:11 f. This concerns an assault, namely the seizing of a man's private parts by a woman. Although it has been argued that assault was a tort which merely involved an action for damages, unquestionably the mutilation of the woman is a punishment inflicted by the state, the man who has suffered the injury apparently taking no part in the action, and receiving no damages. Can these facts be reconciled?

A similar provision is preserved in MAL A 8, which enacts that where a woman crushes one of a man's testicles, one of her fingers is cut off, but where both become infected or she crushes both, then some part of her body is torn out.[71] In view of the retaliatory nature of the Assyrian law, the organ of the woman's body on which mutilation is inflicted is probably a sexual one, and as the word 'both' (*kilalun*) is retained in the text, the plural words 'breasts' or 'nipples' seem to be the best suggestions.[72] The severity of the punishment is due to the fact that the woman has destroyed the man's ability to have children.[73]

It would seem that the same idea is present in the Deuteronomic

---

[68] G. R. Driver, 'Three Notes', *VT*, ii, 1952, p. 356.

[69] But Daube, *VT*, xi, p. 251 expresses doubt as to whether the courts would ever have enforced this law by convicting a man for murder.

[70] See below, pp. 96 ff. [71] ANET, p. 31.

[72] AL, p. 31. [73] Morgenstern, *HUCA*, vii, p. 202.

provision. The Hiph'îl of קִיץ denotes a violent act, and although a euphemism (במבשיו) is resorted to, since what is seized is plural, we may assume that it is the man's testicles. While it is not specifically stated, it must be assumed that this action caused permanent injury, for it would seem unlikely that this mutilation was inflicted merely for the woman's immodesty. However, even if the woman has by her action destroyed the man's ability to procreate, there can be no question of invoking the criminal law of murder. It might therefore be thought that such an assault would be dealt with under the civil law in a similar manner to Exod. 21:22, damages being assessed to the satisfaction of the parties, the husband being liable for his wife's tort. But whereas to cause a miscarriage does not prevent future births, to destroy a man's testicles does. This was a much more serious injury, and while it does not fall directly under the head of murder, it was apparently taken into the criminal law, and thus made a matter of state concern. Perhaps with the knowledge of the Assyrian provision, the Deuteronomist enacts that the offending hand is to be cut off. He has approached this case from the standpoint of the crime of murder, but has been unable to prescribe the death penalty, as there has been no actual death.

(v) *The Priestly Legislation*

Under the pre-exilic criminal law, the murderer was treated like any other criminal, that is a person who had broken one of the covenant stipulations, and was executed to propitiate Yahweh, thereby restoring the covenant relationship. But it has been argued that post-exilic Israel abandoned the death penalty in favour of excommunication.[74] Yet it is clear from the priestly legislation that in contrast to other criminals the murderer was still executed. Thus Num. 35:33 expressly states that only the blood of the murderer can atone for the blood he has shed. The answer to this anomaly cannot lie in the fact that the shedding of blood had a special defiling property (Num. 35:33 f.) not found where other crimes were concerned, for sexual offences also defiled the land, and yet were punished by excommunication (Lev. 18:24 ff.).

The explanation is to be sought in the nature of the crime itself, for murder deprived Yahweh of what was regarded as his property, namely the blood of the deceased, which passed into the control of the murderer. Consequently, even after the death penalty had been otherwise abandoned, Yahweh continued to demand that the community

[74] See above, pp. 28 ff.

should propitiate him by executing the murderer, and it is made plain that by no other means can expiation be made for the crime (Num. 35:33), because only in this way can control over the blood of the murdered be restored to Yahweh (Gen. 9:5 f.). Thus there can be no question of the murderer ransoming his life (Num. 35:31).

But while all blood belonged to Yahweh, it was only the killing of man that constituted murder. This is the significance of the priestly addition to Gen. 9:6 that man was made in the image of God, thereby indicating that only with man could God enter into a direct personal relationship. By this specific reference to the P creation account (Gen. 1:26 f.), the priestly writer confirms that the killing of animals was perfectly legitimate provided that their blood was not appropriated (Gen. 9:2 ff.), for man had been given dominion over them (Gen. 1:28).

(vi) *The Talionic Provisions*

It would seem that the *lex talionis*, which only appears three times in the Old Testament (Exod. 21:23 ff.; Lev. 24:17 ff.; Deut. 19:21), was a post-exilic insertion into Israel's law.[75] Thus it has already been noted that the change in person, and the total lack of connection of the personal injuries outlined in Exod. 21:24 f. with a case of miscarriage, indicate that Exod. 21:23b ff. has replaced an earlier provision.[76] Similarly the excursus on the *lex talionis* in Lev. 24:17 ff. clearly interrupts the case under discussion with which it has no material connection.[77] When the ninth commandment is examined, it will be argued that Deut. 19:16 ff. prescribes execution for anyone who sought to secure the death of another by obtaining on false evidence his conviction to a criminal charge.[78] Thus at first sight the opening talionic provision seems appropriate. But since there is no indication that physical injury of the type set out in the remaining talionic provisions was ever inflicted as a form of punishment in Israel, save in the special case of Deut. 25:11 f., these have no bearing on the precedent under discussion. Further, as there need be no actual death for a man to be convicted of breach of the ninth commandment, even the first talionic provision has in fact no inherent connection with the subject matter of Deut. 19:16 ff.[79] Accordingly, even in Deut. 19:21, the *lex talionis* appears to have been added.

Since these talionic provisions seem to have been deliberately inter-

---

[75] Cf. Sulzberger, *The Ancient Hebrew Law of Homicide*, pp. 118 ff.; Morgenstern, op. cit., pp. 71 ff.   [76] See above, p. 89.   [77] See above, pp. 55 f.
[78] See below, p. 143.   [79] Morgenstern, op. cit., pp. 72 ff.

polated into each of the major legal strands in the Old Testament, namely the Book of the Covenant, Deuteronomy, and the priestly legislation, their insertion must be attributed to the person who brought these strands together, namely the Pentateuchal editor. As there seems to have been a set formula, which in spite of expansion and reinterpretation can be discerned in all three instances, it is probable that this formula, which is preserved in Deut. 19:21, was a current legal maxim. But this is not to be derived from Israel's legal history, which shows no knowledge of punishment by literal retaliation, but must be of foreign origin, presumably Babylonian, and have been taken over by the Pentateuchal editor for his own purpose. In deciding what this was, it must first be considered whether the sudden insertion of these talionic provisions in the post-exilic period indicates that in addition to exacting the death penalty for murder, literal retaliation was now also practised for causing physical injury.

The Code of Ur-Nammu[80] and LE 42 ff.,[81] which prescribe the payment of pecuniary damages for personal injuries, have been contrasted with CH 196 ff. which, at any rate in the case of the leading class, required literal retaliation,[82] and it has been argued that whereas at first the community was satisfied if the parties came to some peaceful settlement, later the state took cognizance of the act, and inflicted its own punishment, which because prisons could not be afforded, took the form of literal retaliation. The *lex talionis* is then understood as a development in the law itself.[83]

Could such a development have taken place in Israel? Apart from the fact that there is no actual evidence of this, Lev. 24:17 f. conclusively indicates that the talionic provisions are not to be interpreted literally. There the talionic phrase concerning life is applied not only to the crime of murder, but also to the tort of killing an animal. Although the use of שלם ('restore') in Exod. 21:34 indicates that for this tort damages in kind must once have been exacted,[84] Exod. 21:34 itself prescribes pecuniary damages. The Pentateuchal editor would hardly have selected this one case in which damages in kind had as early as the Book of the Covenant given way to pecuniary damages, if he had been intent on stressing that now literal retaliation was to be effected. Further, no attempt has been made by him to alter the precedents in the Book of the Covenant requiring the payment of pecuniary

[80] S. N. Kramer, *From the Tablets of Sumer*, Indian Hills, Colorado, 1956, pp. 50 f.
[81] ANET, p. 163.   [82] ANET, p. 175.
[83] A. S. Diamond, 'An Eye for an Eye', *Iraq*, xix, 1957, pp. 151–5.
[84] Morgenstern, op. cit., pp. 96 f.; Daube, *Studies in Biblical Law*, pp. 138 ff.

damages for physical injury. What then does the insertion of the talionic provisions imply?

It has been noted that the purpose in paying damages for tort was to restore the injured party to the position he was in before the injury. It is this idea of *compensation* that allows the first talionic provision to be attached not only to the tort of killing an animal, but also to the crime of murder (Lev. 24:17 f.).[85] The murderer is not executed in order to satisfy the family of the deceased as an act of literal retaliation, but to restore Yahweh to the position he was in before the murder occurred. This can only be achieved by the execution of the murderer, who has appropriated the blood of the deceased. In this way it will be released from his control, and returned to Yahweh, the giver of life (נֶפֶשׁ).[86] In other words the Pentateuchal editor by his use of the *lex talionis* is arguing that Yahweh is in the same position as a man who suffers personal injury, for to lose a man, means, as it were, to lose a limb, for which restoration must be made. Thus though at first sight it looks as if he has introduced into Israel a retaliatory theory of punishment, in fact the Pentateuchal editor's insertions seek to stress the principle of compensation, which is not merely to be confined to the payment of damages for tort, but extends even to murder cases, Yahweh being treated like an injured victim of an assault.

Both in the Book of the Covenant and the priestly legislation the Pentateuchal editor has sought to adapt the talionic provisions to the context in which he has set them. Thus in Exod. 21:25 to the normal clauses dealing with the loss of life and permanent loss of a limb have been added temporary injuries. This has been caused by the fact that the maxim has been inserted at the end of a series of precedents seeking to differentiate between murder and assaults involving temporary, but not permanent, injury.

However in Lev. 24:17 ff., the Pentateuchal editor deliberately used מוּם ('blemish') and שֶׁבֶר ('fracture') in order to refer to the priestly regulations on physical infirmities preventing a man from acting as a priest (Lev. 21:16 ff.).[87] Thus he has suppressed any reference to the hand or foot found in the basic maxim, for it is injury

---

[85] For Daube's full discussion of the *lex talionis*, cf. ibid., pp. 102 ff.

[86] Cf. Alt, 'Zur Talionsformel', *Kleine Schriften zur Geschichte des Volkes Israel*, i, München, 1953, pp. 341 ff. who however sought to link the idea of compensating the deity to both murder and assault. In fact it is only when the נֶפֶשׁ has been destroyed that Yahweh's rights are infringed. For a criticism of Alt's views (*Essays*, pp. 104 ff.) that the *lex talionis* was a specifically Israelite piece of legislation, cf. Rapaport, *PEQ*, lxxiii, pp. 166 f.

[87] Daube, *Studies in Biblical Law*, pp. 112 f.

to the foot or hand which שבר envisages (Lev. 21:19). The purpose of this reinterpretation would seem to be that the Pentateuchal editor is pointing out that damages may not just include the value of something injured or destroyed, for example an ox, or even an arm, but if the injury has other repercussions such as nullifying the right of someone who would otherwise have been eligible to act as a priest, then such loss would cause additional damages to be paid over and above the damages which anyone would receive for the particular personal injury suffered.

(vii) *Suicide*

Suicide is not referred to in the Old Testament legislation, nor in the rare cases where it is described as taking place is there any observation made on its propriety. In view of the Hebrew's attitude to life, it was probably regarded with extreme horror, but as it was the killer taking his own life, no crime was involved. The fact that Hebrew has no word for it, indicates the rarity of suicide.[88] In those cases where it does occur, the person who commits suicide appears anyhow to face certain death (Judg. 9:54; 16:30; 1 Sam. 31:4 f.; 2 Sam. 17:23;[89] 1 Kgs. 16:18).[90]

(viii) *The Cities of Refuge*[91]

Murder was the only crime in Israel which could be committed accidentally, for in every other case intention must accompany act.[92] Whereas initially the criminal law would have made no distinction between premeditated and unpremeditated killing (Exod. 21:12), the Book of the Covenant recognizes the importance of intention in determining the responsibility of the killer. Thus, Exod. 21:13 enacts that if the killer did not hunt out his victim, but God let him fall into his hands, then God will appoint a place (מקום) to which the killer can

[88] L. Nemoy, 'A Tenth Century Disquisition on Suicide according to Old Testament Law', *JBL*, lvii, 1938, p. 412.

[89] This would undoubtedly have been the fate of Ahitophel as a result of his intrigues (Hertzberg, *Samuel*, p. 353).

[90] The two suicides in 2 Macc. 10:13; 14:41 ff. add nothing to this discussion.

[91] Recent discussions have included N. M. Nicolsky, 'Das Asylrecht in Israel', *ZAW*, N.F., vii, 1930, pp. 146–75; David, 'Die Bestimmungen über die Asylstädte in Josua xx', *OTS*, ix, 1951, pp. 30–48; B. Dinur, 'The Religious Character of the Cities of Refuge and the Ceremony of Admission into Them', *Eretz-Israel*, iii, 1954, pp. 135–46 (in Hebrew); Greenberg, 'The Biblical Concept of Asylum', *JBL*, lxxviii, 1959, pp. 125–32; de Vaux, *Ancient Israel*, pp. 160–3.

[92] In contrast to accident, error would provide no excuse to a criminal charge, for though mistaken, the act had been deliberately committed—for instance if A killed B mistaking him for C. Cf. Daube, *RIDA²*, ii, pp. 189 ff.

flee, namely the local sanctuary.[93] This enactment is therefore framed from the standpoint of the covenant relationship, for the only way in which the community could consider itself absolved from its absolute duty to propitiate Yahweh by executing the killer was to hold that the killing had been committed by Yahweh himself. On the other hand, if the elders judged that the killing was premeditated, they were to take the murderer from the altar and execute him (Exod. 21:14).

Exod. 21:13 may therefore be compared with the widely known practice of seeking asylum at the sanctuary, which was no doubt granted at the Canaanite sanctuaries prior to their adoption of Yahwism, and taken over with them. Under this any person in fear of his life could seek asylum at the sanctuary where he might remain until he could enter into a satisfactory arrangement which would allow him to leave in safety. By taking hold of the horns of the altar, he placed himself under the protection of the deity, and could not be forcibly removed.

However, this procedure could never have been resorted to in respect of Israel's criminal law, for the community had an absolute duty to execute the criminal to propitiate Yahweh. Thus even under Exod. 21:13 f. the decision as to whether or not the killing amounted to murder was entirely a matter for the local community, who might enter the sanctuary and remove the criminal for execution. The priests had no power to stop this and should not be introduced into the discussion of this enactment.

It is therefore no surprise that the only actual examples in the Old Testament of persons seeking asylum concern political refugees and not criminals. But whereas Adonijah was able to leave the sanctuary under the protection of a solemn oath (1 Kgs. 1:50 ff.), Joab was summarily executed in the sanctuary itself as an intentional murderer (1 Kgs. 2:28 ff.). He had evidently not envisaged the possibility that Solomon would use the murders of Asahel and Amasa in order legitimately to break sanctuary, or he would never have sought asylum in the royal shrine at Jerusalem.

It is therefore possible to reconstruct the procedure which would have been adopted following an alleged accidental killing. As soon as this had occurred, the רצח ('killer in the covenant community') would seek the protection of Yahweh at the local sanctuary, thereby

[93] Nicolsky, op. cit., pp. 172 ff. understands Exod. 21:13 to refer to one sanctuary only. While this cannot be accepted, it is possible that the wording of Exod. 21:13 does reflect knowledge of the cities of refuge (David, op. cit., p. 37), since it will be shown that they were established prior to the E compilation into which the Book of the Covenant was inserted.

submitting that although he had shed the blood of a fellow member of the covenant community, his act was unpremeditated. The elders would then consider the case, and if they rejected his contention would forthwith remove him from the sanctuary for execution. On the other hand, if they decided that the killing was accidental (an act of God), there was no need to propitiate Yahweh, for the criminal law was not infringed. But in view of Exod. 21:30 which provides for the payment of damages by someone who under earlier law would have been executed for murder, one is probably right in assuming that even though the רצח had not intended to kill his victim, he would have been liable in tort to the family of the deceased. Perhaps damages were assessed by the פללים. Presumably once these had been paid, the רצח would have been free to leave the sanctuary, for even if it were possible, imprisonment there does not seem to have been envisaged.[94]

However, asylum at the sanctuary suffered from a serious defect, namely that the removal of the murderer from the sanctuary was entirely in the hands of the local community, who would have been exceedingly reluctant to judge a killing unintentional for fear that through error on their part, they might find themselves subject to direct divine action for failure to execute a criminal. The only way in which the legislature could ensure that a person who claimed that he had acted unintentionally might receive an impartial trial was to remove the case from the jurisdiction of the local courts. It was to achieve this purpose that the cities of refuge were established.

Since the legislation on the cities is only contained in Deuteronomy (4:41 ff.; 19:1 ff.) and P (Num. 35:9 ff.), on both of which Josh. 20:1 ff. appears to be dependent, it has generally been argued that their establishment resulted from the centralization of the cult at Jerusalem with the abolition of the local sanctuaries at which asylum would have been sought. The list of cities in Josh. 20:7 ff. would then be understood as a later imaginative reconstruction.

But this assertion cannot be maintained for in Hos. 6:8 f. direct allusion is made to two of these cities as *cities of refuge*, namely Ramoth-Gilead (there described as Gilead),[95] and Shechem.[96] The first is pictured as full of those who ought to have been executed, while those who should have been given access to the second are murdered *en route* by the priests.

---

[94] Ibid., pp. 37 f.
[95] Jeroboam II apparently restored to Israel the territory lost since the reign of Solomon (2 Kgs. 14:25), which would have included Ramoth-Gilead (Noth, *History*, p. 250). [96] Dinur, op. cit., p. 142.

Thus as Hosea knew as cities of refuge two of those named in Josh. 20:7 ff., they cannot have been the product of Josiah's reform. In fact their establishment must be attributed to the period of the united monarchy for only then would all these cities have been in Israel's possession. Since it will be shown that the גאל הדם was specifically connected with the cities of refuge, 2 Sam. 14:4 ff. *prima facie* indicates that David rather than Solomon established them. Further confirmation of their pre-Deuteronomic date is given by Deut. 19:12, which by referring to the elders indicates that this legislation ante-dated Jehoshaphat's reform.[97]

There is no precise information as to the subsequent history of these cities, but the fact that Hosea alludes to Ramoth-Gilead as a city of refuge after its recapture, indicates that where cities were lost, no new cities were set up in their place. This is what one would expect, as they were designed to serve the territory surrounding them.

The considerable stress on the cities of refuge in both Deuteronomy and the priestly legislation would seem to indicate that both legislators sought their maintenance or reconstitution. Whether in fact this was achieved, and if so what cities fulfilled this function, cannot be determined, but the detailed priestly legislation makes the existence of such cities in the post-exilic period probable.

From the legislation contained in Deut. 19:1 ff., together with Josh. 20:4 f. which originally formed part of it,[98] can be established the procedure which was adopted when asylum was sought at the cities of refuge.[99] But first it is necessary to consider the identity of the גאל הדם.

It appears from the most recent study of the root גאל that its primary meaning is 'cover', which is applied to two different ideas, namely covering in the sense of protection and covering as a form of defilement.[100] This discussion is only concerned with the former. Accordingly, where a relative is designated גאל, this indicates that he is one's protector upon whom certain prescribed duties are laid. Thus the גאל is found recovering a relative who has sold himself into slavery family property which has become alienated, and the name of a child-less deceased brother by marrying his widow. His function is therefore to restore to the family that which has been lost. In contrast to הדם

---

[97] See above, pp. 18 ff.

[98] Morgenstern, *HUCA*, vii, pp. 204 f. Josh. 20:4 f. is omitted by LXX[B], together with most of verse 6.

[99] Deut. 4:41 ff. adds nothing to the discussion.

[100] Johnson, 'The Primary Meaning of √גאל', VTS, i, 1953, pp. 67–77, *The Vitality of the Individual*, p. 71.

('rescue'), גאל indicates a return of men or things to their legitimate place.[101]

The גאל הדם has been traditionally rendered 'the avenger of blood', and understood as the deceased's nearest male relative who exercised blood vengeance on his behalf. There are, however, insuperable difficulties to this interpretation.

In the first place there is no evidence in the Old Testament for the contention that the blood feud was practised against fellow members of the covenant community. The Book of the Covenant treats murder like any other crime (cf. Exod. 21:12 ff.), and the formula מות יומת must refer to normal communal execution. Had it been desired to stress vengeance, נקם ('avenge') would have been used.

Secondly, it has been argued that blood was considered the personal property of Yahweh to whom it was released on the execution of the murderer. Thus the recovery of the blood of the deceased was not the concern of his relatives, but of Yahweh, the Seeker of blood, from whose control it had been taken.[102]

Thirdly it is strange that where no attempt has been made to designate the גאל by any qualification in respect of his other duties, it has been felt necessary in this case to add הדם ('the blood'). It is inconceivable that this would ever have been done had the גאל and the גאל הדם been intended to apply to the same person. The expression גאל הדם has the distinct appearance of a contrived title which refers to someone other than the person normally designated גאל.[103]

Finally the גאל הדם only appears in connection with the cities of refuge,[104] and must therefore be intimately connected with them. This explains his absence from the Book of the Covenant.

With the institution of the cities of refuge the effective decision as to whether or not the killing was premeditated naturally became vested in the elders of the city of refuge. Consequently when the elders of the killer's city wished to contest his claim to have acted unintentionally, they naturally needed a representative who could plead their case at the city of refuge, and inflict execution on their behalf. This was the function of the גאל הדם. In choosing this title a well-known legal term

---

[101] Daube, *Studies in Biblical Law*, pp. 39 ff., 124, *The Exodus Pattern in the Bible*, London, 1963, pp. 27 f.; Snaith, *ALUOS*, iii, pp. 60 ff.

[102] See above, pp. 85 f.

[103] Sulzberger, *The Ancient Hebrew Law of Homicide*, pp. 55 ff. Although his interpretation is at variance with the one given here, Sulzberger none the less recognized that the גאל הדם was an official, and thus to be contrasted with the גאל.

[104] Only in 2 Sam. 14:4 ff., which has nothing to do with blood vengeance (see above, pp. 83 ff.), is there no specific mention of a city of refuge, but see below, p. 105.

H

has been borrowed to which has been added הדם, thereby indicating that like the גאל, this official, who may be designated the Protector of blood, had the duty of restoring something, namely the blood of the murdered man, to its legitimate owner, Yahweh (the Seeker of blood). Murder being a crime was never the concern of the family of the deceased, but of the community.

It appears probable that provided he could make out a *prima facie* case, the killer had an absolute right to be received at the city of refuge, and could not be turned away. Immediately on arrival he would have notified the elders of the city of refuge of his plight, who would then take him into their city, and give him temporary accommodation until it was known what action the elders of his own city would take (Josh. 20:4).[105] If they decided that the murder was premeditated, previous hostility being the main criterion (Deut. 19:4, 6), they would have dispatched their representative, the גאל הדם, to the city of refuge to recover the killer (cf. Josh. 20:5; Deut. 19:12). While in Josh. 20:5 the גאל הדם fails in his application for the release of the killer for execution,[106] in Deut. 19:11 ff. he succeeds. The wording of Deut. 19:12 is elliptical, but it is clear from Josh. 20:5 that it is the גאל הדם whom the elders of the killer's city send to the city of refuge to receive the murderer on their behalf, and since Josh. 20:5 also indicates that it is the elders of the city of refuge who determine the issue, they must be understood as the subject of ונתנו ('and they shall hand him'). It would seem probable that rather than bring the murderer back to his own city, as in other cases where the גאל הדם encountered him (Deut. 19:6), he would have been executed forthwith. As the officer appointed to act on behalf of the murderer's city, the גאל הדם would have been regarded as an extension of that city, and so death at his hands, rather than at the hands of the elders of the city of refuge, who no doubt supervised the execution, was the appropriate way to propitiate Yahweh.

Since the elders of the killer's city had first to determine whether or not the killing was premeditated before they could dispatch the גאל הדם, the killer would have had a considerable start on him, and in normal circumstances would reach the city of refuge first (Josh. 20:4). But if through his zealousness, or because the killer dallied, the גאל הדם overtook the killer before he reached the city of refuge, and

---

[105] This is the significance of כי ('if') in Josh. 20:5. If it was clearly a case of unpremeditated killing, there was no need to proceed further.

[106] Morgenstern, *HUCA*, vii, pp. 204 f. argues that Deut. 19:10 followed Josh. 20:5.

executed him, he was apparently absolved from any criminal liability
even if it turned out that the killer had in fact acted unintentionally
(Deut. 19:6). The גאל הדם was only fulfilling the commission which
he had received from the court of first instance, namely that the killer
whom that court had found guilty of premeditated murder should be
executed to propitiate Yahweh. It was the killer's fault if he allowed
himself to be caught, and therefore deprived himself of the opportunity of an impartial trial. As has been recognized, the phrase כי-יחם
לבבו need not be understood as describing intense anger or rage
leading to an impairment of judgement.[107] Rather it appears to indicate an inability to hold back, eagerness (cf. Ps. 39:4). This provision
illustrates the tension that existed as a result of the establishment of
the cities of refuge, whose elders could overrule the decision of the
elders of the killer's city, and refuse to surrender to the latter's representative a person whom they deemed should be executed. It was
therefore the legislator's concern that the killer should reach the city
of refuge (Deut. 19:3) in order that he should have the benefit of an
impartial trial.[108] It should, however, be noted that it was *only* the
גאל הדם, that is the duly appointed official of the court of first
instance, and no one else, who had the right to pursue and execute the
killer. He did not act to satisfy a private blood feud, but to fulfil a
decision of the judicature. Presumably, if the killer was at once detained, or did not attempt to flee, perhaps hoping that he would not be
detected, he would have stood trial in his own city, and if found
guilty would have been executed in the normal way, namely by communal stoning.

The situation in 2 Sam. 14:4 ff. now becomes clear. The murderer
has evidently gone into hiding rather than flee to the city of refuge, his
whereabouts only being known to his mother. The local community
has considered the case, and instructed the גאל הדם to find the murderer and execute him. It is specifically from any action on his part
that the mother seeks the king's protection (2 Sam. 14:11, 16).

Although nothing is expressly stated to this effect, it may be
assumed that if the elders of the killer's city decided that the killing
was unpremeditated, and therefore did not commission the גאל הדם
to pursue the killer, the killing would be treated as a tort, and after the
appropriate damages had been paid, the killer would have returned
home. There was no need to propitiate Yahweh, for murder had not
been committed. It was only if the killer had acted with intent to kill

---

[107] Sulzberger, op. cit., pp. 69 f.
[108] Morgenstern, op. cit., pp. 204 f. argues that verse 6 followed verse 3.

that he would have gained possession of the dead man's blood.
Further, it would seem that this would also have been the case once
the elders of the city of refuge had been asked to judge between the
גאל הדם and the killer, and had decided in favour of the latter,
refusing to allow the גאל הדם to execute him. Had it been intended
that the killer should remain at the city of refuge for the rest of his
life, this would surely have been explicitly stated. It is the priestly
legislation which decrees that the unintentional killer shall be imprisoned in the city of refuge, prohibits any payment of damages, and
provides that if the killer illegally leaves the city of refuge, the גאל
הדם may kill him (Num. 35). This must be understood as new legislation. All that the legislation setting up the cities of refuge was intent
on ensuring was that the final decision as to whether or not the killer
had acted intentionally should be removed from the elders of his city.
Thus the cities of refuge are a logical development from temporary
asylum at the local sanctuary. But it should be noted that by the time
of the Deuteronomist at any rate no attempt is made to understand
the unintentional killing as an act of God: instead it is treated as an
accident as the precedent in Deut. 19:5 makes plain.

It would seem that Jehoshaphat's reform[109] would have had very
little effect on the cities of refuge, though presumably the גאל הדם
would now act on the authority of the local state judge(s) rather than
the elders of the killer's city.

It has already been noted that Deut. 17:8 ff. enacts that difficult
cases, murder being specifically mentioned, were to be heard at a
central appeal court in Jerusalem made up of both laity and priests.[110]
It has been contended that this was a deliberate attempt by the Deuteronomic legislation to introduce the hierarchy of the central sanctuary
into the administration of justice in Israel. But it would seem that as a
result of the establishment of this court, the elders of the city of refuge
would have been deprived of their right to decide the fate of the killer
who claimed that he had acted unintentionally, the hearing now taking
place before the central appeal court. This is the position under the
priestly legislation. Further, it may be due to Deut. 17:8 ff. that
Josh. 20:4 f. has been displaced from Deut. 19 owing to the fact that
it clearly refers to the judicial authority of the elders of the city of
refuge. This would also explain their omission from Deut. 19:12,
where they should be understood as the subject of ונתנו.[111] It is only
at this point that Josiah's reform affected the cities of refuge.

---

[109] See above, pp. 18 ff.   [110] See above, pp. 21 f.
[111] In contrast to the elders of the city of refuge, here, as elsewhere, the Deuter-

The priestly legislation (Num. 35:9 ff.; Josh. 20:1–3, 6, 9) continued to recognize the distinction between premeditated and unpremeditated killing, though the elders of the city of refuge no longer determined the issue, but the עֵדָה. It is clear from the fact that the עֵדָה was to return the unintentional killer to his city of refuge (Num. 35:25) that this body was independent of that city. It may therefore be assumed that the עֵדָה was the central appeal court in Jerusalem, now presided over in criminal matters by the high priest (2 Chr. 19:8 ff.).[112] Further Num. 35:25 indicates that the עֵדָה possessed a police force which could recover the killer from the גֹּאֵל הַדָּם and bring him straight to their court. Thus the עֵדָה had the means available to ensure that the killer who claimed that he had acted unintentionally received an impartial trial.

But in contrast to earlier legislation, Num. 35 specifically enacts that even when the עֵדָה judged the killing to have been unpremeditated, the killer was to be imprisoned in the city of refuge for a fixed term. It may be that the term מִקְלָט, usually rendered 'reception', 'in-taking', in fact denotes this, the cities of refuge having become 'prison cities'.[113]

The reason for this new legislation was not that the unintentional killer was understood to have taken possession of the deceased's blood: if he had he would unquestionably have been executed. Rather it is due to the fact that the priestly legislation could not envisage the possibility of someone who had shed blood, even though this was unintentional, taking part in temple worship. By this act he had defiled himself, and as in other cases of inadvertent breaches of the law (Lev. 4 f.; Num. 15:22 ff.), could not be re-admitted to the cult until he had ritually cleansed himself. But the shedding of blood was evidently considered such a serious matter, that it could not be atoned for by mere sacrifice of animals. Indeed, only on the death of the high priest himself was the unintentional killer freed from the city of refuge (Num. 35:25, 28; Josh. 20:6). This provision must be connected to the fact that the high priest had acted as president of the

---

onomic legislation continues to speak of the elders of the criminal's city. Presumably it was not felt necessary to omit any reference to them because the state judges had been in office so long that there was no need to stress their appointment. No one would have thought of the elders of the local community administering justice. See above, pp. 19 f.

[112] See above, pp. 22 f.

[113] Thus Sulzberger, op. cit., pp. 76 f. argued that both מִקְלָט and קָלוֹט (Lev. 22:23) were derived from the same root קָלַט (Cf. BDB, p. 886a), which he held was the antithesis of שָׂרַע ('stretch') (Lev. 21:18; 22:23; Isa. 28:20). קָלַט would then mean 'cabined', 'cribbed', 'confined'. The cities can thus be termed 'prison cities'.

עדה which had determined the question of the killer's responsibility. By deciding that the killer was not a criminal, the high priest must have been understood in some way to have taken upon himself responsibility for the inadvertent act and its expiation.[114] His death was evidently understood to have atoning power for all unintentional shedding of blood, for which during his life he had no means of offering expiation.

Thus imprisonment at the city of refuge should not be understood as expiatory. Its purpose was to detain someone who was ritually unclean until expiation could be made for his inadvertent act, namely the death of the high priest.[115] The idea that Yahweh could have been responsible for the killing is now positively rejected.

As a result of this new understanding of the cities of refuge as prison cities, the priestly legislation had to take into consideration the possibility of escape from the city of refuge before the term of imprisonment was up, that is the death of the high priest. Thus Num. 35:26 ff. provides that even though the killing had been judged unpremeditated, if the גאל הדם encountered the killer outside the city of refuge, he could forthwith execute him. The authority which the גאל הדם had received from the court of first instance was not to be annulled until the killer was declared ritually clean. Further since the unintentional murderer was to be imprisoned in the city of refuge until the death of the high priest, there could be no question of the killing being treated as a tort. Consequently Num. 35:32 forbade the payment of damages to the family of the deceased leading to the return of the killer to his home. Whether damages were paid on his eventual release from the city of refuge, cannot be determined.

Num. 35:16 ff. contain a series of precedents determining whether or not certain action *prima facie* constituted murder. Thus previous enmity or preparation would clearly indicate intention to kill (Num. 35:20 f.), as would the use of an instrument of such a nature that the result of such action must reasonably have been expected to cause death (Num. 35:16 ff.). Pure accident would naturally show lack of premeditation (Num. 35:23), and it is possible that Num. 35:22 contemplates provocation as a defence.

Clearly the priestly legislation still envisages murder as a matter of local concern, the local judge(s) acting as the court of first instance. Presumably if the murderer was immediately apprehended or deliber-

---

[114] Morgenstern, *HUCA*, viii, p. 87.

[115] Num. 35:33 f. should not be placed alongside the provisions on the unintentional killer, but is merely a reiteration of the basic principle of the law of murder (Gen. 9:5 f.).

ately elected to stand trial and was convicted, he would have been stoned by his local community (Num. 35:16 ff., 20 f.), though once he had fled, it was the גאל הדם, and no one else, who was instructed to pursue him, and on encountering him, execute him on behalf of the community (Num. 35:19, 21b).

Num. 35:30 prohibits in any circumstances the execution of a murderer on the evidence of only one witness. It has been noted that the missing subject of ירצח ('he shall kill') must be the גאל הדם.[116] Thus if the court of first instance was unable to obtain the requisite number of witnesses, it was unable to authorize the גאל הדם to pursue the killer and execute him. If he did this on his own initiative, he would himself be treated as a murderer. It has already been recognized that since רצח merely indicates a killing within the covenant community, it can properly be used of the גאל הדם in executing the murderer (cf. Num. 35:27, 30).[117]

In accordance with much exilic and post-exilic legislation, Num. 35:15 (cf. Josh. 20:9) brings the resident alien (גר), together with the temporary resident (תושב), within the scope of the legislation concerning the cities of refuge.

HL 3 f.[118] recognizes the distinction between intentional and unintentional killing. The penalties for the latter were reduced, but in neither case was death demanded. No attempt was made to attribute the accident to God.

CH 206 ff.[119] also recognizes the importance of intention in determining whether murder has been committed. Where death resulted from a blow in a fight, the striker must swear that he did not strike his victim deliberately, and then pay damages. Further, where a surgeon caused the death of a patient, he was not treated as a murderer, but had his hand cut off to prevent him operating again (CH 218).[120]

[116] Reventlow, *Gebot und Predigt*, pp. 73 f.
[117] See above, p. 83.   [118] ANET, p. 189.
[119] ANET, p. 175.   [120] Ibid.

CHAPTER NINE

THE PROHIBITION OF ADULTERY

(Exod. 20:14; Deut. 5:18)

(i) *The Crime of Adultery*

Exod. 20:14 prohibits adultery. Although no object of the verb is expressed, it is clear from Deut. 22:22; Lev. 20:10 that the original commandment restricted adultery to sexual intercourse with the wife of a fellow member of the covenant community.[1] For the purpose of the criminal law, a betrothed girl was treated as if she was already married (Deut. 22:23 ff.).[2] Both the man and the woman were to be executed (Deut. 22:24; Lev. 20:10) by communal stoning (Deut. 22:24).[3]

But originally a woman was not subject to Israel's criminal law, only becoming so as a result of the Deuteronomic reform whereby women were made equal members of the covenant community with men, foreign marriages being prohibited (Deut. 7:3 f.).[4] Thus before the Deuteronomic legislation it was only the wife's lover who could be tried, convicted and executed for the crime of adultery, the injured husband being left with the choice of forgiving his wife or divorcing her. It may have been thought that any wife who committed adultery did so involuntarily, being forced by the man. This would explain why, unlike murder, there is no distinction between voluntary and involuntary adultery in the Book of the Covenant.[5] The execution of the adulterer would have constituted a sufficient deterrent to adultery, besides ensuring that the adulterous wife could never marry her lover. Evidence for this assertion is provided by Hos. 2:4 and Jer. 3:8,[6]

---

[1] In MAL A, 13–14 knowledge of whether the woman was married determined whether the man was punished (ANET, p. 181).
[2] Cf. CH 130 (Ibid., p. 171).
[3] In Babylon execution was by drowning (CH 129: Ibid.).
[4] See above, pp. 15 f.   [5] Cf. Deut. 22:23 ff.
[6] Jer. 3:8, which is dated to Josiah's reign, must be considered older than the Deuteronomic legislation, as subsequently the metaphorical use of divorce for a woman's adultery would have been inapplicable.

where it is indicated that divorce,[7] not execution, was the consequence of a wife's adultery. Indeed it seems from Hos. 2:5 that a special procedure widely known elsewhere was adopted, whereby the wife was stripped naked and driven from the home.[8] By taking off her clothing, the husband showed that he was no longer responsible for his wife's maintenance.[9] Further evidence that initially the wife was not executed for her adultery is provided both by Lev. 20:10 which indicates that originally this enactment was drawn up as if there was only one person to be executed, namely the husband,[10] and Gen. 20:1 ff. in which there is no suggestion that Sarah would have been in any way liable for her adultery with Abimelech.[11] This also explains why Bathsheba is nowhere condemned for her adultery with David.[12]

Accordingly Deut. 22:22 must be understood as new legislation enacting that the wife, as well as her lover, was to be prosecuted and executed for the crime of adultery. There is, however, no indication that before this legislation the husband could himself execute his wife. Even in the case of persons who were not members of the covenant community, those who were had no private rights of life and death over them (cf. Exod. 21:20), although their status could be altered extra-judicially as part of family law (cf. Exod. 21:6). The husband's remedy was to divorce his wife.

The use of the expression עֶרְוַת דָּבָר ('the nakedness of a thing') in Deut. 24:1 is directly due to this new Deuteronomic legislation. Originally the husband had an absolute right to divorce his wife whensoever he wished. But by making the wife's act of adultery a crime, the Deuteronomic legislation removed this act from the sphere of private family law, and made it the concern of the community, though in other respects the husband's freedom to divorce his wife was left

---

[7] Since divorce was not a penalty of the criminal law, but belonged to the realm of family law, which in Israel was of no concern to the courts (cf. Exod. 21:6), it is not proposed to discuss it here. It may however be noted that from earliest times divorce was known in Israel. Whereas a wife could never divorce her husband, the latter had an absolute right to divorce his wife at any time and for any reason whatsoever (de Vaux, *Ancient Israel*, pp. 34 f.; Falk, *Hebrew Law*, pp. 154 ff.). Probably childlessness was the chief cause of divorce (Pedersen, *Israel*, i–ii, p. 71). Since there are no provisions concerning alimony or custody of children, it must be assumed that the former was not paid, and that the latter remained in the custody of the husband (Neufeld, *Ancient Hebrew Marriage Laws*, pp. 123 f.).

[8] Gordon, 'Hos. 2:4–5 in the Light of New Semitic Inscriptions', *ZAW*, N.F., xiii, 1936, pp. 277–80.

[9] *Peake's Commentary*, p. 606a. Cf. Exod. 21:10.

[10] Noth, *Leviticus*, p. 150.

[11] Daube, 'Concerning Methods of Bible-criticism', *ArOr*, xvii, 1949, pp. 93 f.

[12] She may even have encouraged it (Hertzberg, *Samuel*, p. 309).

unimpaired. The Deuteronomist, who was not legislating for divorce in general, but for one specific set of circumstances, therefore inserted ערות דבר to make sure that there should be no ambiguity in his law. That the expression has no moral connotation is confirmed from Deut. 23:15, where it is used of what is unbecoming, but not of what is immoral.[13] It is therefore to be understood as a general expression denoting anything *other than adultery* which the husband found distasteful in his wife.[14]

Confirmation that it was only sexual intercourse with a married or betrothed woman that was prohibited by the Decalogue and so constituted a crime is obtained from Exod. 22:15 f., from which it is clear that the seduction of an unmarried woman was regarded as a tort against her father for which he would bring an action for damages. Since the seduction had made it impossible for the father to make a marriage for his daughter by which he could receive the proper מהר ('bride price'), the seducer was ordered to pay this by way of compensation and take the girl as his wife (Exod. 22:15).[15] Thus

[13] Driver, *Deuteronomy*, pp. 270 f.; Morgenstern, *HUCA*, vii, pp. 155 f.

[14] There is no suggestion in Deut. 24:1 ff. that the husband's rights are in any other way restricted resulting in the necessity to bring a definite charge against his wife before a public body (Yaron, 'On Divorce in Old Testament Times', *RIDA*³, iv, 1957, pp. 127 f.; but cf. Driver, op. cit., p. 272; Neufeld, op. cit., p. 176). Further, unlike Mal. 2:16, Deut. 24:1 ff. expresses no disapproval of divorce, but remains neutral (Yaron, 'CPJud 144 et Alia', *Jura*, xiii, 1962, pp. 172 f.; but cf. J. Modrzejewski, 'Les Juifs et le droit hellénistique: Divorce et égalité des époux (CPJud. 144)', ibid., xii, 1961, pp. 183 f.). The bill of divorce is not to be considered an innovation of the Deuteronomic legislation, but is there presupposed, being already referred to in Jer. 3:8. Certainty that a woman had been divorced was obviously required where sexual intercourse with a married woman would result in a criminal charge leading to execution on conviction. Thus it is probable that the divorce formula of the family law (Hos. 2:4), presumably pronounced by the husband at the door of his house (cf. Exod. 21:6), was either replaced or supplemented by the bill of divorce. Since there is no mention of such a document in either Hosea or the Aramaic papyri from Elephantine, but yet one is referred to by Jeremiah, it is possible that it only became Israelite practice in the period between these prophets, perhaps due to external influence (Yaron, *RIDA*³, iv, pp. 126 f.). The case of Samson's first marriage has been cited as one of uncertainty as to whether the parties were divorced (Daube, *RIDA*², ii, pp. 193 f.), but it is possible that the marriage had never been consummated (BL, i, p. 291). As in Israel, divorce at Elephantine was not a matter for the judiciary, though the announcement of the divorce had to be made before the congregation. Perhaps this took the place of the bill of divorce (Yaron, *Introduction to the Law of the Aramaic Papyri*, Oxford, 1961, pp. 54 f.). Jer. 3:1 is not to be understood as referring to Deut. 24:1 ff., but concerns adultery rather than divorce (*Peake's Commentary*, p. 543a). It would seem that Deut. 24:1 ff. was primarily concerned to protect the second husband (Morgenstern, *HUCA*, vii, pp. 156 f.).

[15] There is no need here to determine whether the father was entitled to absolute possession of the מהר, or only to the usufruct of it (de Vaux, *Ancient Israel*, p. 27). In spite of Gen. 31:15, the fact that labour (Gen. 29:18) or other property (1 Sam.

there was no punitive element in this provision, the father being no better off than if he had arranged his daughter's marriage in the normal way. But Exod. 22:16 reserved for the father the right to withhold his daughter from her seducer, even though the latter must still pay an equivalent sum to the מהר as damages.[16] This was a risk which the seducer ran. The amount of the מהר would, of course, depend on the status of the girl.[17]

In contrast to Exod. 22:15 f., the later legislation of Deut. 22:28 f. both fixed the damages payable for seduction, and apparently compelled the seducer to marry the girl, whom he was subsequently prohibited from divorcing. These provisions are to be understood as deterrent measures, at any rate as far as the daughter of a poor man was concerned.[18] Why the father's right to withhold his daughter from her seducer was abandoned is not clear. It may have been to ensure that she should not be left unmarried, but it is also possible that it was to prevent him trying to pass her off as a virgin (cf. Deut. 22:13 ff.).

It has, however, been argued that whereas force is indicated in Deut. 22:28 f., in Exod. 22:15 f. it is implied that the girl was persuaded by her seducer, and thus consented to the act, which explains why Exod. 22:15 f. does not deprive the husband of his right to divorce.[19] But it would seem that in Deuteronomy the emphasis is on the distinction between a betrothed (22:25 ff.) and an unbetrothed girl (22:28 f.), and not on force or consent.[20] Accordingly, Deut. 22:28 f. should be understood as directly amending Exod. 22:15 f. It has already been indicated that prior to Deuteronomy, the woman may always have been regarded as acting involuntarily in cases of adultery.

On the other hand MAL A 55–6 does seem to distinguish between seduction with and without consent.[21] Where the daughter did not consent, section 55 enacts that if the seducer was married, the father is to take his wife, and use her as a prostitute for his own profit. If the seducer was unmarried, he must pay damages. Thus, as in Israel, it is

---

18:25; 2 Sam. 3:14), which could in no way materially benefit the bride, could be demanded as her price, would seem to indicate that it was in fact an outright gift to the father to compensate him for the loss of his daughter. Whatever the interpretation of Gen. 31:15 is, Laban's daughters cannot refer to any monetary payment by Jacob, because none was made.

[16] Cf. Burrows, *The Basis of Israelite Marriage*, *JAOS* Monograph, xv, 1938, pp. 55 ff.

[17] Cf. 1 Sam. 18:23 ff.

[18] Fifty shekels is probably to be understood as an average bride price (Driver, *Deuteronomy*, p. 258).   [19] Morgenstern, *HUCA*, vii, pp. 118 ff.

[20] AL, p. 53.   [21] ANET, p. 185; AL, pp. 52 ff.

the father who must be compensated for damage to his property. Further, the daughter may be given in marriage to her seducer, who then cannot divorce her. However, the father can withhold her, and still receive damages.[22] Section 56 provides that if the daughter consented, the seducer's wife cannot be touched by the father. The seducer must, however, pay damages, and the father can deal with his daughter as he likes.

Although the only enactment governing such a case now appears in the Holiness Code, it is clear that sexual intercourse with a slave could not be termed 'adultery', since she was the property of her master, and not his wife.[23] The case cited is of a betrothed girl who has not yet received her freedom. Damages[24] are to be paid, and a guilt offering rendered (Lev. 19:20 ff.), thus signifying that only a tort had been committed. It is not specified to whom these damages are payable. It would presumably depend on whether the fiancé had already paid for his bride, either in part or in full.[25]

However in the case of adultery with a betrothed woman, Deuteronomy explicitly recognized that intention determined responsibility. Thus Deut. 22:23 f. provides that when the crime takes place in the city, the woman must be deemed to have consented and therefore must suffer the death penalty because she could have cried for help. On the other hand where the crime takes place in the open country, no such presumption can be made, for even if the woman called for help, there would be no one to hear her (Deut. 22:25 ff.).[26] But in view of the order of the Deuteronomic legislation which first deals with a wife, then a betrothed virgin and then an unbetrothed virgin, it is possible that this concession was not extended to include a married, as well as a betrothed woman.

[22] Ibid., pp. 60 f. interprets section 55 to mean that if either the married or unmarried seducer is not compelled to marry the daughter, he must pay further damages in addition to providing the father with his wife for prostitution, or, if unmarried, damages.

[23] Thus Job. 31:10 assumes that a female slave will be the subject of promiscuous sexual intercourse. The offence which Job states that he has not committed (verse 9) is the attempted seduction of a married woman. Until sexual intercourse had taken place, there was no crime, but evidently some action could be taken against the attempted seducer. Presumably this would have been brought by the husband. Perhaps it resulted in the infliction of whipping (see below).

[24] This is the significance of בקרת (Speiser, 'Leviticus and the Critics', *Yehezkel Kaufmann Jubilee Volume*, pp. 33 ff.; Noth, *Leviticus*, p. 143).

[25] Cf. LE 31 (ANET, p. 162). The damages payable in this case are more than those demanded for the death of a slave (LE 55: ANET, p. 163). Cf. Goetze, *The Laws of Eshnunna*, p. 89.

[26] Cf. HL 197 (ANET, p. 196) and note on consent LE 26 (ANET, p. 162), CH 130 (ANET, p. 171) and MAL A 12, 23 (ANET, pp. 181 f.).

The cases so far examined have involved the married or betrothed woman as the accomplice of the man, but in Deut. 22:13 ff. the woman alone is made the subject of the legislation. This enacts that a bride who cannot prove her virginity at the consummation of her marriage can be executed for her 'adultery', even though at the time she lost her virginity she might not have been betrothed (Deut. 22:20 f.). She has married under false pretences. But if the husband fails to substantiate this charge against his wife, the law provides that he is to be whipped and must pay damages to his father-in-law. Further, he is deprived of his right to divorce his wife (Deut. 22:13 ff.).

The only crime under discussion in Deut. 22:13 ff. is adultery. If this is not proved the charge is treated as a tort, namely slander of a woman. Thus, as in the case of seduction of an unbetrothed virgin (Deut. 22:28 f.), fixed damages are payable to the injured party, that is the father, for the charge imputes fraud on his part. It is as if a warranty which he had given on the sale of goods had been called into question, and it has been found that the goods were in fact of the quality which the warranty had asserted. Here, however, the damages are excessively severe, being double those prescribed for seduction of an unbetrothed virgin. Further they were presumably additional to the bride price which in the case of money was probably paid over on betrothal.[27] These damages, together with the provision concerning whipping, and the prohibition of divorce, are designed as deterrent measures to ensure that no attempt should be made to bring false charges.[28]

Since Deut. 22:13 ff. envisages the local elders as the administrators of justice, this provision must ante-date Jehoshaphat's reform,[29] which probably explains why it heads the Deuteronomic law on marriage, since, as has already been recognized, Deut. 22:22–29 represents the new Deuteronomic legislation. But since the Deuteronomist recognized the woman's criminal liability, it was necessary for

[27] de Vaux, *Ancient Israel*, p. 33.
[28] When the ninth commandment is discussed it will be held that it was concerned with false evidence in a criminal action by which it was hoped to secure the judicial murder of the accused. Since the Deuteronomist regarded women as equal members of the covenant community with men, a husband who brought false charges against his wife's lack of virginity on marriage might have been thought to have been guilty of this crime. But the law here specifically prevents this possibility by regarding his action as a tort. With this provision should be compared CH 127 (ANET, p. 171), which prescribes that through shaving half his hair and probably his beard, the slanderer should become an object of ridicule (BL, i, p. 278 f.). For a discussion as to whether he was also flogged, see BL, ii, p. 213 f. Cf. MAL A 18–19 (ANET, p. 181).
[29] See above, pp. 18 ff.

him to amend Deut. 22:13 ff. to take cognizance of the new situation
he had created. To do this he added Deut. 22:20 f., as the Deuteronomist's 'purging' formula makes plain.[30] Prior to this, if the parents
could not prove their daughter's virginity on marriage, the husband
would presumably have divorced his wife, and perhaps sued the father
for recovery of the מהר. Further, the damages and the prohibition of
divorce by a husband who fails to justify his charge (Deut. 22:19) may
also be an additional measure to be attributed to the Deuteronomist
(cf. Deut. 22:29).

Deut. 22:13 ff. is the only offence for which whipping is actually
prescribed, but it would seem from Deut. 25:1 ff. that the practice was
not uncommon. One can only guess as to the kind of occasion which
would result in this action, but it would seem that it was probably
administered by the court for any activity which was likely to cause a
breach of the peace. It was certainly not a penalty of the criminal law,
which in all cases demanded that the guilty man should be executed by
communal stoning to propitiate Yahweh. But the criminal law only
dealt with a limited scope of offences and contained no provisions for
the maintenance of law and order. Evidently discretionary powers
were given to the elders to inflict corporal punishment where they
deemed it necessary.[31] Thus as Deut. 22:13 ff. with its reference to
tort makes plain, whipping should not be regarded as part of the
criminal law proper, though it was inflicted at the order of the local
community, for there was nothing sacral about it. Deut. 25:1 ff.,
which by its mention of judges reflects Jehoshaphat's reform, probably
limits the stripes to forty in order to avoid any permanent injury to the
recipient.[32]

Deut. 22:21 provides that if the woman is convicted of the loss of
her virginity prior to her marriage, then she is to suffer execution in the
normal way, save that it is to be outside her father's house. This is
not an additional punishment of the woman, but a punitive measure
directed against the father. Had the charge failed, it would have been
he who would have received damages. It was only right that attention
should be drawn to the fact that even though he may have been un-
aware of the circumstances, he was guilty of fraud, for he had received the מהר for a bride who was not a virgin. He should have
proved a better guardian of his property.

---

[30] See below, p. 182.
[31] Alternatively, people who were likely to cause a breach of the peace could be
detained in the stocks (Jer. 20:2 f.; 29:26; 2 Chr. 16:10).
[32] Cf. MAL B 8 (ANET, p. 186) which prescribes one hundred strokes.

It is too simple a view of the law of adultery to regard the wife as merely part of her husband's property, for, in distinction from a daughter, by virtue of the marriage, she became an extension of the husband himself (Gen. 2:24), and it was through her that his name was continued. The purpose of the legislation prohibiting adultery was therefore to protect the husband's name by assuring him that his children would be his own.[33] This explains why the law of adultery is restricted to sexual intercourse with a married woman, but does not seek to impose sexual fidelity on the husband. There is no thought of sexual ethics as such, but of paternity. This is the reason why once women were brought within the scope of the criminal law by the Deuteronomist, he extended the crime of adultery as far as they were concerned to include lack of virginity on marriage (Deut. 22:20 f.). Thus the act of adultery was a crime which involved the person of a fellow member of the covenant community, and not a tort on his property. The Sinai Decalogue was concerned with persons not property. But as adultery was a crime, it was regarded as a repudiation of Yahweh (Gen. 20:6; 39:8 f.) and, therefore, like other crimes, threatened the covenant relationship. Consequently it demanded state, not private, action which culminated in the execution of the criminal in order to propitiate Yahweh. Thus there could be no pardon of the adulterer or, after the Deuteronomic revision, of the adulteress. The husband who had been injured could take no private act of revenge, nor could he settle for damages, as in the case of a tort committed to his property.[34] The only thing which concerned him, as it did the community, was that the criminal must be publicly tried, convicted and executed.

The position in Israel is thus significantly different from that in other ancient Near Eastern countries where the purpose of the law is solely to redress the husband for the wrong inflicted upon him. It is he who determines the fate of his wife and, in consequence, that of her lover, for if he forgives the former, the latter must also be pardoned.[35] Thus adultery elsewhere in the ancient Near East was regarded as a secular offence against the husband and not, as in Israel, a sacral offence against God, which in view of the covenant concept

[33] For the importance of the continuance of the name, cf. Johnson, *The One and the Many in the Israelite Conception of God*, Cardiff, 1942, pp. 7 f. Cf. Deut. 25:5 f.

[34] Gen. 38:24 might be held to indicate that in patriarchal times adultery was a matter of private vengeance, though in this case it is the *paterfamilias* who orders the execution of the offending woman. But see below, p. 129.

[35] Cf. CH 129 (ANET, p. 171), MAL A 14–16, 23 (ANET, pp. 181 f.), HL 198 (ANET, p. 196).

resulted in communal liability and the absolute duty to execute the
adulterer. Even when the non-Israelite state took notice of the adultery
by itself punishing the wife, rather than leaving this to the husband
himself,[36] it still remained primarily a matter of personal vengeance
on his behalf. It is the religious background of Israel's criminal law
which distinguishes this law from that of all other ancient Near
Eastern countries.[37]

But in spite of this difference between Israel and other Near Eastern
countries, it appears that adultery was widely termed 'the great sin',
this expression being found in certain Egyptian marriage contracts,[38]
and in the Akkadian documents of Ugarit,[39] in addition to its literal[40]
and metaphorical[41] use in the Old Testament.

Num. 5:11 ff. prescribes the procedure to be adopted by a husband
when he suspects that his wife has committed adultery, but who has
no concrete evidence, and so cannot prosecute her lover in the local
criminal court. Instead, he is to bring her before the priest and subject
her to an אלה ('curse'), the private use of which was prohibited by
the third commandment.[42] It is in fact probable that a prosecution
for adultery could only have been brought if there were actual eyewitnesses who had caught the couple *in flagrante delicto* (Num. 5:13).[43]

Although this procedure is now contained in P, it would appear to
be ancient, and originally to have existed without reference to Yahweh.
Thus at one time it was evidently thought that the water which the
woman was made to drink itself implemented the spell (המאררים),[44]

---

[36] Punishment by the husband was evidently no longer envisaged by CH 129, but
traces of it can clearly be recognized in MAL A 14–16, 23, though 12–13 seem to imply
state execution. It is probable that the law was in a state of transition whereby the
husband's powers of acting extra-judicially were being limited, but there is no indication of any new attitude to his right to have his wife executed or pardoned as he pleased.
HL 197 f. (ANET, p. 196) would seem to reflect a similar situation. It has recently
been argued that LE 28 (ANET, p. 162) in fact legislates for the death of the lover, the
fate of the wife being left to the husband or father (Yaron, 'Matrimonial Mishaps at
Eshnunna', *JSS*, viii, 1963, pp. 8 f.).

[37] W. Kornfeld, 'L'adultère dans L'Orient Antique', *RB*, lvii, 1950, pp. 92 ff.;
Greenberg, *Yehezkel Kaufmann Jubilee Volume*, pp. 12 f.

[38] Rabinowitz, 'The "Great Sin" in Ancient Egyptian Marriage Contracts', *JNES*,
xviii, 1959, p. 73.

[39] W. L. Moran, 'The Scandal of the "Great Sin" at Ugarit', ibid., pp. 280 f.

[40] Gen. 20:9.   [41] Exod. 32:21, 30 f.; 2 Kgs. 17:21.

[42] See above, pp. 54 f. Cf. Brichto, *The Problem of 'Curse'*, pp. 49 ff. It would seem
that the verb שבע ('swear') and the noun שבועה ('oath') are used here, because by
consenting to the אלה, the woman turns the curse into a self-inflicted oath, swallowing
the imprecatory words (cf. Exod. 32:20).

[43] Cf. the use of מצא ('find') in Deut. 22:22 and note CH 129 (ANET, p. 171; BL,
i, p. 281).

[44] Speiser, *JAOS*, lxxx, pp. 198 f.; Brichto, op. cit., pp. 111 f.

and so inflicted harm on the guilty wife, but that later this was attributed to Yahweh's direct action (Num. 5:21), the rite being incorporated into Yahwism.[45] Perhaps it was inherited from Canaan.

In a recent discussion of this rite,[46] which has noted that the order of the afflictions in Num. 5:21 and 27 is not the same, it has been suggested that in fact two alternative afflictions are envisaged. Whereas the guilty wife who was already pregnant was to have a miscarriage, the womb of the guilty wife who had not yet conceived was to grow dry, resulting in her sterility. The unique Hebrew word צבה is held to be identical with a Syriac word for 'was dry'. The ritual itself was designed to frighten the guilty wife and so encourage the appropriate punishment. While accepting that sterility is referred to, another recent view notes that it is nowhere stated that the woman was already pregnant, and suggests that it is the state of 'false pregnancy' which is envisaged.[47] In any event, if the wife was innocent she had nothing to fear, for she would be capable of conceiving and bearing a child.

Whatever was contemplated as the exact result of the spell, the ritual, whose consequence would not have been known for some time, did not constitute a judicial trial,[48] for its purpose was not to convict the criminal (the adulterer), who remained undetected, but to ascertain whether a crime had in fact been committed, with the sole purpose of establishing the legitimacy of any child subsequently born. Even if the woman was found guilty, there is no indication that any further physical action was taken against her, though presumably her husband would divorce her. She was to become an אלה (Num. 5:27), that is the subject of an imprecation, among her people (Jer. 29:22). Thus Num. 5:31 is not to be understood as referring to the possible punishment of the wife by the community.[49] תשא את-עונה ('she shall bear her

---

[45] Gray, *Numbers*, p. 47; Blank, *HUCA*, xxiii. 1, p. 88. On the question of the possible conflate nature of the text, see Gray, op. cit., pp. 49 ff.; R. Press, 'Das Ordal im alten Israel', *ZAW*, N.F., x, 1933, pp. 122 ff.

[46] G. R. Driver, 'Two Problems in the Old Testament Examined in the Light of Assyriology', *Syria*, xxxiii, 1956, pp. 74 ff. He also suggests (pp. 73 f.) that the usual translation of the water of 'bitterness' should be replaced by the water of 'contention', 'dispute', based on the Hebrew מרה 'was rebellious'. A handful of dust would not have made the water bitter.

[47] Brichto, op. cit., p. 49.

[48] Trial by ordeal does not seem to have been part of Israel's judicial system. The only mention of it occurs in Exod. 22:6 ff., where the different procedure of Exod. 22:9 ff. shows that Exod. 22:6 ff. was taken over by Israel. See below, pp. 135 ff.

[49] It has been argued that before the Deuteronomic legislation no criminal charge could have been brought against her. Through the priestly reform, the wife would have suffered excommunication rather than the execution first prescribed by Deut. 22:22.

I

guilt') simply means that the wife must bear the consequences of her act, namely direct divine punishment as set out in verse 27.[50] Further, the man referred to in verse 31 is not the suspected adulterer, but the jealous husband.[51] Unlike the husband in Deut. 22:18 f., he is to suffer no penalty should his suspicion have proved unfounded.

In contrast to this primitive paternity rite, CH 131 in exactly similar circumstances provides that a wife shall affirm her innocence by taking an oath and then may return to her home.[52] By taking the oath she declared herself innocent, and must be accepted as such. If she refused to take the oath, she would have been judged guilty, and drowned. But if the charge is made by someone other than her husband, for his sake she must submit to the river ordeal (CH 132), and so risk her life.[53] Similarly under MAL A 17, when one man informs another of his wife's repeated adultery, they go to the river for the water ordeal.[54]

Finally, it seems probable that originally as with some manuscripts of the LXX, the Nash Papyrus and Philo, the commandment on adultery preceded that on murder,[55] for this would give to the Decalogue a logical development of its crimes. The point of connection between the fifth and seventh commandments is, of course, future generations. Whereas the fifth deals with the possible repudiation of parents by sons, the seventh ensures for a father the paternity of children born to his wife, and so protects his name. If this is in fact the correct order, then these two commandments would be followed by the three commandments which sought to protect the person of an individual member of the covenant community, that is the commandments governing murder, mantheft[56] and false evidence in a criminal action.[57] This change of order may have resulted in the loss of an original object to the commandment against adultery (Lev. 20:10) caused by the influence of the now surrounding commandments.[58]

[50] See above, pp. 30 f.

[51] Noth, *Numbers*, E.T., London, 1968, p. 52. But Noth wrongly imagines that the adulterers were stoned.

[52] ANET, p. 171. Her home seems to refer to her quarters in her husband's house (BL, i, p. 284; S. A. Cook, *The Laws of Moses and the Code of Hammurabi*, London, 1903, p. 109.

[53] ANET, p. 171.

[54] ANET, p. 181. The ordeal would have been by the woman alone (AL, pp. 68 f.). The informer was not treated as a slanderer if the woman was found innocent (Cf. MAL A 18–19).

[55] Cf. D. Flusser, ' "Do not Commit Adultery", "Do not Murder" ', *Textus*, iv, 1964, pp. 220–4.

[56] See below, pp. 130 ff.   [57] See below, pp. 142 ff.

[58] Luke 18:20 and Rom. 13:9 would support this change of order.

Further, it will be argued that the tenth commandment is to be connected with the administration of justice, thus forming a logical development from the ninth.[59]

(ii) *The Extension of the Crime*

While it will be argued that the priestly legislation extended the crime of adultery to include all unnatural sexual offences, neither the Book of the Covenant nor Deuteronomy were interested in sex *per se*. Thus it has already been recognized that adultery was not prohibited as a sexual crime, but to guarantee the paternity of any child born to a married woman. Similarly extra-marital intercourse was not forbidden, though a man might find himself liable for damages under the civil law for seduction of a virgin.

At first sight Exod. 22:18 might be thought to refute this contention. But the prohibition of bestiality should not be understood as an extension of the crime of adultery, but as the condemnation of a practice associated with Canaanite ritual. Though precise evidence is lacking, it may not unreasonably be conjectured that the aim of bestiality was to attempt a physical union with the deity through a sacral animal, perhaps culminating in its sacrifice.[60] This submission receives support from HL 187 f., 199 f.,[61] concerning which it has been suggested that the reason that it was only copulation with cattle, sheep and pigs which constituted bestiality, and not horses or mules, was that the former were sacred animals.[62]

If this view is correct, then since the first commandment prohibited relations with any deities other than Yahweh, it is union with him that is the concern of Exod. 22:18. But it has already been recognized that it was a condition of the covenant relationship that Yahweh remained outside the control of man, Israel being forbidden a פסל ('image'), and the use of his name for magical purposes. It therefore seems that bestiality was made a criminal offence in order to ensure Yahweh's freedom. Such a practice was not to be performed in his sanctuaries.

Since sexual practices were not the concern of the criminal law, there need be no surprise that sodomy is neither prohibited in the

---

[59] See below, pp. 149 ff.

[60] E. C. B. MacLaurin, *The Figure of Religious Adultery in the Old Testament*, Leeds University Oriental Society Monograph, vi, 1964, n. 53 and pp. 10 f. suggests that the prohibition of bestiality could be related to the Canaanite ritual of the intercourse between Baal and Anath (cf. G. R. Driver, *Canaanite Myths and Legends*, Old Testament Studies, iii, Edinburgh, 1956, pp. 117 ff.). This suggestion is taken up by Good, *Stanford Law Review*, xix, p. 961.

[61] ANET, pp. 196 f.

[62] Neufeld, *The Hittite Laws*, London, 1951, p. 188.

Book of the Covenant nor Deuteronomy, in spite of the fact that a story of attempted sodomy is twice used to illustrate utter depravity (Gen. 19; Judg. 19), though in each case the emphasis falls not on the proposed sexual act *per se*, but on the terrible violation of the customary law of hospitality.[63] One cannot, of course, be certain that all Israel's criminal law has been preserved in the Old Testament codes, but there appears no reason to doubt that such an act was first made criminal by the priestly legislation (Lev. 18:22; 20:13).

Comparative law codes may indicate a similar situation. Both sodomy and bestiality are omitted from CH, but, while it does not refer to bestiality, MAL A 20 prescribes that he who performs an unnatural offence on another male child shall be so used himself, and then made into a eunuch.[64] For slander of a man, MAL A 19 provides that the slanderer shall be flogged, condemned to forced labour for a month, castrated and fined.[65] It is thus probable that between the compilation of CH and MAL a new attitude to sodomy arose similar to the development which is found in the Old Testament.[66] While HL governs adultery, bestiality and certain prohibited sexual relations with relatives, only in this latter case is there a reference to sodomy, namely between a father and his son.[67]

The only sexual prohibition besides the crime of adultery and the tort of seduction recorded in Deuteronomy, outside the liturgy of Deut. 27:15 ff.,[68] is that a man should not marry or have sexual relations with his father's wife, that is his step-mother (Deut. 23:1). This enactment thus renders illegal the ancient right of the heir to inherit his father's wives and concubines, and, save in the case of his mother, to have sexual relations with them (Gen. 35:22; 49:4; 2 Sam. 3:7; 12:8; 16:22; 1 Kgs. 2:22; 1 Chr. 2:24).[69] Even though no

---

[63] It would appear that these two accounts are based on the same story, but it is not certain when this was incorporated into the existing narratives. Thus it seems from Isa. 1:10; Jer. 23:14; Ezek. 16:49 that Sodom's sin was not primarily associated with this crime (von Rad, *Genesis*, p. 213). Further, in Judg. 19–21, where it is connected to Gibeah, it now appears as a Deuteronomic illustration of the anarchy that existed before the inauguration of the monarchy, and has been combined with other ancient material in the story of the rape of the daughters of Shiloh. Hosea by his references to Gibeah (9:9; 10:9) might be thought to refer to this incident, but it is possible that he was referring to the inauguration of Saul as the first king of Israel (1 Sam. 10:26). The story would therefore appear to be both ancient and unattached.

[64] ANET, p. 181.   [65] Ibid.   [66] AL, p. 71.

[67] HL 189 (ANET, p. 196). It is possible that Ham was guilty of an improper sexual act with regard to Noah (Gen. 4:24).

[68] See below, pp. 187 f.

[69] Robertson Smith, *Kinship and Marriage*, pp. 104 ff. A man would have had to be well off to have had two wives. A son by a first marriage would often be the same age as a later wife of his father. By taking possession of his father's wives and concubines,

penalty is prescribed, it would seem from its position at the conclusion of a series of laws on adultery that Deut. 23:1 is to be understood as an extension of this crime, and thus would have demanded execution. Further, it would appear that the priestly legislators adopted this Deuteronomic expansion, and, in reaction to what was conceived as the immorality of Canaan, reinterpreted the crime of adultery to include all unnatural sexual unions. Thus in Lev. 18:6 ff.; 20:10 ff. can be discerned the working out of a fully comprehensive code of all sexual crimes for the post-exilic period. There is, however, no mention of the tort of seduction, the priestly law here only being concerned with what ultimately would involve excommunication from the elect community of post-exilic Israel, namely crimes.

Before examining the growth of the priestly legislation, one must consider whether there were any prohibitions on sexual relations under customary family law. These can in fact be discerned from Lev. 18:6 ff., which has clearly been modelled on a concrete situation. This situation is the patriarchal family of three or four generations living together under one roof among whom customary law forbade any casual sexual relations outside marriage.[70] This would comprise one's mother (verse 7),[71] step-mother (verse 8),[72] full sister (verse 9),[73] daughter,[74]

---

the heir gave notice that he had displaced his father. This explains the importance of the royal harem to the man who would usurp the throne (cf. Tsevat, 'Marriage and Monarchical Legitimacy in Ugarit and Israel', *JSS*, iii, 1958, pp. 237–43).

[70] Cf. K. Elliger, 'Das Gesetz Leviticus 18', *ZAW*, N.F., xxvi, 1955, pp. 1–25; Noth, *Leviticus*, pp. 135 f.; Porter, *The Extended Family in the Old Testament*, Occasional Papers in Social and Economic Administration, vi, London, 1967.

[71] Cf. CH 157 (ANET, p. 172); HL 189 (ANET, p. 196). Porter, op. cit., pp. 13 f. argues that the phrase 'the nakedness of your father' has been added with reference to Gen. 9:20 ff. Sexual intercourse with one's mother is prohibited not because she is one's father's wife (verse 8), but simply because she is one's mother.

[72] Cf. HL 190 (ANET, p. 196). However CH 158 (ANET, pp. 172 f.) has been interpreted as referring to the chief wife who was not to be inherited (BL, i, pp. 321 f.).

[73] Although a half-sister through a common father would have been found in the patriarchal home (verse 11), a half-sister through a common mother would not (cf. Elliger, op. cit., p. 10). She would have remained with her father or his family. The full sister would have been unmarried, for on marriage she would have left home (Lev. 21:3). However, Porter, op. cit., pp. 11 ff. criticizes Elliger for his rigid assertion that a daughter always left her father's home on her marriage. But the only real example of a husband going to live with his wife's family is that of Jacob, and there special circumstances operated (cf. C. S. Rodd, 'The Family in the Old Testament', *BT*, xviii, 1967, p. 23). Further, as comparison with the Nuzu texts seems to confirm (Gordon, *BA*, iii, pp. 5 ff.; Jack, *ET*, xlviii, p. 549), Laban appears to have adopted Jacob as his son. Consequently Rachel's relatives would have been regarded not merely as in-laws, but as full relations, thus gaining the protection of the customary family law.

[74] The daughter must have been accidentally omitted from Lev. 18. Cf. Gen. 19:30 ff.; CH 154 (ANET, p. 172); HL 189 (ANET, p. 196).

grand-daughter through one's son (verse 10),[75] half-sister through one's father (verse 11),[76] paternal aunt (verse 12),[77] paternal uncle's wife (verse 14),[78] daughter-in-law (verse 15),[79] and sister-in-law (verse 16).[80] Other than the daughter, the only female relative whom one might have expected to have been included in the list is the wife of one's grandson. A grandmother is not included as she would constitute no temptation to her grandson.[81] But while marriage with full blood relations would certainly have been forbidden under customary law,[82] this would not have extended to other relatives, provided that they were in a position to marry.[83] Indeed custom decreed that a man should marry his deceased brother's childless widow.[84] There is, however, nothing distinctively Israelite about this customary law, which probably formed part of an ancient body of family law inherited from primitive times, and which was no doubt widely observed. Nor need it be assumed that it ever existed in a written form such as is now employed in Lev. 18:6 ff. Customary family law simply forbade sexual relations outside marriage with any female relative normally found in one's tent or house: no one needed to have these relatives spelt out one by one. Lev. 18:6 ff. is the work of the priestly legislator who uses the customary law for his own extended purposes.

The order in which the priestly legislation evolved can be deter-

[75] The inclusion of the grand-daughter through a daughter is due to the priestly legislator. Since a daughter would have left home on her marriage, her daughter could not have formed part of the family unit.

[76] Cf. 2 Sam. 13:12. This does not mean that marriage was forbidden (Gen. 20:12; 2 Sam. 13:13).

[77] The paternal aunt would be unmarried. On marriage she would leave her home, and become part of her husband's family. The inclusion of the maternal aunt (verse 13) is due to the priestly legislator. Normally she would not have been found in her married sister's dwelling.

[78] Brothers did continue to live together after marriage, but with the birth of children, younger brothers would usually leave the family dwelling to form their own. Thus nieces and cousins would not have fallen within the scope of customary family law (Gen. 11:29). Indeed the person most often selected for one's bride was one's cousin (Gen. 24:48; 28:2) (Köhler, *Hebrew Man*, p. 90). An uncle could be as young as or younger than his nephew, for his father could have married a new young wife in his old age, and produced a son when his other sons were already grown up.

[79] Cf. Gen. 38; CH 155 f. (ANET, p. 172) (BL, i, pp. 318 f.).

[80] Cf. HL 195 (ANET, p. 196).

[81] Elliger, *ZAW*, N.F., xxvi, pp. 9 f.

[82] Mother, full sister, daughter, grand-daughter.

[83] Widowed step-mother or sister-in-law, half-sister through a common father etc.

[84] Cf. Deut. 25:5 ff. (AL, pp. 240 ff.). Cf. HL 193 (ANET, p. 196). In his discussion of Gen. 38, Pedersen, *Israel*, i–ii, p. 79, indicates that in an emergency the duty of raising up a son for the deceased may have extended to his father. Accordingly in Gen. 38 the irregularity would not be that Judah fathered a child through his union with Tamar, but that he did so while a son of his was still alive.

mined by referring to the penalties prescribed, for it has already been recognized that in the exilic situation execution was replaced by reliance on divine activity to inflict punishment, which in turn was replaced by the post-exilic punishment of excommunication.[85]

Thus in view of the execution formula, Lev. 20:10 ff. can be isolated as the first stage of the reinterpretation of the crime of adultery to include all unnatural sexual unions. This coda subsumes under that crime sexual intercourse with one's step-mother or daughter-in-law, sodomy,[86] marriage with a mother and daughter,[87] and bestiality, which is now extended to include women.[88] Thus whereas Lev. 20:11 repeats the Deuteronomic enactment prohibiting sexual relations with one's widowed step-mother (Deut. 23:1), Lev. 20:12 extends this to one's widowed daughter-in-law with whom marriage had once been regarded as legitimate (Gen. 38). The penalty of burning in Lev. 20:14 is clearly a later interpolation,[89] and it is possible that the whole section was interpolated.[90] Presumably Lev. 20:14 does not just prohibit simultaneous marriage, but would include marriage with one's mother-in-law after the death of one's wife.

Those provisions which rely on divine activity to effect punishment must constitute the second stage of the reinterpretation of the crime. At first sight these appear to comprise Lev. 20:17, 19–21. These enactments will be examined in reverse order.

Lev. 20:21 apparently renders illegal the ancient custom of levirate marriage (Deut. 25:5 ff.), the punishment of childlessness being particularly apt.[91] Lev. 20:20 prohibits marriage with a paternal uncle's widow. That in this case a permanent union is also envisaged

---

[85] See above, pp. 28 ff.

[86] Homosexual relations between women are nowhere prohibited.

[87] Cf. HL 191, 195 (ANET, p. 196).

[88] Since women were not liable under the pre-Deuteronomic criminal law, Exod. 22:18 would only have applied to men. Lev. 20:15 f. also enacts that the animal must be killed as well.

[89] See below, p. 129.

[90] Cf. Daube, *Studies in Biblical Law*, pp. 78 ff. While Daube is certainly correct in asserting that Lev. 20:17 f. does not form part of the original coda Lev. 20:10 ff., his assertion that Lev. 20:10–16 is itself made up of two codas, Lev. 20:10–13; 14–16, seems doubtful, for it would seem that since bestiality was already a crime in the Book of the Covenant, Lev. 20:15 f. would have formed part of the original coda. Daube's preference for recognizing new additions to existing law by means of tacking on rather than insertion has been criticized by H. Kosmala, 'The So-called Ritual Decalogue', *ASTI*, i, 1962, p. 58 and cf. pp. 44 f. Kosmala argues that both methods were used, insertion being the later.

[91] However, Porter, *The Extended Family*, p. 19 argues that this enactment merely prohibits marriage with one's sister-in-law when she has *already* borne a son to one's deceased brother.

can similarly be recognized from the nature of the punishment. Although Lev. 20:19 also places reliance on divine intervention for its enforcement, it would seem that the entirely different form of this provision from that of the remainder of Lev. 20:10 ff. indicates that it has been subsequently interpolated being a conflation of Lev. 18:12 and 13.

This leaves Lev. 20:17. This verse is heavily overloaded, both marriage and unnatural sexual lust being mentioned, together with two punishment formulas. But like Lev. 20:20 f. it may be assumed that it also originally prohibited a formerly legitimate marriage relationship with someone whom one could have expected to find in one's home. This must have been one's half-sister through a common father (Gen. 20:12; 2 Sam. 13:13). The half-sister through a common mother has been subsequently inserted, together with a reference to unnatural lust and the excommunication formula.[92] Thus Lev. 20:17 (minus the reference to the half-sister through a common mother), 20 f. formed the second coda to the reinterpretation of the crime of adultery.

The third stage in the development of the law on sexual offences in the Holiness Code would appear to be the reinterpretation and codification of the old customary law of the patriarchal family to prohibit absolutely all sexual relations, *whether within marriage or not*, with any relative who could be described as 'near of kin' (שאר), a term which included even relatives by marriage (Lev. 18:17b).

Thus in addition to those relatives whom one would have found in the ancient patriarchal home of three or four generations under one roof, the grand-daughter through a daughter and the maternal aunt find their way into the priestly legislator's list. But the half-sister through a common mother was not yet introduced into Lev. 18:6 ff., for had this been the case, Lev. 18:11 would never have appeared.

Lev. 18:17a seems to envisage the same situation as Lev. 20:14, which in Lev. 18:17b is extended to the second generation as well.[93] As has been noted in connection with Lev. 20:14, it would seem that marriage after one's wife's death would also have been prohibited. On the other hand, while Lev. 18:18 specifically prohibits simultaneous marriage with two sisters (cf. Gen. 29:21 ff.), it does not forbid subsequent marriage with a deceased wife's sister.[94]

The reinterpretation and codification of the old customary law in

---

[92] The singular עונו ישא ('he shall bear his iniquity') is odd, when elsewhere in Lev. 20:10 ff. all parties to the crime are held liable. The LXX reads the plural.
[93] Cf. HL 195 (ANET, p. 196).   [94] Cf. HL 191, 192, 195 (Ibid.).

Lev. 18:6 ff. is therefore a logical development from the two codas which have already been isolated in Lev. 20:10 ff. Further, the fact that Lev. 20:19, itself a conflation of Lev. 18:12 and 13, relies on divine intervention to secure the punishment of the offender, indicates that this reinterpretation took place during the exilic situation, and prior to the development of excommunication as the penalty for breach of the post-exilic criminal law. It is probable that Lev. 20:19 was interpolated into Lev. 20:10 ff. due to the recognition that it prohibited two formerly legitimate marriage relationships, one of which concerned someone whom a man might expect to find in his home (cf. Exod. 6:20).

The final additions to Lev. 20:10 ff. can be recognized from their use of the excommunication formula. These consist of the insertion of Lev. 20:18, which prohibits sexual intercourse with a woman during her menstrual period, and the expansion of Lev. 20:17. In spite of the fact that the punishment of burning appears to have replaced an earlier punishment formula in Lev. 20:14, it would seem that, in view of the retention of the earlier punishment formula in Lev. 20:17, in addition to the new punishment of excommunication, it is unlikely that in Lev. 20:18 excommunication replaced a previous formula similar to that in Lev. 20:19. Accordingly Lev. 20:18 must be understood as a new provision. Sexual intercourse with a woman in her menstrual period had probably long been considered improper (Ezek. 22:10), though not criminal. It would seem that it was inserted last because it did not specifically concern sexual intercourse with a *relative*.[95]

The position of Lev. 20:18 has, however, been determined by the desire of its interpolater to emend Lev. 20:17. It is at this point both in Lev. 20:17 and Lev. 18:9 that the half-sister through a common mother was introduced into the list of prohibited sexual relationships, Lev. 20:17 being adapted to indicate unnatural sexual lust, and the excommunication formula being added. Thus the final clause of Lev. 18:9 refers to the half-sister through a common mother, and indicates that wherever she is born, sexual intercourse with her is prohibited.

---

[95] However, Daube, *Studies in Biblical Law*, pp. 78 ff. argues that Lev. 20:17 f. was added before Lev. 20:19 ff. on the basis that while Ezek. 22:10 f. contained references to sexual intercourse with one's half-sister through a common father, and with a woman during her menstrual period, it did not refer to any of the instances set out in Lev. 20:19 ff. But he fails to recognize that Lev. 20:17 has two punishment formulas, the latter one of which links the verse to Lev. 20:19 ff., and shows that Lev. 20:18 was later inserted at the same time as Lev. 20:17 was expanded to include the excommunication formula.

This was the last relative of whom the priestly legislation took cognizance, for it never extended its law to include nieces.

Finally, all sexual crimes found in Lev. 20, including the ritual to Molech, were added to the list of relatives in Lev. 18:6 ff. to constitute a complete code of all such crimes for the post-exilic period. This addition (Lev. 18:19 ff.) was followed by a hortatory passage (Lev. 18:24 f.), which concluded with the excommunication formula (Lev. 18:29).

Thus for the post-exilic period, the crime of adultery was reinterpreted to include any of the offences specified in Lev. 18:6 ff., breach of any of which would involve excommunication.

The ritual לַמֹּלֶךְ associated with a shrine in the valley of Ben-Hinnom outside Jerusalem has generally been understood to refer to child sacrifice.[96] It has been held to derive from Phoenician influence, and reference has been made to the Punic term *molk*, which apparently indicates a particular type of sacrifice, namely that of a child, for which an animal could be substituted.[97] This has led to the hypothesis that מלך does not refer to a deity, but to the sacrifice itself.[98] However, Lev. 20:5 (cf. 2 Kgs. 17:31) confirms beyond doubt that in מלך one is to recognize the designation of a deity, which Jer. 7:31; 19:5; 32:35 indicates is Yahweh himself.[99] The introduction of Baal in Jer. 19:5; 32:35 (cf. Deut. 12:31) represents a later editing showing the complete impropriety of the ritual. Thus by מֹלֶךְ one is to understand the noun מֶלֶךְ ('king') with the vocalisation of בֹּשֶׁת ('shame') to denote abhorrence. This ritual was evidently frequently practised and is therefore not to be compared with 2 Kgs. 3:27 and associated with a time of national danger.

While Ezek. 16:21; 23:37 would appear to confirm that child sacrifice was practised, the position of Lev. 18:21 amid a series of unnatural sexual offences would imply that it is similarly to be understood. Thus the LXX and Samaritan versions gave this verse a sexual connotation, apparently understanding it to refer to cultic prostitution. While they may have read עבד ('serve') for עבר ('pass over'),[100] it is

---

[96] Reference to the ritual may be found in Lev. 18:21; 20:2 ff.; Deut. 12:31; 18:10; 2 Kgs. 16:3; 21:6; 23:10 (cf. 2 Kgs. 17:31); Jer. 7:31; 19:5; 32:35; Ezek. 16:21; 20:31; 23:37. Cf. Isa. 30:33. In 1 Kgs. 11:7 מֹלֶךְ should be corrected to מִלְכֹּם ('Milcom').

[97] de Vaux, *Ancient Israel*, p. 445, *Studies in Old Testament Sacrifice*, Cardiff, 1964, pp. 73 ff.

[98] Eissfeldt, *Molk als Opferbegriff im Punischen und Hebräischen und das Ende des Gottes Molech*, Beiträge zur Geschichte des Altertums, iii, Halle a. Saale, 1935.

[99] Albright, *Archaeology and the Religion of Israel*, pp. 162 ff.; J. Gray, *The Legacy of Canaan*, VTS, v, 1957, p. 126; Eichrodt, *Theology*, i, pp. 149 f.; Noth, *Leviticus*, pp. 147 f.   [100] G. Quell, BH, p. 172.

more probable that they understood עבד to mean 'have sexual intercourse', 'mate', as in Job 21:10.[101]
But since the LXX nowhere else understands the ritual in this manner, this cannot be its original interpretation.[102] It would seem that the most satisfactory solution to the nature of the rite so far produced, and one which takes into account both the apparent sacrifice of the children (Ezek. 16:21; 23:37) and the ritual's obvious sexual connotation (Lev. 18:21), is that those who were sacrificed were the offspring of cultic prostitution.[103] If this is so, then Ezek. 16:20 ff.; 23:37 ff., may have a literal application. Since the king would appear to have been connected with the practice of the Jerusalem cultus, there is no *prima facie* reason for rejecting this suggestion in connection with Ahaz and Manasseh.

The presence of sacred prostitutes in the cult was a continual problem for Judah in the period of the monarchy (1 Kgs. 14:24; 15:12; 22:46).[104] They were finally condemned by Deut. 23:18, and action taken against them by Josiah (2 Kgs. 23:7). Similarly the ritual למלך was declared illegal by Deut. 18:10, and the high place at which this was practised destroyed by Josiah (2 Kgs. 23:10), though after his death the ritual was revived.[105]

Finally it may be noted that on the basis of Gen. 38:24 it has been thought that in patriarchal times the penalty for adultery was burning.[106] There is no other indication that such a penalty was ever prescribed save in two provisions of the Holiness Code, namely for marriage with a mother and a daughter (Lev. 20:14), and prostitution by a priest's daughter (21:9), which is probably to be understood as cultic prostitution.[107] It would seem probable that during the exile the penalty of burning, which appears to mean burning alive rather than branding or cremation after execution, was borrowed from two similar enactments of Babylonian law (CH 110,[108] 157).[109] But that it was ever exercised in post-exilic Israel which relied on excommunication rather than execution appears to be very unlikely. Thus Judah's order that Tamar should be burnt before he has even heard her defence may in fact be a priestly gloss reflecting this Babylonian type of punishment, which had been incorporated into the Holiness Code.[110]

---

[101] G. R. Driver, *VT*, ii, p. 356, 'Babylonian and Hebrew Notes', *WO*, ii, 1954, p. 19.
[102] Snaith, 'The Cult of Molech', *VT*, xvi, 1966, pp. 123 f. argues that Lev. 18:21 does refer to the giving of children for cultic prostitution. But he fails to consider Ezek. 16:21; 23:37.   [103] Elliger, *ZAW*, N.F., xxvi, p. 17.
[104] Cf. Hos. 4:14.   [105] See above, p. 30.
[106] de Vaux, *Ancient Israel*, p. 36.   [107] Noth, *Leviticus*, p. 156. Cf. Lev. 19:29.
[108] ANET, p. 170.   [109] ANET, p. 172.   [110] BL, i, pp. 495 f.

CHAPTER TEN

THE PROHIBITION OF THEFT

(Exod. 20:15; Deut. 5:19)

(i) *The Crime of Manstealing*

As will be made clear,[1] theft of property in Israel was not a crime, but a tort resulting in an action for damages by the injured party. But since the Decalogue contains an enactment against theft, then, if the contention that this was ancient Israel's criminal law code is to be maintained, it must be shown that there was a category of theft in pre-exilic Israel for which, on conviction, the offender would suffer the criminal law penalty of execution. This is the crime of manstealing referred to in both the Book of the Covenant (Exod. 21:16) and Deuteronomy (24:7), which aimed at preventing the sale of an Israelite not within the covenant community, but outside it.[2]

The case of Joseph appears to supply an example of the kind of situation envisaged by this crime, namely the sale of the victim outside his community, and indicates the ease with which the criminal could dispose of him (Gen. 37:25 ff.).[3] Once a man had been sold to slave traders, there was very little hope of his recovery. Thus in its outcome, manstealing was very little different from murder. Indeed in Deut. 24:7 the thief is described as גנב נפש ('the stealer of life').[4] It is for this reason that Exod. 20:15 is absolute, for as in the case of murder, it seeks to protect not only adult males, but also women and children. Once any of these were sold outside the community, they were effect-

---

[1] See below, pp. 132 ff.

[2] Alt, 'Das Verbot des Diebstahls im Dekalog', *Kleine Schriften*, i, pp. 333 ff.; Reventlow, *Gebot und Predigt*, pp. 80 f. On the originality of Alt's contention, cf. M. H. Gottstein, 'Du sollst nicht stehlen', *TZ*, ix, 1953, pp. 394 f.; J. J. Petuchowski, 'A Note on W. Kessler's "Problematik des Dekalogs" ', *VT*, vii, 1957, pp. 397 f.

[3] Gen. 37:25 ff. appears to preserve two accounts of Joseph's fate, in one of which he is sold by his brothers, and in the other he is stolen from the pit in their absence (von Rad, *Genesis*, p. 348). L. Kopf, 'Arabische Etymologien und Parallelen zum Bibel-wörterbuch', *VT*, viii, 1958, p. 169 argues that Gen. 40:15 does not refer to manstealing. But this would seem to be the crime to which Judah alludes in Gen. 44:16.

[4] On the use of נפש, see above, pp. 85 f.

ively lost to Yahweh for ever. Thus the absence of an object to this commandment is not to be understood as a later development. The effect of the commandment was to guarantee the residence of every individual Israelite within the covenant community.

The fact that the Deuteronomist felt it necessary to set out the crime, which he specifically connects with members of the covenant community, shows that the commandment still had relevance in the last years of the monarchy. There was always the risk that Israelites might be sold to invading foreign powers. Thus both Hos. 4:2 and Jer. 7:9, which clearly reflect the Decalogue, should be understood as referring to manstealing, and not to theft in general.

It has been recognized that Exod. 21:16 has been expanded by the addition of נמצא בידו ('and he is found in his presence'), and it has been argued that whereas originally the crime could only have been proved if the victim had actually been sold (that is passed out of the hands of the thief), by virtue of this addition, merely to be found in wrongful possession of a fellow Israelite was sufficient evidence to enable conviction for this crime to be obtained.[5] Another examination has, however, suggested that the clause might refer to the proceeds of sale, rather than to the man himself.[6] There would, however, seem to be no reference to permanent possession, such as enslavement.[7]

The meaning of התעמר in Deut. 24:7 is uncertain. The same word only occurs elsewhere in Deut. 21:14, again in the Hithpaʻēl, where an Israelite is forbidden to sell a wife whom he has taken from a conquered enemy, and in whom he has ceased to have pleasure. To this is added לא תתעמר בה apparently in apposition to מכר ('sell').

Basing its derivation on an Arabic word meaning 'cherish enmity', 'rancour', 'malice', התעמר has been translated 'deal tyranically with'.[8] But placed alongside מכר, this is tautologous. While the LXX renders Deut. 24:7 by καταδυναστεύω ('oppress', 'dominate', 'exploit someone'), in Deut. 21:14 it uses ἀθετεω ('deal treacherously with', 'break faith with'), perhaps indicating uncertainty as to the exact meaning of the word. It has been suggested that the verb might be emended to read התעשר ('enrich oneself'),[9] but since the same spelling appears in two separate and distinct enactments in Deuteronomy, it would appear that the MT must preserve the correct reading. It would therefore seem best to understand התעמר as a commercial

---

[5] Daube, *Studies in Biblical Law*, p. 95.
[6] Noth, *Exodus*, p. 180.
[7] Cf. Morgenstern, *HUCA*, vii, p. 189, viii, pp. 125 f.
[8] BDB, p. 771b; K-B, p. 717a. [9] J. Hempel, BH, pp. 296, 300.

term,[10] the precise meaning of which has now been lost. This is the interpretation of the Targum, which uses the verb תגר ('treat as merchandise').

CH 14 provides the death penalty for kidnapping a seignor's young son.[11] What 'young' means is nowhere defined.[12] The section does not mention what the kidnapper intends doing with his victim. There is no recorded offence of stealing an adult. HL 19–21 prescribe punishments for the theft of a man, woman or slave.[13] None involve the infliction of the death penalty, though in the case of theft of a free man or woman the compensation that has to be paid is more severe than that for murder.[14]

(ii) *The Tort of Theft*

In ancient Israel theft of property was not regarded as a crime, but a tort, the injured party being restored as far as possible to the position he was in before the damage of which he complains occurred. Thus where an ox gored another ox to death, the living ox was sold, and the proceeds of sale, together with the dead animal's carcass, were divided between the parties (Exod. 21:35).[15] Each party must share in the misfortune. But if the owner of the living ox knew that his beast had a propensity to gore, then he must give to the owner of the dead animal another ox of the same monetary value as the dead animal, and would himself take the carcass (Exod. 21:36). The goring ox would, of course, have lost its value being a dangerous animal, and was, therefore, not given to the plaintiff as compensation for his loss.[16]

But in the case of theft of animals, a prospective thief would not have been deterred by the knowledge that if he were caught, he would only have to return to the plaintiff an animal of the same value as the stolen beast. Consequently the law enacted that in the case of an ox the thief must restore fivefold, and for a sheep fourfold (Exod. 21:37; 22:2b).[17] These punitive damages are not to be regarded as a fine, for

---

[10] Daube, op. cit., p. 95; David, '*hit'āmēr* (Deut. xxi. 14; xxiv. 7)', *VT*, i, 1951, pp. 219–21. Cf. further Alt, '*zu hit'ammēr*', ibid., ii, 1952, pp. 153–9.

[11] ANET, p. 166.   [12] BL, i, p. 105.   [13] ANET, p. 190.

[14] Neufeld, *The Hittite Laws*, pp. 138 f.

[15] Cf. LE 53 (ANET, p. 163).

[16] It has already been noted on p. 97 that in Exod. 21:34 monetary damages have replaced restitution in kind, perhaps because they were easier to assess.

[17] The reason that the damages for stealing an ox are greater than those for stealing a sheep is probably that the owner of the ox was also being compensated for loss of services which the ox could perform, such as ploughing (Daube, *Studies in Biblical Law*, p. 133). Cf. the often excessive punitive damages prescribed under HL 57 ff. ANET, p. 192) for theft of animals.

they are paid to the plaintiff and not to the state, which had laid down their amount, and would secure their payment. A thief who could not pay the requisite damages was to be sold (Ex. 22:2b).[18] The poorer the potential thief, the greater was the deterrent value of these measures, which would hardly have affected the rich.

The major difficulty in legislating against theft is to determine at what moment the offence is committed. Thus if an animal belonging to the plaintiff is found among the defendant's flock, it is always open to the latter to plead that it strayed there. Initially it appears that the tort was not committed until the animal had been either killed or sold, but that later it was extended to include being in wrongful possession of another's beast.[19] In this latter case, the punitive damages were fixed at twofold (Exod. 22:3).[20]

The damages for theft of property other than animals is nowhere explicitly stated, but from Exod. 22:6 it may be deduced that in all other cases punitive damages amounting to double the value of the stolen articles had to be paid.

It is only by distinguishing between the criminal and civil law that David's reaction to Nathan's parable can be understood (2 Sam. 12:5 f.).[21] The offence which the rich man in Nathan's parable had committed was the theft of a sheep for which the poor man could sue him in tort for fourfold restitution (2 Sam. 12:6). The LXX here reads sevenfold. While it is possible that the punitive damages were later increased,[22] it is more likely that sevenfold is a later proverbial expression indicating that perfect restitution must be made.[23] While a later scribe might have altered the MT to fourfold to conform with the law,[24] it would seem more probable that the LXX rendering is due to a recollection of the proverbial saying preserved in Prov. 6:31, which also reads sevenfold. What then is the meaning of 2 Sam. 12:5?

It has already been noted that the punitive damages prescribed for

---

[18] There is no justification for the contention that this provision protected the thief from more serious action by the injured party (cf. Daube, op. cit., p. 93), for the only course open to him under the civil law was to sue the tortfeasor in damages. The thief would have been placed in the same position as an insolvent debtor.

[19] Ibid., pp. 90 f.

[20] The inclusion of the ass, which is not mentioned in Exod. 21:37, is a later addition. The LXX reflects the confusion in the list of animals by omitting the ox.

[21] Cf. my short note, 'The Interpretation of 2 Samuel xii. 5–6', VT, xvi, 1966, pp. 242–4.

[22] Cook, The Laws of Moses and the Code of Hammurabi, pp. 215 f.; Morgenstern, HUCA, vii, p. 98.

[23] de Vaux, Ancient Israel, p. 160.   [24] Driver, Samuel, p. 291.

theft would have been little deterrent to the rich. It would therefore seem reasonable to suppose that David's angry outburst, in which he describes the rich man as a בן־מות ('son of death'), reflects the inadequacy of the civil law in this particular case.

The expression בן־מות occurs elsewhere only in 1 Sam. 20:31 and 26:16 (in the plural). In 1 Sam. 20:31, Saul indicates that David has acted so badly that he deserves to die, but when Jonathan challenges him to specify the offence, Saul cannot. David has done nothing to which Saul can legally take exception.[25] In 1 Sam. 26:16 David accuses Abner and Saul's men of such negligent behaviour that they deserve to be executed as criminals for their failure to guard the Lord's anointed. But there is no suggestion that they have committed any crime for which the death penalty could have been exacted. Similarly, David, when he uses the term בן־מות, indicates that the rich man in Nathan's parable had committed such a heinous offence that he deserves to be indicted on a criminal charge and suffer the penalty of the criminal law, capital punishment (2 Sam. 12:5), but that because he has in fact committed no *crime*, the state cannot intervene, and so the injured party is left to sue for full compensation under the civil law (2 Sam. 12:6). David thus contrasts the criminal and civil law, state prosecution and an action by the plaintiff, capital punishment and damages. The rich man deserved death for his callous act, but was protected by the law itself.

With the expression בן־מות should be compared the phrase איש מות ('man of death') found in 2 Sam. 19:29 (in the plural) and 1 Kgs. 2:26, which also indicates those who should certainly die. 2 Sam. 19:29 refers to Saul's family. The speaker is Mephibosheth who seeks to flatter David into again showing him mercy by recalling that, although in David's eyes all Saul's family deserved death, Mephibosheth himself had been previously spared.[26] In 1 Kgs. 2:26 Abiathar, who had supported Solomon's rival Adonijah in the succession struggle, though worthy of death is given a free pardon.[27]

Both בן־מות and איש מות are therefore emphatic expressions, indicating those who in the eyes of the speaker should without doubt

---

[25] Saul had already attempted to murder David, both directly (1 Sam. 18:10 f.) and indirectly (1 Sam. 18:25).

[26] As 2 Sam. 21 appears to be presupposed by 2 Sam. 9, it is probable that Mephibosheth is making a specific reference to the seven sons of Saul whom David handed to the Gibeonites to execute. Similarly, Shimei also appears to refer to this event (2 Sam. 16:5 ff.) (Hertzberg, *Samuel*, pp. 299 ff., 345 f., 381 ff.).

[27] Similarly Joab is not executed for his support of Adonijah but on a criminal charge of murder (1 Kgs. 2:32). See above, p. 85.

be executed. Accordingly, this would appear to be another case where מות is used superlatively,[28] though as in other cases where מות has been treated as a superlative,[29] its primary meaning is still apparent. The expressions are first understood as referring to those who ought to be executed, being 'death's men' or 'sons', that is, they already belong to that realm of weakened life which the Hebrew understands as the state of מות.[30] Because of their emphatic use, they can then come to be understood in a superlative sense, and thus mean 'the deadly man', 'the arch villain'.

Thus in 2 Sam. 12:5 f. David describes the rich man as an arch villain who is morally guilty, but regretfully notes that the criminal law cannot touch him. There is therefore no need to regard 2 Sam. 12:6 as an interpolation,[31] nor to hold that both penalties were exacted.[32]

The climax of the narrative is now reached with Nathan's dramatic disclosure to David that he is the rich man of the parable. But he is not simply a בן-מות, a man who deserves to die, but who can only be sued in tort: he is, by his murder of Uriah, an actual murderer who should suffer execution under Israel's criminal law. It is due to Yahweh's direct pardon that David is to be spared (2 Sam. 12:13).[33]

It would seem that theft of property continued to be treated as a tort under the priestly legislation, and so did not involve excommunication from the cult (cf. Lev. 5:21 ff.), and that it is to this and kindred torts that Lev. 19:11–13 refers, these verses having in effect a close relationship with the various situations envisaged in Exod. 21:37–22:12.

Exod. 22:6 ff. contains a series of enactments about property dispute cases in which the court has no means of deciding the issue, and so exceptionally orders that the matter should be resolved at the sanctuary by means of an oath. These provisions will be examined in reverse order.

Exod. 22:9 ff. governs the liability of a depositee for animals

---

[28] Winton Thomas, 'A Consideration of Some Unusual Ways of Expressing the Superlative in Hebrew', *VT*, iii, 1953, pp. 219 ff.; S. Rin, 'The מות of Grandeur', ibid., ix, 1959, pp. 324 f.; Winton Thomas, 'Some Further Remarks on Unusual Ways of Expressing the Superlative in Hebrew', ibid., xviii, 1968, p. 123.

[29] Eg. Judg. 16:16; 2 Kgs. 20:1; Isa. 53:12.

[30] Johnson, *The Vitality of the Individual*, pp. 88 ff.

[31] Morgenstern, *HUCA*, vii, p. 98; Daube, *Studies in Biblical Law*, p. 153.

[32] Hertzberg, *Samuel*, p. 313.

[33] While the king was subject to the criminal law, and therefore could suffer divine punishment for breach of it, it is possible that as head of the judiciary he was outside the jurisdiction of the courts, and therefore could not be indicted and tried on a criminal charge.

K

entrusted to his care, and provides that if an animal died, was injured, or, perhaps, driven away[34] while in his possession, in the absence of any witness, the depositee must take an oath before Yahweh if he is to absolve himself from his liability to make restitution. Such an oath would of course have been sworn at the sanctuary. The owner of the animal has no option but to accept the oath,[35] for it is assumed that if the depositee had sworn falsely, divine punishment would inevitably fall upon him.[36] This is not a case of trial by ordeal, for like the paternity rite in Num. 5:11 ff.,[37] no judgement is given, nor is any future action by the complaining party contemplated.[38]

But in contrast to Exod. 22:9 f., Exod. 22:8, which is not confined to relations between an owner and a depositee, but concerns property disputes in general, clearly deals with a case of trial by ordeal. This provides that where two parties contest the ownership of property, they shall come before הָאֱלֹהִים, who will determine the issue, the guilty party being treated as a thief, and so liable for twofold restitution. How the decision was obtained is not stated. Here there is both a judgement and the implementation of that judgement in the payment of damages. The use of אֱלֹהִים, first with the definite article and then as the subject of a plural verb, indicates that originally this enactment did not refer to Yahweh, which, together with the fact that nowhere else in Israelite law is there any reference to trial by ordeal, confirms that it is of foreign origin.

Exod. 22:7 provides that where money or goods have been stolen from the house of a depositee, and the thief has not been found, then

---

[34] It is possible that אוֹ נִשְׁבָּה ('or is driven away') should be deleted from verse 9, for it is clear that verse 11, which deals with theft, is in contrast to verse 9. Further, these words also appear in verse 13 in the LXX. But it has been suggested that אוֹ נִשְׁבָּה refers to a raid by an external party, traces of which would be found, whereas verse 11 deals with theft within the local community (Morgenstern, *HUCA*, vii, pp. 107 f.).

[35] The verb לָקַח ('accept') refers to the oath (BDB, p. 543a), and not to the dead or wounded animal (Morgenstern, op. cit., p. 108).

[36] This declaratory type of oath is found elsewhere in ancient Near Eastern law. Cf. LE 37 (ANET, p. 163); CH 103 (ANET, p. 170), 249, 266 (ANET, pp. 176 f.); HL 75 (ANET, p. 192).

[37] See above, pp. 118 ff.

[38] However, where an animal was stolen, the depositee was judged negligent, and had to make restitution (Exod. 22:11), though if the beast had been killed by wild animals he could escape this provided he produced the carcass or part of it as evidence (Exod. 22:12). Whereas the LXX and Vulgate contemplate the owner being taken to the carcass, the MT understands the carcass being brought to the owner, which interpretation is supported by Gen. 31:39; 1 Sam. 17:34 f., and Amos 3:12 (Fensham, "*d* in Exodus xxii. 12', *VT*, xii, 1962, pp. 337–9). In such a case no oath would have been needed. Cf. CH 244, 266 (ANET, pp. 176 f.; BL, i, pp. 438 ff.). There is no mention of any oath in the sections concerning damage or loss to borrowed animals in Exod. 22:13 f.

the depositee must draw near to האלהים to ascertain whether or not he has himself appropriated the deposited property. Since אלהים with the definite article is again used, *prima facie* Exod. 22:7 should be understood as referring to the same procedure as Exod. 22:8, namely trial by ordeal, and not to the declaratory oath of Exod. 22:10.[39] This is confirmed from the Nuzu tablets, in one of which identical wording to Exod. 22:7 has been found. These tablets indicate that the ordeal consisted in swearing an oath before the *ilāni*, which it has been earlier noted are the etymological equivalent of אלהים, and as in Gen. 31 are to be identified with the *teraphim*.[40] While a person who refused to submit to an oath before the *ilāni* naturally lost his case, the Nuzu tablets show that even if he did so swear, the case might still be decided against him.[41] This confirms that the oath was an ordeal and not a declaratory oath as in Exod. 22:10.[42] In contrast to Exod. 21:6, it would have been sworn before the sanctuary *teraphim*.

There are accordingly two different procedures for dealing with property dispute cases in Exod. 22:6 ff. But with the abolition of the *teraphim* in the Deuteronomic reform (2 Kgs. 23:24), trial by ordeal oath became impossible, and as Lev. 5:21 ff. seems to confirm, an oath before Yahweh was sufficient to determine the ownership of any disputed property, including that which was lost. But since trial by ordeal was not an Israelite method of obtaining justice, it is possible that even before the Deuteronomic reform the declaratory oath before Yahweh replaced this foreign procedure, and that Exod. 22:7 f. was understood in terms of Exod. 22:10.

In spite of the increased severity of the priestly legislation in respect of the cult, false oaths were still not made criminal because to do so threw doubt on the efficacy of the oath itself. Where orthodoxy asserted that a false oath would result in direct divine punishment, for the state itself to inflict punishment, instead of leaving it to the deity himself, amounted to an admission that the deity was incapable of action. Thus the punishment for false oaths in general continued

---

[39] Cf. Morgenstern, *HUCA*, vii, pp. 114 ff. Both the LXX and Vulgate insert the equivalent of ונשבע ('and he shall swear') in Exod. 22:7 after האלהים.
[40] See above, pp. 60 ff.   [41] Gordon, *JBL*, liv, p. 142.
[42] While admitting the equation of the *ilāni* of the Nuzu tablets with אלהים and *teraphim* in Gen. 31, this identification in Exod. 22:7 f. has been challenged by reference to LE 37 (ANET, p. 163) from which it has been held that אלהים refers to the god of a particular sanctuary, Tishpak in Eshnunna, Yahweh in Israel (Fensham, *JBL*, lxxvii, pp. 160 f.; Loretz, *Bibl.*, xli, pp. 167 ff.). But this argument fails to recognize that the oath in LE 37 is of the declaratory type, and that accordingly the procedure outlined in that section is similar to Exod. 22:10, and not to Exod. 22:7 f.

to be left to the deity to inflict when he would. This is confirmed from Lev. 5:21 ff.

But the possible presence in the cult of those who had sworn falsely was obviously invidious to the authorities. This explains the desire of the priestly legislation to encourage voluntary confession to such an act, illustrated by the smallness of the punitive damages compared with those prescribed elsewhere in the Book of the Covenant. Thus Lev. 5:21 ff. requires the restoration of the appropriated property, the payment of punitive damages to the value of one fifth of that property, and the rendering of the necessary guilt offering by which atonement might be made (cf. Num. 5:5 ff.). The offence is regarded primarily as a sin against Yahweh, rather than a tort against one's neighbour.[43] Lev. 19:12a, as the context makes clear, must also refer to false oaths in property dispute cases.[44]

Another practice of the civil law of theft connected with the sanctuary was the אלה ('curse') placed on an unknown thief by the injured party through public proclamation at the sanctuary. This is specifically mentioned in Judg. 17:2 and Prov. 29:24.[45] That the mother who had lost her silver had first to pronounce the אלה publicly is confirmed by the addition of וגם אמרת באזני ('and also spoke (it) in my ears'). Since she suspected her son, she subsequently recounted to him the curse which she had pronounced publicly, and which was in consequence already in operation, in order to induce him to confess. Naturally this was now as much in her interest as in his, for she must have feared that disaster would strike him. Prov. 29:24 indicates that not only the thief himself, but also a receiver would be subject to the curse.

Further, it is this institution to which Lev. 5:1 alludes. The witness who has heard the public proclamation of the curse on the unknown thief, and subsequently fails to testify, brings himself within the area of divine punishment, that is under the curse itself.[46] He is counted as an accessory after the fact.

---

[43] Cf. further Ps. 24 discussed on p. 187 below. Lev. 5:4 shows the same desire to encourage confession for an oath rashly uttered.

[44] Mal. 3:5 also refers to the oppression of the hireling in respect of his wages in conjunction with false swearing.

[45] Cf. Brichto, *The Problem of 'Curse'*, pp. 42 ff. For a criticism of Brichto's interpretation of the third commandment, see below, pp. 146 f.

[46] Brichto, op. cit., p. 43 renders קול אלה by 'a public summons backed by a contingent curse'. It should, however, be understood as a 'public proclamation of the curse (on the unknown thief)'. Further, there is no suggestion in the MT that the קול אלה itself was directed at the witness. The RSV unjustifiably imports 'to testify' into its translation.

There need be no hesitation in restricting the אלה to cases of theft with which Judg. 17:2 and Prov. 29:24 specifically connect it, for in the first place it is pronounced by the injured party, thus signifying that a tort and not a crime has been committed, and secondly breach of the criminal law would in any event have automatically resulted in the criminal coming under the curse of Yahweh. Accordingly to place an אלה upon him would have been meaningless. But in contrast to a criminal, a thief had only committed a tort, and therefore his sole liability if he was caught was a civil action for damages. By placing him under the אלה, the thief, like the unknown criminal, was now subject to divine punishment, and so long as he refused to confess his act, could no longer have any enjoyment in life (Prov. 29:24). But it should be noted that whereas in the case of murder by an unknown person no אלה was placed on the criminal, in that case the community had to propitiate Yahweh, for a crime, unlike a tort, broke the covenant relationship between Yahweh and the community (Deut. 21:1 ff.).

The אלה was in effect a prayer to Yahweh, and consequently would have been proclaimed at the sanctuary in the presence of the priests, the guardians of the cult.[47] This is confirmed from 1 Kgs. 8:31 f. (2 Chr. 6:22 f.), which cannot be understood as referring to oaths sworn in property dispute cases (Exod. 22:7 ff.), for whereas an אלה was implicitly contained in every oath (שבועה), nowhere does the verb אלה mean 'swear on oath'.[48] Accordingly אלה must be given its proper meaning of 'curse' and 1 Kgs. 8:31 f. understood as referring to the curse placed on an unknown thief. Thus one should read with the LXX נשא ('take'), rather than the MT's נשא ('exact'),[49] and understand the neighbour as the subject of both this verb and the remainder of the sentence. ואלה ('and he pronouces the curse') should also be read with the LXX. It was the person who had suffered the injury who pronounced the curse at the sanctuary. Accordingly 1 Kgs. 8:31 may be rendered: 'If someone injures his neighbour, and the latter takes up a curse against him to bring him under the curse, and comes and pronounces the curse before your altar in this house. . .'[50]

Both a false oath in a property dispute case and an אלה placed on an unknown thief are referred to in Zech. 5:3 f.[51] In both cases the אלה

---

[47] Cf. the paternity rite in Num. 5:11 ff. (see above, pp. 118 ff.) and oaths in property dispute cases (Exod. 22:7ff.).

[48] Brichto, op. cit., pp. 22 ff.   [49] BDB, p. 670b; K-B, p. 638a.

[50] Brichto, op. cit., pp. 52 ff. while substantially giving the same interpretation, understands אלה as the subject of ובא.

[51] Although לשקר only occurs in verse 4, it is clearly to be understood in verse 3. Zech. 8:17 also refers to false swearing.

is depicted as going forth to bring disaster. Whereas in the case of the unknown thief, the אלה would have had to have been specifically pronounced at the sanctuary, in the case of the man who had sworn falsely it would have been self-inflicted being implicit in his oath.

The normal verb for 'steal' is גנב, but both גזל and עשק are also used of the illegal acquisition of property. While גזל means 'to seize by force', and is usually rendered 'rob',[52] עשק indicates the withholding of property which rightfully belongs to another, and is generally translated 'oppress'.[53] Both verbs thus describe torts.

While CH provides no general enactment on the law of theft, it may be deduced that the usual penalty both for the thief and the receiver of stolen goods was death.[54] If the thief was dead, damages were payable from his estate.[55] A similar fate awaited the man who falsely alleged that he was the owner of lost property.[56] But to constitute theft, it would seem that the property had to be taken from the possession of another.[57] Thus if the property in question was already in the hands of the offender before his appropriation of it, then this did not amount to 'theft', but to a breach of trust for which compensation was ordered.[58] In Israel there was no need to make such a distinction for either action would have amounted to a tort for which the injured party would sue for damages (Exod. 21:37; 22:2b–3, 6 ff.). It has been held that CH 8[59] indicates that later damages replaced the death penalty,[60] though these are so high that death would still have normally been inflicted. Perhaps even in other cases the thief was able to come to an extra-judicial arrangement with the injured party,[61] for there was no 'religious' significance in the execution. While MAL hardly alludes to theft,[62] HL prescribes that damages

[52] Eg. Deut. 28:29; Judg. 9:25; Job 20:19; 24:2; Mic. 2:2.

[53] Eg. Deut. 24:14; Hos. 12:8; Mal. 3:5. A nation could be the subject of oppression, that is have its freedom withheld (Jer. 50:33; Hos. 5:11), or oppress another (Isa. 52:4).

[54] Cf. CH 7, 9, 10, 22, 25, 34 (ANET, pp. 166 f.).

[55] CH 12 (ANET, p. 166).

[56] CH 11 (ANET, p. 166).   [57] BL, i, pp. 80, 450 f.

[58] Cf. CH 112, 120, 124–5, 254–5, 265 (ANET, pp. 170 f., 176 f.). In the case of appropriation of farm implements (CH 259 f.) (ANET, p. 177), where the compensation is small, it has been suggested that this appropriation may have been treated as an act of illegal borrowing, rather than theft (BL, i, p. 450). Exceptionally CH 253 requires mutilation (ANET, p. 176). Cf. CH 256 (ANET, p. 177).

[59] ANET, p. 166.

[60] Meek, *Hebrew Origins*, p. 66.   [61] Ibid., pp. 81 ff.

[62] Cf. MAL A 3–6 (ANET, pp. 180 f.) which govern theft by a married woman, and are to be understood as a supplement to CH (AL, pp. 22 ff.), and MAL C+G 8, F 1 f. (ANET, pp. 187 f.) from which it would seem that theft of animals was not punished by death.

should be paid. However, it has already been noted that even for murder HL did not exact the death penalty.[63]

The result of this discussion should make it plain that, in contrast to Babylonian law, in discussing theft in Israel the crime of man-stealing and the tort of theft of personal property must be distinguished. It is failure to do this that has led to erroneous attempts to discern a development in the law of theft in Israel. Thus it has been held that originally the penalty for all kinds of theft was death, but that, either in contrast to CH,[64] or in a similar manner to that Code's alleged development,[65] this was later reduced to damages. In fact there was no development in the Israelite law, for execution was exacted for the crime of manstealing and damages were payable for the tort of theft of personal property. Israel's criminal law was concerned with the protection of persons not of property, and in no case would it regard the latter as more important than the life of a member of the covenant community.

Finally, it cannot be maintained that there was in Israel a crime of theft of sacred objects[66] comparable to CH 6 and 8.[67] No mention is made of such a crime in the law codes themselves, nor can the case of Achan be used to support it, for Achan and his family were not exe-cuted for theft, but because he had brought himself and his family within the area of the ban to which Jericho was already subject.[68] Indeed there would have been no need to legislate against theft from a sanctuary, for to lay hands on Yahweh's property could only have led to direct divine action (2 Sam. 6:6 f.). There was no necessity to legislate for that which no one would contemplate undertaking.

---

[63] Only in two instances (HL 123, 126) (ANET, p. 194) in the many sections on theft in the Hittite Laws is there any mention of a death penalty. Neufeld, *The Hittite Laws*, p. 176, suggests that the theft of the bronze lance in HL 126 may amount to an act of sacrilege, the lance having had a ritual purpose. HL 95 (ANET, p. 193) in the case of a slave exceptionally provides for mutilation.

[64] Mendenhall, *BA*, xvii, pp. 38 f.

[65] Meek, *Hebrew Origins*, pp. 66 ff.; Daube, *Studies in Biblical Law*, p. 94.

[66] Cf. Ibid., pp. 201 ff.   [67] ANET, p. 166.

[68] See above, p. 40. The other cases cited in support of this contention are Rachel's theft of Laban's household gods (Gen. 31:17 ff.), the alleged theft of Joseph's divining cup (Gen. 44:1 ff.), and the theft of the contents of Micah's shrine (Judg. 18:14 ff.). The fact that Jacob orders the death of the person with whom Laban's household gods are found discloses the absolute power of the head of the clan in patriarchal times, but says nothing about any special category of theft. As regards Joseph's cup, there is no suggestion that Joseph or his steward thought that death was the appropriate penalty for its theft. This only enters the discussion because the brothers were so certain of their innocence that they were able to make this extravagant offer. Whether any more can be made of these accounts than the natural pursuit of thieves on the discovery of the loss of property seems very doubtful.

CHAPTER ELEVEN

THE PROHIBITION OF FALSE WITNESS

(Exod. 20:16; Deut. 5:20)

(i) *Judicial Murder*

That the ninth commandment is not a general injunction against lying,[1] but specifically concerns the giving of false evidence in legal proceedings may readily be recognized both from the use of the noun עֵד ('witness'), and the verb עָנָה ('testify').[2] The עֵד would indicate anyone who gave evidence in a case, which under Israelite legal procedure could even include those who were to judge it.[3]

Whereas in Exod. 20:16 the witness is described as of שֶׁקֶר ('falsehood', 'deception'), in Deut. 5:20 he is called שָׁוְא, which indicates that which is groundless, worthless, or lacks substance. It has been held that while Exod. 20:16 only covered a testimony which included actual lies, Deut. 5:20 related to any evidence which was calculated to mislead or deceive the court, even though no direct lie was told.[4] But this seems much too subtle. שֶׁקֶר indicates quite generally the broad idea of causing deception, the means of which need not be confined to a lie.[5] Accordingly there would seem to be no material distinction between the two words so far as the scope of this commandment is concerned (cf. Isa. 59:4).[6] Whereas Exod. 20:16 simply refers to what the witness does, namely causes deception, Deut. 5:20 seeks to stress what the witness is, that is a worthless, empty man.[7]

---

[1] Köhler, *Old Testament Theology*, E.T., London, 1957, p. 251; Stamm, *TR*, N.F., xxvii, p. 300; Stamm and Andrew, *The Ten Commandments*, pp. 108 f.

[2] Cf. Exod. 23:2; Num. 35:30; Deut. 19:16 ff.; 1 Sam. 12:3; Mic. 6:1 ff., and the case of Job (Köhler, *Hebrew Man*, pp. 158 ff.).

[3] Ibid., p. 157; de Vaux, *Ancient Israel*, p. 156; Stamm, *TR*, N.F., xxvii, p. 301.

[4] Ibid., pp. 199, 300; Stamm and Andrew, *The Ten Commandments*, pp. 15, 107 f.

[5] Andrew, 'Falsehood and Truth', *Interpr.*, xvii, 1963, pp. 429 ff.; Stamm and Andrew, *The Ten Commandments*, p. 110.

[6] Deut. 5:20 is the only occurrence of the phrase עֵד שָׁוְא, whereas עֵד שֶׁקֶר is found in Deut. 19:18; Ps. 27:12; Prov. 6:19; 12:17; 14:5; 19:5, 9; 25:18. Rowley, *BJRL*, xxxiv, p. 114 argues that the variation is due to a copyist.

[7] M. A. Klopfenstein, *Die Lüge nach dem Alten Testament*, Zürich, 1964, pp. 18 ff.

But it has not generally been recognized that the proceedings envisaged by this commandment are to be limited to criminal cases, though if the Decalogue was in fact Israel's criminal law code, this is what one might expect. This is confirmed by Deut. 19:16 ff., which is to be understood as a longer version of the original commandment.[8] In the first place the 'purging' formula (Deut. 19:19) is only used in connection with capital punishment,[9] and therefore indicates that since the false witness is to be treated as he had attempted to treat his brother, he must have sought the latter's execution through conviction to a criminal charge.[10] Secondly, this is the implication of the term סרה, which generally indicates revolt against Yahweh, that is apostasy. Since the covenant relationship was secured by obedience to the criminal law contained in the Sinai Decalogue, and not by the civil law, it was only breach of the former which could properly be termed סרה. Therefore in Deut. 19:16 סרה should be rendered 'crime'.

Thus once more it is the person of the individual member of the covenant community, and not his property, that is the concern of the criminal law, which protects him from what is here termed 'judicial murder'. There is, however, one important point in which this crime is to be distinguished from murder itself, namely that the death of the victim is not required for the crime to be constituted. Thus even though there was in fact no miscarriage of justice which resulted in the execution of the accused, the false witness would be guilty of a criminal offence, and so liable to the death penalty (Deut. 19:19).

But this crime should not be termed 'perjury', that is the giving of false evidence under oath, for there is no indication at all in the Old Testament that evidence was given under oath.[11] Thus in addition to the commandment itself, neither Exod. 23:1–3, 6–9; Deut. 19:15 ff. or Lev. 19:15 f. make any reference to a false *oath*. The swearing of an oath (שבועה) was a cultic action which properly had to be undertaken at the sanctuary in the presence of the priests, whereas the administration of justice was conducted at the city gate before the elders. It was only in property dispute cases where the elders had no means of deciding the issue, that an oath was exceptionally required to be sworn at the sanctuary, which oath decided the issue (Exod. 22:9 ff.; Lev. 5:21 ff.). Such a procedure would have been quite meaningless if the parties had already given evidence under oath.

[8] Morgenstern, *HUCA*, vii, pp. 76 f.

[9] Deut. 13:6; 17:7, 12; 21:21; 22:21, 22, 24; 24:7. Cf. 19:13; 21:9.

[10] It has already been argued on p. 96 that the talionic provision contained in verse 21 is a post-exilic addition.

[11] Greenberg, 'Witness', IDB, iv, 1962, p. 864.

Indeed had an oath been necessary in order that evidence might be given, then there would have been no need for the ninth commandment itself, since every oath contained a self-curse (אלה), which if that oath was false would immediately have resulted in direct divine action. As has already been noted in the discussion of the third commandment, false oaths were not expressly prohibited under the Decalogue, for there was no need to make provision for something which everyone knew could only result in disaster.[12]

It has earlier been argued that originally a single witness would have been sufficient to secure a conviction.[13] Consequently where the court had the right to exact the death penalty on the unsworn evidence of this witness, it was imperative that it should be able to rely on the truth of that evidence. No greater precaution could be conceived than the commandment which declared that the giving of false evidence in a criminal case would itself be a crime punishable by death. The motive for this crime could either be to secure the murder of someone whom one wished disposed of, as in the classic example of the judicial murder of Naboth (1 Kgs. 21), or to avoid conviction oneself for a crime which one had committed, and for which one had not yet been accused. It is probable that under Israelite procedure a man was assumed guilty until proved innocent.[14] The term רֵע ('neighbour'), as its similar use in the tenth commandment makes clear, would originally have referred to a fellow male member of the covenant community, as before the Deuteronomic reform women were not subject to the criminal law, and therefore could not have been prosecuted.

The manual of justice contained in the Book of the Covenant (Exod. 23:1–3, 6–9) refers to the crime of judicial murder, though its emphasis is ethical rather than judicial, being concerned with promoting the right attitude to justice, rather than the infliction of punishment for breach of the criminal law.[15] Thus Exod. 23:7 enjoins the Israelite to keep far from a דבר־שקר, that is an action based on false evidence, by which, as the verse states, those innocent of any criminal act might be convicted and executed.

The same crime is referred to in Exod. 23:1, where, however, the witness is described as עֵד חמס. This is not to be understood as a witness of violence,[16] but as a witness who promotes violence,[17]

[12] See above, pp. 53 f.   [13] See above, p. 23.
[14] von Rad, *Deuteronomy*, p. 59.   [15] For further discussion, see p. 158 below.
[16] Cf. Reventlow, *Gebot und Predigt*, p. 83, who cites Lev. 5:1 in support of his contention that the עֵד חמס is someone who witnesses a violent action, and who has in consequence a duty to bring this to the notice of the community, as this harms their

namely the execution of an innocent person. The phrase עֵד חָמָס is therefore a stronger alternative form to the עֵד שֶׁקֶר, the witness who promotes deception, both of which are used in Deut. 19:16ff. Similarly Ps. 27:12 describes the עֵדֵי־שֶׁקֶר as breathing out[18] חָמָס against the Psalmist, and Ps. 35 depicts עֵדֵי חָמָס (verse 11) seeking the Psalmist's life (verse 4) by bringing false accusations against him (דְּבְרֵי מִרְמוֹת) of which they proclaim themselves eyewitnesses (verses 20 f.).

Though at first sight it might appear that Exod. 23:1a refers to the repetition of rumours as hearsay evidence,[19] comparison with Lev. 19:16 seems to indicate that these rumours are in fact repeated outside the court, perhaps with the aim of creating a climate of opinion in which a false charge might succeed, or of encouraging someone else to institute a prosecution (cf. Ezek. 22:9). Whether Exod. 23:1 indicates that this was to be regarded as an extension of the original commandment, and therefore constituted a criminal offence, cannot be determined.

The priestly legislation continued to regard the giving of false evidence in criminal actions as a crime, Lev. 19:16 forming a very similar combination to Exod. 23:1. That there is a reference here to the activity of a witness rather than a general injunction not to cause death can be recognized from the use of the verb עָמַד ('stand'), for witnesses stood to give evidence.[20]

Under CH[21] punishment for acting as a false witness was based on the logical application of the *lex talionis*, the offender suffering the same penalty as that which would have been inflicted on the accused had the charge been proved.[22]

(ii) *'False Swearing' in Two Alleged References to the Decalogue*

Hos. 4:2 would appear to reflect ancient Israel's criminal law, as set out in the Decalogue, and to list those crimes which directly concerned the protection of members of the covenant community. Thus

relationship with Yahweh. But no mention is made of any act of violence in Lev. 5:1, and it has been shown on p. 138 above that in fact this verse refers to a particular procedure in connection with the civil law of theft.

[17] BDB, p. 329b.; Driver, *Deuteronomy*, p. 235.

[18] Reading וְיָפֵחַ (W. O. E. Oesterley, *The Psalms*, London, 1955, p. 195; Kissane, *Psalms*, i, p. 121. Cf. F. Buhl, BH, p. 997). Cf. Prov. 25:18.

[19] Morgenstern, 'The Book of the Covenant'—Part IV', *HUCA*, xxxiii, 1962, pp. 89 f.

[20] Köhler, *Hebrew Man*, p. 155.   [21] CH 1-4, 11 (ANET, p. 166).

[22] In the case of an unproved charge of sorcery, however, the accused himself must first suffer the river ordeal (CH 2) (BL, i, pp. 61 ff.).

there are set out in succession murder, (man)stealing,[23] adultery, and a reference to burglary (Ex. 22:1–2a), which is intended as a deliberate substitution for the original tenth commandment.[24] These crimes are preceded by the words אלה וכחש, which have generally been understood zeugmatically, being rendered 'false swearing', with the implication that they referred to the ninth commandment.[25]

Quite apart from the fact that this translation would have to be rejected as far as that commandment was concerned, for evidence was not given under oath, there is, however, no indication anywhere that אלה means 'swear'.[26] Consequently, if the ninth commandment is referred to, then this must be governed by כחש alone. Since the word means quite generally 'deceive', 'dissemble', one may conclude that in fact this verse does so.[27] Presumably this word has been selected in order to express the idea of the commandment by one verb.

Therefore אלה וכחש must indicate two crimes, and one need not hesitate to give אלה its usual meaning 'curse', and understand it to refer to the third commandment. Although the purpose of that commandment was to prevent the manipulation of Yahweh by the improper use of his name, it is the only other commandment which directly concerned the person of every individual Israelite, for it ensured that no one could be subjected to magical practices. It is, therefore, entirely intelligible that this commandment should be referred to here.

But it has, however, been argued that there was in Israel a form of legitimate conditional curse, which could be used by an individual in an accusation of wrongdoing against a specific person where there was no proof of his guilt. The following example is cited: 'If A has taken my such-and-such, may Yahweh do this-and-that to him'. Because of the conditional 'if', the declarer could act with impunity, and thus, even though he knew that A was innocent, effect his 'character assassination'. The same examination then goes on to argue that it was against misuse of this institution that Exod. 20:7 was enacted, the fraudulent use of which is found mentioned in Pss. 10:7; 59:13 and Hos. 4:2, and forms the background to Ps. 24.[28]

But it has already been held that the use of an אלה by a private individual was prohibited by the third commandment. In the dis-

---

[23] See above, pp. 130 ff. Even the Deuteronomist found it necessary to refer to this crime (Deut. 24:7), though he nowhere mentions the tort of theft.

[24] See below, pp. 149 ff.

[25] W. R. Harper, *Amos and Hosea*, ICC, 1905, p. 250.

[26] Brichto, *The Problem of 'Curse'*, pp. 22 ff.

[27] Ibid., pp. 57 f.   [28] Ibid., pp. 56 ff.

cussion of adultery and theft, its exceptional use both in the rite to
establish a child's paternity (Num. 5:11 ff.)[29] and in the case of theft
by an unknown person has been noted.[30] But in each case the אלה
was a specifically cultic instrument, which had to be publicly pronounced at the sanctuary. Further, in the case of theft by an unknown
person, even when the person who had suffered the loss had suspicions
as to whom the thief might be (Judg. 17:2), there is no indication that
the אלה pronounced at the sanctuary was directed at a *named* subject.
Thus Lev. 5:1, Prov. 29:24 and Judg. 17:2 cannot be used to support
the existence of an alleged conditional curse directed at a *particular*
person, whereby his character might be ruined with impunity.

Both Pss. 10 and 59 appear to envisage the practice of magic by the
Psalmist's enemies, who imagine that Yahweh is powerless to act.
This is the significance of the terms מרמות ('deceits)', תך ('oppression'), עמל ('trouble'), and און ('iniquity'), which in the MT of Ps.
10:7 are all equivalent expressions to אלה ('curse').[31] It would seem
that כחש ('deceit') in Ps. 59:13 should also be understood as referring
to magical devices.[32] There is no necessity to render the conjunction
of the two terms in Ps. 59:13 and Hos. 4:2 in the same way, for where
a word carrying a general meaning like כחש is used, its interpretation
must be determined by the context of the passages in which it appears.

The suggestion that the third commandment was aimed at the
fraudulent use of a legitimate conditional curse directed at a named
person, an instrument of whose existence the Old Testament gives no
indication, must therefore be rejected. Consequently it could not have
formed the background to Ps. 24, which it will be held served a very
different purpose.[33] There is thus no ground at all for setting aside the
conclusion reached in Chapter 5 that the third commandment was
enacted to protect the divine name from being used for magical
purposes.

Hos. 4:2 is then to be understood as referring to those crimes which

---

[29] See above, pp. 118 ff.   [30] See above, pp. 138 ff.

[31] This would still appear to be the interpretation of the psalm even if אלה is to be
taken with verse 6, the most attractive reading being לדר ודר אֲשָׁרַי לֹא תַכְרִיעַ אלה
(Buhl, BH, p. 983), which has been rendered, 'From generation to generation my steps
shall not draw down a curse' (E. A. Leslie, *The Psalms*, New York, 1949, p. 222). The
wicked feel so sure of themselves in their apostasy that they reject the possibility of the
infliction of the divine אלה. Other suggestions are that אלה should be omitted (Oesterley,
The Psalms, p. 144) or that it should be emended to read אָלַֽיִךְ, the text being altered
to read אֲשֶׁר לֹא כָרַע אֲלֵךְ which is then translated 'with unfaltering step shall I walk'
(Kissane, *Psalms*, i, p. 41).

[32] Oesterley, op. cit., pp. 295 f. and cf. Mowinckel, *The Psalms in Israel's Worship*,
i, E.T., Oxford, 1962, pp. 199 f.   [33] See below, p. 187.

secured the protection of the individual Israelite. It was because Israel entered into the exclusive covenant relationship at Sinai that these actions became crimes, and not through any universal religious beliefs, for they formed part of the covenant stipulations laid on her by Yahweh, breach of which led to the repudiation of the covenant itself. It is, therefore, a natural corollary of Israel's lack of awareness of Yahweh (verse 1) that these crimes should be openly committed. Further, the covenant law not only ensured Israel's sole allegiance to Yahweh, but also the wellbeing of the community and the land itself (verse 3). Once the law was disregarded, anarchy reigned.

As evidence was not given under oath, וְהִשָּׁבֵעַ לַשֶּׁקֶר ('swear falsely') in Jer. 7:9 cannot refer to the ninth commandment.[34] Although this wording is used of false oaths in property dispute cases (Lev. 5:22, 24; 19:12; Zech. 5:3 f.), it is unlikely that these are referred to here, and it must accordingly be considered whether any other action could have been envisaged which would both fit the context and for which support might be found in Jeremiah's use of שבע ('swear') elsewhere.

While an oath was in effect a confession of faith,[35] and consequently had to be sworn in Yahweh's name (Deut. 6:13; 10:20. Cf. Josh. 23:7), swearing was a part of routine worship,[36] the oath of allegiance evidently amounting to a form of creed (Hos. 4:15; Isa. 48:1). Thus, whereas to swear by Yahweh was synonymous with true worship (Ps. 63:12; Isa. 45:23), to swear by another deity amounted to a direct act of apostasy, and so to breach of the first commandment. It would seem that it is to this form of apostasy that Jer. 7:9 refers. Just as incense was being burnt to Baal, and relations entered into with other gods, so those deities were being acknowledged by oaths in the cult. Actual instances of such apostasy are mentioned in Amos 8:14; Zeph. 1:5,[37] and are also referred to by Jeremiah himself (4:1 f.; 5:7; 12:16). Frequently such apostasy did not amount to a total rejection of Yahweh for another deity, but either to the recognition of other gods alongside him (Jer. 44:25 f.; Zeph. 1:5) or to an insincere acknowledgement of Yahweh without any intention of fulfilling his demands (Isa. 48:1; Jer. 5:2).

[34] Since Jeremiah appears to envisage crimes rather than torts, for his concern seems to be with those actions which might result in repudiation of the covenant, he must understand theft to refer to manstealing (cf. Deut. 24:7).

[35] Driver, *Deuteronomy*, pp. 94 f.

[36] Harper, *Amos and Hosea*, p. 184.

[37] Reading בְּמִלְכֹּם ('by Milcom') with the Versions. For the deity Milcom, cf. 1 Kgs. 11:5, 33; 2 Kgs. 23:13.

CHAPTER TWELVE

THE PROHIBITION OF DEPRIVING AN ELDER OF HIS STATUS

(Exod. 20:17; Deut. 5:21)

If the Decalogue is Israel's criminal law code, then the tenth commandment cannot merely refer to some mental attitude, but must indicate some overt action for which a man could be prosecuted.

Since it has been argued that all the commandments originally consisted of a short apodictic clause, one may proceed with the discussion of this commandment on the assumption that originally it only concerned the בית ('house'), the second clause being a subsequent expansion. That the Deuteronomist understood the בית to refer to a building is plain from Deut. 5:21 where it is listed alongside other items of property. But even in Exod. 20:17 בית is to be understood in this sense, and not as a collective term for the family or household, for there is no mention of children, and animals can hardly be reckoned part of the household.[1] Further, since the escaped Egyptian slaves who became the covenant community did not adopt a nomadic way of life, but settled at the first suitable place they encountered, Kadesh,[2] it can be assumed that they dwelt there in permanent buildings. Indeed tradition asserts that these slaves were brick-makers (Exod. 5:7 f.). Consequently the argument as to whether בית can include a tent seems irrelevant.[3]

Most recent discussions of this commandment have sought to maintain that the verb חמד, traditionally rendered 'covet', should not be restricted to mental desire but must govern the steps necessary

[1] J. Herrmann, 'Das zehnte Gebot', *Sellin-Festschrift*, Leipzig, 1927, pp. 75 ff.; Reventlow, *Gebot und Predigt*, pp. 87 f.

[2] See above, pp. 8 f. I. Lewy, 'Auerbachs neuester Beweis für den Mosaischen Ursprung der Zehngebote Widerlegt', *VT*, iv, 1954, pp. 313 ff. has conclusively shown that the suggestion that the commandment is to be connected with Rechabite philosophy, its purpose being to prevent a renunciation of the nomadic way of life by desiring houses, cannot be maintained, for the commandment would then have also had to forbid agriculture and viticulture, as well as prohibit the building of houses.

[3] Herrmann, op. cit., p. 76; Weiser, *Introduction*, p. 121; Noth, *Exodus*, p. 166.

to implement that desire.[4] While חמד is followed by לקח ('take') in Deut. 7:25 and Josh. 7:21, and by גזל ('seize by force', 'rob') in Mic. 2:2, it is argued that its absolute use in Exod. 34:24 and Ps. 68:17 confirms that activity is included in the verb. Thus it is held that in the former case what the Israelites fear is not that someone might merely desire their lands, but set about seizing them. Similarly it is argued that in Ps. 68:17, Yahweh does not just desire to live on the mountain, but takes steps to realize that desire. Indeed the use of לבב ('heart') in Prov. 6:25 could indicate that חמד has been deliberately qualified to show that no action was contemplated.

But can this in fact be maintained? In the first place, on etymological grounds, it has been pointed out that there is no indication of any other meaning than 'desire', 'delight' in the nouns derived from the root חמד.[5] Nor do cognate languages necessarily support the contention that חמד indicates activity. Thus in Arabic the root denotes praise,[6] and the Phoenician inscriptions from Karatepe do not positively confirm that there the root *must* include action.[7] Secondly, in order to indicate change of possession, an additional verb is undoubtedly needed (Deut. 7:25; Josh. 7:21; Mic. 2:2). Surely if the Decalogue had sought to prohibit dispossession of property it would have used such words as לקח or גזל, and not resorted to חמד. Further it has been recognized that Exod. 34:24 need not necessarily refer to invasion by those who have been driven out, but could indicate that the expulsion will be on such a scale that there will be no one left within Israel to desire the pilgrims' land when they go up to the central sanctuary.[8] Finally, the Deuteronomist certainly understood חמד to indicate desire alone, and not activity, as his use of אוה in Deut. 5:21b confirms. It would therefore seem that one should first consider whether חמד does not in fact indicate mental desire, though if this is so, then Exod. 20:17a in its present form could not have been part of Israel's criminal law.[9]

[4] Kennett, *Deuteronomy and the Decalogue*, p. 67, *The Church of Israel*, Cambridge, 1933, p. 143; Herrmann, op. cit., pp. 69 ff.; Köhler, *TR*, N.F., i, p. 183; Alt, *Kleine Schriften*, i, pp. 333 ff.; Keszler, *VT*, vii, p. 13; Reventlow, op. cit., pp. 85 ff.; Stamm, *TR*, N.F., xxvii, pp. 301 ff.; Stamm and Andrew, *The Ten Commandments*, pp. 101 ff.

[5] J. R. Coates, 'Thou shalt not covet', *ZAW*, N.F., xi, 1934, pp. 238 f.

[6] Ibid.

[7] Alt, 'Die phönikischen Inschriften von Karatepe', *WO*, i, 1949, pp. 274 f., 278 f. Cf. Gray, *The Legacy of Canaan*, p. 65.

[8] Cf. Jacob, *JQR*, N.S., xiv, p. 169.

[9] While it is not denied that ancient peoples understood the significance of coveting (J. P. Hyatt, 'Moses and the Ethical Decalogue', *Encounter*, xxvi, 1965, p. 205), what is denied is that such an idea would find any place in what so far has been shown to be Israel's criminal law code, for no prosecution could have been brought for its breach.

But let it be assumed that the original commandment did prohibit seizure of one's neighbour's house, some other verb than חמד being used. It has, however, been contended that Israel's criminal law was not concerned with the protection of property, but of persons. Therefore if this assumption is correct, it would seem that the primary concern of the commandment could not have been the house as such, but the effect that dispossession would have had on the houseowner.

It has earlier been argued that the senior male member of each house held the office of elder, and that the elders would have been responsible for the government of the local community's affairs, among which the administration of justice was the most important feature.[10] Dispossession would have meant loss of that status. Can it be that the purpose of the original commandment was to guarantee the democratic nature of the administration of justice in Israel, and so of the covenant law itself, including the decision to inflict the death penalty for its breach? This would make very good sense coming after the commandment against acting as a false witness, and would also explain why it was the house alone, and not land in general, which was the object of the prohibition against dispossession.[11]

But it will at once be asked why Exod. 20:17a does not refer explicitly to taking possession of one's neighbour's house, but instead uses חמד. The answer to this question lies in the change in the administration of justice brought about by Jehoshaphat's reform,[12] for with the appointment of royal judges in place of the local elders (2 Chr. 19:5) the *raison d'être* for the commandment was lost. Consequently it became redundant, since it was not the purpose of the criminal law to protect property itself. Thus as prosecution under this commandment was no longer contemplated, it was spiritualized by the substitution of חמד for the original verb which would have

---

Thus Gordon's contention ('A Note on the Tenth Commandment', *JBR*, xxxi, 1963, pp. 208 f., 'The Ten Commandments', *Christianity To-day*, viii, 1964, p. 628) that the commandment is to be understood as a reaction to Canaanite religion, since the Ugaritic texts show that Baal coveted, cannot be accepted. Further, while the original commandment will be shown to have been connected with the administration of justice in Israel, there seems no justification for Hyatt's contention (pp. 205 f.) that by prohibiting covetousness, the commandment ensured that bribes should not be taken by officials and judges.

[10] See above, pp. 17 f.

[11] It is possible that this commandment gave rise to the Israelite conception of the ownership of realty in perpetuity. But since the commandment only applied to houses, it could not properly be used in connection with land. It would, therefore, seem that Ahab's request to Naboth to sell him his vineyard was in no sense improper, but that Naboth used an appeal to filial piety to get out of an awkward situation (1 Kgs. 21:1 f.).

[12] See above, pp. 18 ff.

L

denoted taking possession of the house. As a result the commandment could still be recited in the cult.

All this is confirmed by Hos. 4:2. For although there is no indication that the elders were deprived of their judicial authority in the northern kingdom, it would seem that while Hos. 4:2 lists those crimes which affect the person, and specifically refers to the third, sixth, seventh, eighth and ninth commandments,[13] either Hosea himself or a subsequent scribe deliberately avoids mentioning the tenth commandment. Instead another provision concerning one's neighbour's house, namely the enactment on burglary contained in Exod. 22:1–2a,[14] concludes the list.

Since the amplification of the commandment by the addition of Exod. 20:17b is clearly older than the Deuteronomic version of the commandment, it is probable that this is also the work of the author of the other expansions referred to earlier. He apparently wanted to include in the commandment all other property which an Israelite might have acquired by agreement, purchase or gain, namely his wife, servants, larger livestock, and other personal property. This explains why children are omitted.[15]

Although for the purpose of damages for tort the Deuteronomist still regarded a woman as her father's (Deut. 22:29) or, presumably, her husband's property, he none the less raised her status to that of membership of the covenant community. This accounts for the inversion in Deut. 5:21 of house and wife, which order is followed by the LXX in both versions of the Decalogue, and also by the Nash Papyrus. In addition the field is inserted after the house, perhaps under the influence of Isa. 5:8 and Mic. 2:2. Instead of חמד being used in both clauses, אוה is substituted in Deut. 5:21b, apparently as no more than a stylistic variation,[16] as is confirmed by the LXX which renders both חמד and אוה in both versions of the commandment by ἐπιθυμέω ('desire').[17]

---

[13] See above, pp. 145 ff.   [14] See above, pp. 92 f.

[15] Jacob, *JQR*, N.S., xiv, p. 175. Thus Exod. 20:15 cannot properly be contrasted with Exod. 20:17, the former being held to refer to the theft of a freeborn Israelite himself, the latter to the theft of his dependants (cf. Alt, *Kleine Schriften*, i, pp. 333 ff.). Exod. 20:15 has been left absolute by intention, and governs the theft of any Israelite, whether man, woman or child (see above, pp. 130 ff.). Further, there would seem to be no justification for Reventlow's contention (*Gebot und Predigt*, pp. 90 ff.) that there was originally a code using the verb חמד.

[16] Driver, *Deuteronomy*, p. 86.

[17] Mark 10:19 probably refers to this commandment, though ἀποστερέω means 'defraud', 'deprive'.

PART III

THE HISTORY OF ISRAEL'S CRIMINAL LAW

CHAPTER THIRTEEN

FROM SINAI TO SHILOH

The detailed examination of the ten commandments has confirmed the hypothesis that in contrast to all other ancient Near Eastern legal codes, Israel technically distinguished the legal concept 'crime', the Decalogue being pre-exilic Israel's criminal law code. Indeed ancient Israel's law can only be understood if it is recognized that she clearly distinguished between crime and tort. Further, it has been shown that Israel's criminal law had a distinctive religious background. It was not haphazardly selected over a period of years to meet the different conditions which faced her in her history, nor was it inherited from a tribal nomadic past or another legal system. It was in fact a conscious creation at a specific point in time, being the stipulations of the covenant entered into at Sinai resultant on the exodus from Egypt. It thus belongs to a particular situation in history, and must be understood against that background. It was these covenant stipulations which brought Israel into being as a distinct community initially resident at Kadesh, and it was their observance which guaranteed her future existence. Since breach of any of these stipulations threatened the covenant relationship itself, the community treated their breach as crimes and executed the offender to propitiate Yahweh. It was only for breach of the covenant stipulations that the death penalty was exacted, and this was never a matter of private vengeance, but of community action. Further, while the covenant concept remained in force, that is throughout the pre-exilic period, no new crimes were added to Israel's criminal law which could not be derived from the Decalogue. Thus the commandments are to be thought of neither as ethical norms nor as regulations for the good ordering of society, but as the stipulations whose observance maintained the covenant relationship.

It has been shown that the first five commandments were particularly concerned to ensure the permanent relationship of each individual Israelite with Yahweh, whose vassal he became by taking part in the festival of the ratification of the covenant. Thus members of the covenant community were to have relations with no other god but Yahweh, whose absolute freedom from manipulation by men was ensured by the prohibition of images and of the use of the divine name for magical purposes. To remind Israel of her unique existence, a special day, the sabbath, was to be regularly observed, and absolute obedience to parents was ordained to prevent the renunciation of one's ancestral faith.

The final five commandments protected the person of a fellow vassal, that is of every other Israelite, by protecting his life, the future of his name, his residence within the covenant community and his right to play his part in the community's affairs. In no case does the protection of property *per se* concern Israel's criminal law.

Since each individual was deemed to have entered into the covenant relationship (Exod. 24:3 ff.), all men were therefore treated as equal before Yahweh, and as each family was represented by its head in the community's affairs (Exod. 24:1a, 9 ff.), no family could be considered more important than another. Thus the covenant community was of necessity both an egalitarian and a democratic society which owed allegiance to no one other than Yahweh. Naturally, as Mendenhall has recognized, such a society would have proved exceedingly attractive to those under subjection to political powers. It is in this attraction that Mendenhall finds the explanation for the extreme rapidity of 'the conquest', which he argues is not to be primarily understood as a successful invasion from without, but as a peasants' revolt from within, whereby the serfs of Trans-Jordan and Canaan rebelled against their masters, and identified themselves with the covenant community, thereby adopting their traditions.[1] Only when a city state or king resisted this revolt was armed force necessary.[2] One should therefore speak of the conversion, rather than the conquest, of Canaan.

Mendenhall argues that the term *Habiru*, or the alternative *Apiru*, which was widely known throughout the ancient Near East,[3] was used to describe those who withdrew from an existing political society. From this it follows that in the Amarna letters,[4] the *Habiru* are to be

---

[1] *BA*, xxv, pp. 71 ff.

[2] This would both confirm Noth's negative view of the use of archaeology in dating the conquest (*History*, pp. 82 f.), and also take into account the destruction of such cities as Lachish and Hazor (Vriezen, *The Religion of Ancient Israel*, pp. 158 f.).

[3] Cf. Meek, *Hebrew Origins*, pp. 7 ff.   [4] Cf. DOTT, pp. 38 ff.; ANET, pp. 483 ff.

understood neither as an ethnic group, nor as invaders, but as part of the indigenous population of Canaan, who rebelled against those city states loyal to Egyptian domination. Naturally the term *Habiru*, which there can be little doubt is reflected in the Old Testament word 'Hebrew',[5] was eminently suitable to describe the escaped Egyptian slaves who transferred the concept of suzerainty from the realm of politics to that of religion, thereby renouncing any form of political domination. Such domination would have involved the acknowledgement of foreign gods, which the first commandment itself prohibited (Exod. 20:3). This explains how a term used widely throughout the ancient Near East came in particular to designate membership of the Yahwistic covenant community. Thus the term Hebrew is to be understood as synonymous with 'Israelite'.[6] However, 1 Sam. 14:21 provides an instance of its use in the technical sense of those who had withdrawn from existing society when it denotes the rebel Israelites who had joined the Philistines.

Since the Amarna letters ante-date the establishment of the covenant community at Kadesh, what was then the political situation in Canaan is uncertain. It is, however, probable that in view of the extreme complexity of the history of the twelve tribes, the process described in the Amarna letters continued, and that the Shechemite tribes should be understood as representing those members of the agricultural population of Canaan who had already succeeded in gaining their independence from the Canaanite city states,[7] and before the entry of Yahwism into Canaan established themselves as an amphictyony centred on Shechem. Certainly this shrine possessed a pre-Yahwistic covenant tradition, as the name of its god, Baal-berith or El-berith indicates (Judg. 8:33; 9:4, 46).[8] It would however seem that it was Yahwism, based on the covenant stipulations of the Decalogue, which provided the necessary cause to unite the agricultural population of Trans-Jordan and Canaan in opposition to all political domination, and with which the Shechemite amphictyony was able to identify itself.

[5] Noth, op. cit., pp. 33 ff.; Winton Thomas (Ed.), *Archaeology and Old Testament Study*, Oxford, 1967, pp. 11 ff.

[6] Cf. Morgenstern, *HUCA*, vii, pp. 38 ff.; David, *OTS*, v, p. 64; and Rapaport, *PEQ*, lxxiii, pp. 160 ff., who specifically attacks the views of Alt, *Essays*, pp. 93 ff.

[7] Cf. Mendenhall, op. cit., pp. 73 f. who recognizes that the tribes pre-existed the conquest.

[8] G. E. Wright, *Shechem*, London, 1965, pp. 136, 140 f.; Winton Thomas (Ed.), *Archaeology*, p. 365; Clements, *Abraham and David*, SBT², v, 1967, pp. 84 ff. Cf. further Albright, *Archaeology and the Religion of Israel*, p. 113; F. Willesen, 'Die Eselsohne von Sichem als Bundesgenossen', *VT*, iv, 1954, pp. 216 f.

The climax of this spread of Yahwism was its adoption by the tribes gathered at Shechem and recorded in Josh. 24.[9] Like the Sinai pericope this narrative is also to be attributed to E, and is set out in the Hittite suzerainty treaty form.[10] Thus verses 2 ff. constitute the historical prologue, which represents the 'official' history of Israel including 'the conquest', and incorporates the traditions of the fathers, that is of the tribes themselves.

This is followed by the order to renounce foreign gods (verses 14 ff.), whose acknowledgement was symbolized by their idols, which would have been the only tangible obstacles to the acceptance of the covenant stipulations.[11] Until such images were destroyed, their owners could not be incorporated into the covenant community. Verses 14 ff. betray the fact that it was not until after the exodus from Egypt that Yahwism was adopted.

The covenant is then inaugurated, though the covenant stipulations are now omitted. It has been argued that the terms of the covenant would no longer have been relevant to the conditions of the period of the judges, and attempts have been made to find the missing legislation elsewhere in Israel's legal corpus.[12] In fact it would seem that E placed the Book of the Covenant here,[13] which is probably reflected in the use of the phrase חק ומשפט ('laws and precedents') in verse 25. But this code is not to be equated with the original covenant legislation of the Shechemite amphictyony, but reflected current legislation at the time E wrote.[14] The law which the amphictyony accepted could only have been the covenant stipulations of the Sinai Decalogue, upon which the covenant community was founded, and obedience to which determined its existence. The reference to the writing down of the covenant stipulations (Josh. 24:26) must be attributed to E's insertion of the Book of the Covenant at this point, for it must be assumed that with the inauguration of the Yahwistic Israelite amphictyony the ark with the two tablets of the law was brought from Kadesh to Shechem, thus obviating any necessity to record the covenant stipulations.[15] The ceremony at Shechem does not describe the creation of a new relationship, but the incorporation into an existing relationship of

---

[9] The LXX reading of Shiloh for Shechem in verses 1 and 25 cannot be accepted.

[10] Mendenhall, *BA*, xvii, pp. 62, 67 ff.; Muilenburg, *VT*, ix, pp. 357 ff.; Thompson, *Ancient Near Eastern Treaties*, pp. 22, 34.

[11] Cf. circumcision (see above, pp. 14 f.).   [12] Mendenhall, op. cit., p. 68.

[13] Weiser, *Introduction*, pp. 121 f.   [14] See below, pp. 159 f.

[15] Reference has already been made on p. 7 above to the stone set up as a witness to the covenant (Josh. 24:27).

new clans.[16] Shechem thus became the centre of a large complex of tribes all of whom were members of the Yahwistic covenant community and were therefore bound to Yahweh and each other in respect of the covenant stipulations, but who otherwise continued to possess a certain measure of internal freedom.

From time to time further tribes or city states would have joined the amphictyony, an example of which is provided by the covenant with the Gibeonites (Josh. 9:3 ff.).[17] As in Exod. 18:10 ff., Yahweh's historic acts on Israel's behalf are referred to, and the proceedings culminate with a covenant meal between the parties.

For some reason which can no longer be determined Shechem ceased to be the central amphictyonic shrine, and after Bethel[18] and Gilgal (at least) had fulfilled that function, Shiloh became the last centre of the amphictyony.[19] But the capture of the ark (1 Sam. 4) and the destruction of that sanctuary marked the end of an era for Israel, and led directly to the inauguration of the monarchy.

[16] Bright, *History*, pp. 145 f.; Beyerlin, *Origins and History*, pp. 151 ff.
[17] See above, pp. 84 f.
[18] For a discussion of the later pilgrimage from Shechem to Bethel based on the interpretation of Gen. 35:1 ff., cf. Alt, 'Die Wallfahrt von Sichem nach Bethel', *Kleine Schriften*, i, pp. 79 ff. Cf. further Beyerlin, op. cit., pp. 111 f.
[19] Noth, *History*, pp. 94 ff.

CHAPTER FOURTEEN

THE BOOK OF THE COVENANT

Although Exod. 20:22–23:33 is usually termed the Book of the Covenant, it is clear that this is not a unity. If a law code is to be isolated, then Exod. 23:20 ff. cannot be included in it, but must constitute a later addition. The origin of this addition will be investigated later.[1] But it has also been argued that the series of provisions on what has been described as 'humaneness and righteousness' (Exod. 22:20–26; 23:1–9) are to be understood as a later addition to the law code, for unlike the criminal and civil enactments of Exod. 21–22:19 no action is envisaged for their breach.[2] They are ethically rather than juridically based, being particularly concerned to ensure a right attitude to the helpless, that is the weaker members of society, and animals. Thus even the manual of justice in Exod. 23:1–3, 6–9, though it refers to the crime of false witness, is more concerned with the impartiality of justice than punishment of the criminal guilty of breach of the ninth commandment.[3] If this contention is correct, then Exod. 22:27 would have followed Exod. 22:19, and would have formed the conclusion to a small additional criminal law coda (Exod. 22:17 ff., 27). Further, it seems that Exod. 21:1 was once intended to constitute the introduction to the law code. It will in fact be argued that the provisions in Exod. 20:23 ff. have been subsequently placed there in order to give them emphasis.[4] Thus it would seem that the original code consisted of Exod. 21–22:19; 22:27–29 (30);[5] 23:10–19.

The opening provisions deal with slaves (Exod. 21:2–11). These are followed by an examination of those crimes which particularly needed to be distinguished from torts. Thus there is a detailed examination of the law of murder, which apart from introducing the idea of asylum (Exod. 21:12–14), aims at differentiating between the tort of

[1] See below, p. 174.
[2] Lewy, 'Dating of Covenant Code Sections on Humaneness and Righteousness', *VT*, vii, 1957, pp. 322 ff.
[3] See above, pp. 144 f.　　　　　　　　[4] See below, p. 174.
[5] It is probable that Exod. 22:30 was a later insertion (Lewy, op. cit., p. 322; Noth, *Exodus*, p. 188).

assault which would result in an action for damages, and the crime of murder for which the death penalty would have been exacted (Exod. 21:18–32; 22:1–2a).[6] The law on repudiation of one's parents is also included to show that an assault, which would only amount to a tort if committed on someone else, constituted a crime if inflicted on parents (Exod. 21:15, 17).[7] Similarly reference is made to the crime of manstealing (Exod. 21:16) so that this crime should not be confused with the tort of theft.[8] The next group of laws concern theft or damage to personal property, which being torts require payment of damages (Exod. 21:33–37; 22:2b–16). There then follows the small criminal law coda (Exod. 22:17–19, 27), and finally a list of positive obligations to Yahweh which every member of the covenant community must perform (Exod. 22:28 f.; 23:10–19).[9] This explains why the criminal law provision on sabbath observance appears in this section.

It would therefore seem that the Book of the Covenant is a collection of laws arranged in a systematic order, and thus reflects a particular moment in Israel's legal history. Can one have any idea, either from external or internal evidence, when this was? Now legal precedents tend to be collected when there is a substantial change in the constitution of the community.[10] Since the Shechemite covenant (Josh. 24) merely amounted to the incorporation of additional tribes into the existing covenant relationship, such a change did not in fact occur until the inauguration of the Davidic monarchy. Is it then possible to understand the Book of the Covenant as the legislation of the new Davidic state, which would, of course, have existed alongside the Decalogue, which continued to be recited in the cult (Pss. 50; 81)?

Internal evidence is notoriously difficult to evaluate, but it would seem that Exod. 21:2 ff. supplies one with a conclusive affirmative answer. It has already been shown that this opening provision of the Book of the Covenant is to be understood as the secularization of the right of the Hebrew male slave to his release at the end of the seventh year in order that he might be able to take part in the seven year covenant festival at the central amphictyonic shrine, which festival

---

[6] It has already been noted on p. 92 above that this provision has been displaced from its original position, and set among the precedents on theft of property.

[7] See above, p. 80.

[8] See above, pp. 130 ff. Although the tort of seduction is included in the Book of the Covenant (Exod. 22:15 f.) among those precedents which concern damage to personal property, since, in contrast to theft, there was a special verb to distinguish the crime of adultery from this tort, it was evidently felt unnecessary to refer to the crime.

[9] In view of this, it seems unlikely that the law of the altar (Exod. 20:24 ff.) was once included among these enactments.   [10] Mendenhall, *BA*, xvii, pp. 32 ff.

ceased to be celebrated following the capture of Shiloh.[11] Thus Exod.
21:2 ff. provides a fixed point from which to date the Book of the
Covenant, and confirms that in its present form it cannot be attributed
to the pre-monarchical period. In addition it has also been suggested
in the discussion of the fifth commandment that the precedent Exod.
21:15, which in effect marks a distinct change in emphasis of that
commandment, directly arose out of the establishment of Yahwism as
the state religion under David.[12]

Thus it now becomes probable that the term נשיא in the concluding enactment of the additional criminal law coda refers to the
king.[13] As a matter of fact this makes very good sense, for it would
appear that faced with the difficulty of inserting Exod. 22:27 into his
pre-monarchical narrative (Josh. 24), the E compiler excized an
original מלך ('king'), which properly occurs in 1 Kgs. 21:10, and
invented the phrase 'נשיא of your people' as a circumlocution for
'king', the word נשיא being derived from the root נשא meaning
'bear', that is 'bear rule'.[14] This would explain why this expression
only occurs in Exod. 22:27 in the pre-exilic material.

Indeed it is quite possible that the additional criminal law coda is to
be attributed to David himself. Thus Exod. 22:17 may represent his
reaction to Saul's over-zealous action in barring the necromancers from
Israel (this was as far as the criminal law could be stretched),[15] and
Exod. 22:19,[16] if not 22:18,[17] may reflect the incorporation into
Yahwism of the Jebusite shrine of Jerusalem.

Like CH,[18] the Book of the Covenant appears to have been issued
by the king in the name of his deity for although only breach of the
criminal law directly involved Yahweh, every department of life was
none the less understood to be his concern. But it is not to be interpreted as an exhaustive statement of all the law of the Davidic state:
it does not reduce existing customary law to writing, nor, apart from
Exod. 21:1–11 does it deal with family law such as divorce or adoption.
No doubt there were additional cultic provisions besides Exod.
23:14 ff. The reason why only the pre-exilic criminal law receives an
exhaustive treatment is that by virtue of the Mosaic covenant this
alone was capable of a direct theological interpretation. This probably
also explains the curious fact that there is no further detailed treatment

---

[11] See above, pp. 73 f.   [12] See above, p. 81.   [13] See above, pp. 42 f.
[14] Cazelles, *Code de l'Alliance*, p. 82.
[15] See above, pp. 56 ff.   [16] See above, pp. 39 ff.   [17] See above, p. 121.
[18] On the comparison of the legislative roles of the Babylonian and Hebrew kings on
their accession, cf. Wiseman, 'The Laws of Hammurabi Again', *JSS*, vii, 1962, pp.
161 ff.

of civil law precedents in the Old Testament. Since the civil law was not at the basis of the covenant relationship it was of no great interest to the various authors of the Old Testament material.

Of course, the bulk of the enactments of the Book of the Covenant are not the product of the Davidic state, but primarily consist of the law of the amphictyony, though no doubt the principle of compensation for tort was also practised by the covenant community at Kadesh. Further, since it has been argued that 'the conquest' was in fact a process of conversion, naturally the tribes who were now incorporated into the covenant relationship brought into that situation certain practices which were not incompatible with the covenant law of the Decalogue. This would include their own law, which was accordingly amended where necessary to conform with the principles of the covenant law. It is this fact which accounts both for the similarity of the Book of the Covenant to other ancient Near Eastern law, and also for its distinctive Israelite features,[19] a fact which some commentators have failed to recognize largely due to their reliance on a false antithesis between apodictic and casuistic law, and their desire to decide for or against the Israelite origin of the Book of the Covenant.[20]

The role of the so-called minor-judge has already been examined and it has been suggested that they may have been responsible for the precedents differentiating murder from assault.[21] Further it would appear from 1 Sam. 12:3 that they also heard appeals in civil actions, for this verse seems to indicate the withholding of an individual's rights to justice, thereby indicating that reference is being made to the civil law. Be this as it may, it is probable that there was already a considerable measure of uniformity of the civil law throughout the amphictyony. But whether punitive damages for theft were exacted prior to the establishment of the David monarchy, and if so whether these were standardized, cannot be determined.

---

[19] Meek, *Hebrew Origins*, pp. 69 ff.

[20] Cf. Alt, *Essays*, pp. 81 ff. with Rapaport, *PEQ*, lxxiii, pp. 158 ff. It is failure to distinguish between Israel's criminal and civil law which leads Fensham ('The Possibility of the Presence of Casuistic Legal Material at the Making of the Covenant at Sinai', *PEQ*, xciii, 1961, pp. 143 ff.) to place the casuistic law in the *covenant* at Sinai. Eissfeldt, *Introduction*, p. 219 points out, though he admits that this is an argument from silence, that the Book of the Covenant apart from secondary additions makes no reference to having been enacted at Sinai.

[21] See above, pp. 20 f.

CHAPTER FIFTEEN

THE DAVIDIC COVENANT

There can be no doubt that it was external pressure in the form of the Philistine military successes which caused the covenant tribes to seek a king. But initially it appears that he was intended to be no more than a permanent charismatic leader, and therefore to have no part in the religious functions of the amphictyony presided over by the so-called minor-judge who acted as mediator of the covenant.[1] It was only after the capture of Jerusalem by David that the offices of charismatic leader and minor-judge were effectively combined, and a philosophy of the monarchy formulated.

The loss of the ark on which Yahweh was supposed to manifest himself, and the destruction of the amphictyonic shrine of Shiloh, followed by the defeat and death of Saul at the battle of Mount Gilboa, must have resulted in considerable uncertainty as to the nature of Israel's covenant relationship with Yahweh. Undoubtedly what was needed was confirmation of Yahweh's presence within the state and a guarantee of his approval of it. This was provided by the Davidic covenant by which Yahweh was held to have explicitly selected Mount Zion as his dwelling-place, and the Davidic dynasty to rule over his people in perpetuity (2 Sam. 7:8 ff.; 23:5; Pss. 89:4 f., 20 ff.; 132:11 f.).[2] Thus both in the temple and in the person of the king, Israel was to recognize her own divine election.

One cannot overestimate the importance of the pre-Yahwistic traditions of Jerusalem as a divine dwelling-place in the formulation of this covenant.[3] Indeed it appears probable that the Jebusite shrine itself, together with its cult image, Nehushtan, and priest, Zadok, was taken over by David,[4] and until the temple was built by Solomon

[1] For the tension between Samuel and Saul, see above, p. 55, n. 12, and Mendenhall, *BA*, xvii, pp. 40 f.; Newman, *The People of the Covenant*, pp. 132 ff. As covenant mediator, Samuel could both select and reject Saul as king.

[2] Clements, *Prophecy and Covenant*, pp. 56 ff.

[3] Clements, *God and Temple*, Oxford, 1965, pp. 40 ff.

[4] Rowley, 'Zadok and Nehushtan', *JBL*, lviii, 1939, pp. 113 ff., 'Melchizedek and Zadok (Gen. 14 and Ps. 110)', *Bertholet-Festschrift*, pp. 461 ff. On the basis of 1 Chr.

acted as the royal Yahwistic shrine. But in order to confirm Yahweh's election of Mount Zion, David brought the ark to Jerusalem (2 Sam. 6:12 ff.), thus signifying that the Davidic state was the legitimate successor to the amphictyony.[5]

To what extent the Abrahamic covenant influenced the formation of the Davidic covenant remains an open question. It has been argued that this ancient covenant associated with Hebron from which David first ruled Judah (2 Sam. 2:1 ff.) was deliberately taken over and used of David.[6] But it is possible that the treatment of the Abrahamic covenant is to be ascribed to the southern writer J who makes the reign of David the fulfilment of an earlier promise to Abraham. Whatever the true position is, there is no need to investigate it further here.

The major distinctions between the Mosaic and Davidic covenants are obvious. First the emphasis is now placed not on human obligation, but on divine commitment. While in the Mosaic covenant it was the clans who bound themselves to Yahweh by agreeing to obey his commandments, in the Davidic covenant it was Yahweh who specifically undertook certain future action. Secondly, whereas the Mosaic covenant was made between Yahweh and all the people, the Davidic covenant simply involved Yahweh and an individual, the nation being treated as a third party. For this reason it would seem erroneous to hold that the Mosaic covenant was superseded by the Davidic covenant.[7] Rather the two covenants were intended to exist alongside

---

12:29, C. J. Hauer ('Who was Zadok?', *JBL*, lxxxii, 1963, pp. 89 ff.) argues that Zadok was a deserter from Jerusalem who joined David at Hebron. This explains his later high office.

[5] Kraus, *Worship in Israel*, pp. 181 ff.

[6] Clements, *Abraham and David*. On pp. 33 f., Clements raises the possibility that the Abrahamic covenant originally involved responsibilities for Abraham and his descendants, but that through the Yahwist's desire to heighten the divine promise, these were dropped. On the other hand Newman, op. cit., would connect the ideas behind the Davidic covenant with a particular understanding of the Mosaic covenant which he alleges was operative at Hebron. This understood that covenant to have been made with Moses himself, and to be both for ever and unconditional. However Newman's thesis depends on a literary analysis which divides the material rigidly between the sources J and E, and which at any rate in the case of Exod. 24 (see above, pp. 5 f.) and 34 (see below, pp. 168 ff.) will be rejected in this study.

[7] Mowinckel, *He that Cometh*, E.T., Oxford, 1956, pp. 73 f.; A. H. J. Gunneweg, 'Sinaibund und Davidsbund', *VT*, x, 1960, pp. 335 ff.; Porter, *Moses and Monarchy*, pp. 11 ff.; de Vaux, 'Le Roi D'Israël, Vassal De Yahvé', *Mélanges Eugène Tisserant*, i, Città del Vaticano, 1964, pp. 119 ff.; Clements, *Prophecy and Covenant*, pp. 62 ff.; McCarthy, 'II Samuel 7 and the Structure of the Deuteronomic History', *JBL*, lxxxiv, 1965, pp. 136. But cf. L. Rost, 'Sinaibund und Davidsbund', *TLZ*, lxxii, 1947, cols. 129 ff.; Mendenhall, *BA*, xvii, pp. 70 ff., IDB, i, p. 718.

each other, for they were made with different parties. It is perfectly true that in contrast to the house of Saul (1 Sam. 13:13 f.; 15:26 ff.) the Davidic covenant ensured that the particular faults of an individual king would not lead Yahweh to renounce the Davidic dynasty (2 Sam. 7:14 f.), but this did not mean that Yahweh did not continue to demand the *nation's* obedience to the Mosaic covenant law, which the king was to maintain. Thus 2 Kgs. 11:17 records the renewal of both the Davidic and Mosaic covenants.[8] Further, it is probable that one should understand 'the testimony' (הָעֵדוּת) (2 Kgs. 11:12) handed to Joash at his coronation as a copy of the Mosaic tablets of the law containing the covenant stipulations, obedience to which determined the existence of the state.[9] Responsibility for their observance was placed directly on the king as the vassal of Yahweh[10] and fountain of justice (Ps. 132:11 f.; 1 Kgs. 8:25). The Deuteronomic law of the king (Deut. 17:18 ff.) would then reflect this procedure. It has already been noted that the Decalogue apparently came to be recited in the cult at the annual autumnal royal festival in Jerusalem (Pss. 50; 81).[11]

Thus the covenant stipulations of the Sinai Decalogue continued to act as Israel's criminal law throughout the period of the Davidic

[8] Gray, *Kings*, pp. 523 f.

[9] Widengren, 'The Ascension of the Apostle and the Heavenly Book', *UUÅ*, 1950.7, pp. 24 f., *JJS*, ii, 1957, pp. 6 f. Cf. Ps. 132:12 where the same word appears in the plural alongside בְּרִית ('covenant'). Others have suggested that this word refers to the divine protocol handed to the king at his coronation together with his crown, which protocol, in addition to the conditions of his office, would contain his coronation name and divine commission to rule as the adopted son of Yahweh (cf. Ps. 2:6 ff.). Such a divine protocol was known in Egypt. Cf. von Rad, 'The Royal Ritual in Judah', *Essays*, pp. 225 ff.; Mowinckel, *The Psalms in Israel's Worship*, i, pp. 62 f.; de Vaux, *Ancient Israel*, p. 103; Johnson, *Sacral Kingship in Ancient Israel*[2], Cardiff, 1967, pp. 23 ff.; Gray, *Archaeology*, pp. 141 ff., *Kings*, pp. 518 f.; Weiser, *The Psalms*, E.T., London, 1962, pp. 781 f. In addition some have thought that the testimony was a document actually worn by the king (May, 'A Key to the Interpretation of Zechariah's Visions', *JBL*, lvii, 1938, p. 181; Johnson, *Sacral Kingship*, pp. 23 f.), and it has been connected with the *Urim* and *Thummim* (G. Östborn, *Tōrā in the Old Testament*, Lund, 1945, pp. 80 ff.; Widengren, *UUÅ*, pp. 25 f.).

[10] De Vaux (*Mélanges Eugène Tisserant*, i, pp. 119 ff.) argues that through his anointing the king became the vassal of Yahweh. He compares this rite with the Egyptian practice of anointing great functionaries, and in particular the Canaanite kings who became vassals of Pharaoh.

[11] But Ps. 50:18 ff. does not in fact refer to breach of the Sinai Decalogue itself, but to general improper conduct, which does not of itself prevent the participants taking part in the cult. Thus the Psalmist only refers to those who associate with thieves and adulterers, and not to those who themselves commit theft and adultery. Nor do verses 19 f. refer to the crime of giving false evidence in a criminal action. Thus the Psalmist's concern is to condemn spiritual insincerity. Even though those who are addressed have not broken the covenant law, and so can take part in the festival, yet they are unworthy of taking the covenant stipulations upon their lips.

monarchy, and therefore remained distinct from her civil law. This explains why there was no Davidic state criminal law other than that which could be directly derived from the ten commandments (Exod. 22:17–19, 27). Thus the criminal law was not secularized, and the death penalty continued to be exacted in order to propitiate Yahweh. The continuation of the Davidic dynasty, as well as the existence of the state, was dependent on the observance of the Mosaic covenant law (cf. 1 Sam. 12:14 f.).[12] Therefore unlike the situation in other ancient Near Eastern countries, the king was not an absolute monarch, since his rule was subject to an already existing constitution, that is the Mosaic covenant, which he was powerless to renounce (1 Sam. 10:25).[13]

But by virtue of the Davidic covenant the king had become a constitutional monarch, and those who would challenge his authority by rebellion found that they were in fact rebelling against Yahweh who had established the royal dynasty. There was only one way of renouncing the Davidic covenant, and that was to return to the pre-monarchical traditions for the appointment of a leader. Infuriated by an arrogant and excessive use of royal power the northern tribes did precisely this. At the old amphictyonic centre of Shechem the Davidic dynasty was rejected, and with prophetic backing (1 Kgs. 11:29 ff.) a separate kingdom founded, the king being held to have been designated by Yahweh in accordance with the ancient concept of charismatic leadership. Even though both Omri and Jehu founded dynasties, this concept was never entirely lost in the northern kingdom.[14] As a result, whereas in the southern kingdom the prophets could only plead with the Davidic monarch for a change of heart, in the northern kingdom they could openly encourage rebellion in Yahweh's name (2 Kgs. 9).

Naturally the northern kingdom inherited from the united monarchy the Book of the Covenant, which was already its law, and which it continued to enforce. But it seems that there was no real attempt to return to the tribal conditions of the amphictyony. Indeed with the incorporation of so much foreign territory and its peoples into the Davidic empire, this would presumably have been impossible. Thus

[12] Cf. Muilenburg, *VT*, ix, pp. 360 ff. Even though this passage may have been written from the standpoint of post-exilic Israel, it seems that it preserves a genuine tradition of the parallel nature of the two covenants.

[13] Mendenhall, *BA*, xvii, p. 38 asserts that 1 Sam. 10:25 preserves the tradition that a king was only accepted provided that he agreed to maintain the existing law. Cf. further David's adultery with Bathsheba and subsequent murder of Uriah for which David acknowledges his liability (2 Sam. 12:13).

[14] For an examination of the contrast in the constitution of the two kingdoms, cf. Alt, 'The Monarchy in the Kingdoms of Israel and Judah', *Essays*, pp. 241 ff.

the seven year covenant festival was not restored, but instead a royal festival, rival to that instituted at Jerusalem, was inaugurated by Jeroboam (1 Kgs. 12:32).

There can be little doubt that the Davidic kings and the Jerusalem court came to rely more and more on the promise contained in the Davidic covenant to the exclusion of the threat inherent in the Mosaic covenant. It was the recognition that this threat was still a reality which led to Hezekiah's reform.

CHAPTER SIXTEEN

HEZEKIAH'S REFORM

Although later generations specifically attributed Hezekiah's reform to the influence of the prophet Micah (Jer. 26:17 ff.), there can be no doubt that it was the fall of the northern kingdom which provided the Davidic king with the requisite evidence of the validity of the eighth century prophetic message that failure to observe the Mosaic covenant law could only lead to an irrevocable breach of the covenant relationship.[1] This resulted in Hezekiah's recognition that the apparent security offered by the Davidic covenant was illusory, and so led to the institution of his reform.

As a result of Ahaz's appeal to Tiglath-pileser, even if Assyrian gods were not actually installed in the temple, Judah was at least forced to acknowledge by her vassaldom that Yahweh was dependent on the Assyrian deities (2 Kgs. 16:10 ff.). This was a direct negation of the covenant concept (Exod. 20:3).[2] Thus Hezekiah's reform had to begin with the repudiation of Assyrian suzerainty, which could, of course, only take place when the political situation made it possible. The detailed history of this period is notoriously difficult to evaluate, and in view of the fact that this study is primarily concerned with the history of law, it is not proposed to discuss the various views as to the dating of Hezekiah's revolt and its consequences. It is sufficient to point out that this must have provoked Sennacherib's campaign against Judah, and since the latter, whether or not there was a later campaign, can be dated to 701, it must be assumed that the revolt took place shortly before this.[3]

[1] The importance of the eighth-century prophets is that they recovered the idea that Yahweh's judgement would fall not merely on specific individuals or towns, but on the covenant community as a whole (cf. C. Westermann, *Basic Forms of Prophetic Speech*, E.T., London, 1967).

[2] It was for this reason that the eighth-century prophets advocated political neutrality in an attempt to maintain the independent political position guaranteed by the covenant itself (cf. H. Donner, *Israel unter den Völkern*, VTS, xi, 1964, pp. 168 ff.).

[3] For a full discussion of this problem and the literature on it, cf. Rowley, 'Hezekiah's Reform and Rebellion', *BJRL*, xliv, 1961/2, pp. 395 ff., who argues that the date of Hezekiah's revolt was 703 by amending ארבע עשרה ('fourteenth') in 2 Kgs. 18:13 to read ארבע ועשרים ('twenty fourth').

M

But Hezekiah's campaign is not merely to be understood as a national movement for independence.[4] Understanding that it was Israel's apostasy, particularly to be recognized in syncretism with Canaan, which had caused Yahweh to break the covenant relationship with the northern kingdom, Hezekiah, at the same time as he threw off Assyrian suzerainty, deliberately launched a full scale attack on the Canaanite elements in Judah's religion (2 Kgs. 18:4). Thus the elaborate altars with their cult apparatus of *maṣṣeboth* and *'asherim* were destroyed,[5] along with the bronze serpent Nehushtan, whose creation was attributed to no less a person than Moses himself. This was probably the cult object associated with the original Jebusite shrine at Jerusalem, and taken over by David after his conquest, Num. 21:8 f. being created as an aetiological account to justify its presence in the Solomonic temple.[6] In addition the Chronicler records that Hezekiah celebrated the Passover festival at the purified temple in Jerusalem, and that men were bidden to attend from all over Judah, and even Israel (2 Chr. 30:5).

Even though Assyria quickly reasserted her supremacy over Judah, who remained her vassal throughout the long reign of Manasseh, Hezekiah's reform none the less had a tremendous effect on the history and literature of Judah, an effect which has not hitherto been recognized. For it is the contention of this study that the nature of Hezekiah's reform has in fact been summarized in Exod. 34:10 ff., which has been created as the climax to the pre-priestly Sinai material by the JE redactor writing in Judah in the light of that reform.

This contention is in sharp contrast to the once common view that Exod. 34:14 ff. was to be described as 'the ritual Decalogue' and attributed to J, while Exod. 20:3 ff. contained 'the ethical Decalogue' which was the work of E.[7] Recent scholarship has, however, shown increasing scepticism as to whether any Decalogue can be isolated from Exod. 34:14 ff.[8] Further, although Exod. 34:14a and 17 have usually

---

[4] Vriezen, *Religion*, pp. 205 ff.

[5] While this stone pillar had been interpreted by Israel as manifesting a theophany, it originally represented a male deity, and therefore constituted an obvious danger. Thus בסל and *maṣṣebah* are found in conjunction in Mic. 5:12; Lev. 26:1; Deut. 7:5; 12:3, though it should be noted that earlier Hosea had felt no need to condemn the *maṣṣebah* (3:4). In contrast the *'asherah* was probably always regarded as improper, being a representation of a female deity (Eichrodt, *Theology*, i, pp. 115 ff.).

[6] See above, pp. 162 f.

[7] Thus Rowley, *BJRL*, xxxiv, 1951/2, pp. 99 ff. argued that whereas 'the ritual Decalogue' was to be derived from the Kenites, 'the ethical Decalogue' was the work of Moses himself.

[8] Bentzen, *Introduction*, ii, p. 57; Weiser, *Introduction*, p. 105; Zimmerli, *The Law and the Prophets*, p. 33; Nielsen, *The Ten Commandments*, pp. 14 f.; and especially

been treated as two of the commands of the supposed 'ritual Decalogue', the remaining verses, like Exod. 23:20–33 with which they have much in common, have been termed 'deuteronomistic'.[9] But modern Pentateuchal criticism has indicated that one should not expect to find the hand of the Deuteronomist in the Tetrateuch.[10] In fact Exod. 34:11–17 should be read as a whole.

Exod. 34:11–17 deals with the exclusive relationship which Israel is to have with Yahweh, particularly ensuring that she should not be contaminated by fraternizing with the Canaanites. Thus Exod. 34:11 f. warns against any contact with the six indigenous peoples, and above all orders Israel to avoid entering into a covenant with them. This would involve the acknowledgement of their gods. Instead Israel is charged to destroy certain cult apparatus at the Canaanite shrines, for by the first and fundamental commandment, Israel is to worship no other god but Yahweh (Exod. 34:13 f.). The author fears that if such action is not taken the Israelites will end up eating food sacrificed to foreign gods (verse 15). Further, the Israelites are warned against taking Canaanite wives who may tempt their husbands to worship their gods (verse 16).[11] Finally there is the command to make no molten gods. Clearly Hezekiah's action as recorded in 2 Kgs.18:4 is exactly in accord with this passage, both in his attack on the high places with their cult apparatus of *maṣṣeboth* and *'asherim* (cf. Exod. 34:13), and also in his destruction of the bronze serpent Nehushtan (cf. Exod. 34:17).

But whoever composed Exod. 34:10 ff. understood the first and second commandments as one, for there is now no longer any concern with images of Yahweh as such, but with images of foreign deities whom Israel might be tempted to worship. It has, however, already been shown that the person who expanded and reinterpreted the second commandment also understood the first two commandments as one,[12] and since both the expansion of the second commandment and Exod. 34:14 specifically refers to Yahweh as jealous, the probability is raised that they are the work of the same author. This is further supported by the fact that the expansion of the second commandment is primarily concerned with images from nature, of which,

---

Kosmala, *ASTI*, i, pp. 31 ff., though unlike Kosmala, this study will treat Exod. 34:10–28 as a unit.

[9] Cf. Noth, *Exodus*, pp. 192, 261 ff.

[10] For a summary of recent study, cf. Rowley (Ed.), *The Old Testament and Modern Study*, Oxford, 1951, pp. 63 ff.

[11] See above, pp. 15 f.   [12] See above, p. 51.

of course, Nehushtan forms an example. But this was not the only nature image which attracted the condemnation of eighth century Yahwism.

It has already been noted that Hezekiah's reform resulted from the fall of the northern kingdom, which vindicated the eighth-century prophetic preaching. A new feature of that preaching was Hosea's attack on the cult bulls of the northern kingdom (8:5 f.; 10:5; 13:2),[13] the most notable of which had been erected by Jeroboam at Bethel and Dan (1 Kgs. 12:28 f.).[14] His selection of the bull, the cult animal associated with the indigenous religious practices of Canaan, as the cult object within his royal sanctuaries was no doubt deliberate. But whereas in non-Yahwistic Canaan and in Syria the figure of Hadad-Ramman had been placed upon such cult bulls, Jeroboam left them riderless. In this way the invisible and unrepresentable Yahweh was held to be seated upon them, as in Solomon's temple he was thought to be enthroned upon the cherubim.[15] The bulls therefore constituted the throne or pedestal of Yahweh,[16] which explains why Elijah felt no need to condemn them, nor Jehu to destroy them (2 Kgs. 10:29). Thus Jeroboam's action cannot be understood as a repudiation of Yahwism as his choice of Abijah for his son's name confirms (1 Kgs. 14:1).[17] Indeed it has already been argued that in rebelling against Judah, the northern tribes were specifically rejecting the Davidic monarchy in order to return to the more primitive amphictyonic position.[18] It was later generations that misunderstood Jeroboam's purpose, which was simply to provide the northern kingdom with a suitable national cultic symbol in place of the ark. Further, it would seem highly probable that it was at this time that the original story of

[13] Hos. 12:12 may contain another reference to the cult bulls, though שׁוֹר is nowhere else used of bull worship (Harper, *Amos and Hosea*, p. 390).

[14] L. Waterman, 'Bull Worship in Israel', *AJSL*, xxxi, 1914/15, p. 253 arguing from the use of the plural עֲגָלוֹת ('calves') in Hos. 10:5, holds that there were in fact two calves at Bethel in imitation of the cherubim in the temple, Dan being a later insertion in 1 Kgs. 12 due to an older tradition of an improper image there. But the remainder of the MT in Hos. 10:5 refers to a calf in the singular, as does the LXX.

[15] It would seem that the cherubim were not part of the ark of the wilderness period (cf. Clements, *God and Temple*, pp. 28 ff.).

[16] Obbink, *ZAW*, N.F., vi, pp. 267 ff.; Albright, 'Proceedings, December 28th, 29th and 30th 1937', *JBL*, lvii, 1938, p. xviii, *From the Stone Age to Christianity*, pp. 203, 229.

[17] Newman, *The People of the Covenant*, pp. 179 f. Cf. Meek, 'Some Religious Origins of the Hebrews', *AJSL*, xxxvii, 1920/1, pp. 119 ff., *Hebrew Origins*, pp. 135 ff., who argues that Jeroboam re-established the ancient bull cult associated with the tribe of Joseph, which had been suppressed during the period of the united monarchy, when Israel was under the domination of southern Yahwism.

[18] See above, p. 165.

the making of the golden calf at Sinai under Aaron's instructions was created to act as an aetiological account justifying Jeroboam's action, and to indicate that the calf image was as ancient a cult object as the ark itself. This story now underlies Exod. 32.[19] Thus by his religious innovations, Jeroboam sought to ensure that members of the northern kingdom should no longer go up to Jerusalem (1 Kgs. 12:28).

However in popular usage the bulls came to be associated with Yahweh himself, and as a result the identity of Yahweh was assimilated with that of Baal (Hos. 2:16 f.). This may have in part been due to the fact that whereas the cherubim in the temple were hidden from public view, the bulls were not.[20] Confirmation that Yahweh could be associated with the bull has been supplied by the ostraka discovered at Samaria, and now dated to the reigns of Jehoahaz[21] or Jeroboam II,[22] in which the divine name יו was found compounded with 'bull'.[23] Further, it is probable that Yahweh's title as אֲבִיר ('Mighty One') used of Jacob in Gen. 49:24; Isa. 49:26; 60:16; Ps. 132:2, 5, and Israel in Isa. 1:24 was a conscious development from an earlier designation of אַבִּיר ('bull'), later, like the appellation Baal, considered improper.[24] Hadad-Ramman was frequently called 'Bull'. But Hosea himself does not equate the bull statues with images of Yahweh.[25] It is the improper veneration which they receive which is the ground of his complaint. The people confuse the god with the god-bearer, and in their confusion merge the worship of Yahweh with that of Baal. This led to Yahweh being treated as a nature deity.[26]

[19] Newman, op. cit., pp. 181 ff. Cf. Kennett, 'The Origin of the Aaronite Priesthood', *JTS*, vi, 1904/5, pp. 165 f.

[20] Wright, 'The Present State of Biblical Archaeology', *The Study of the Bible To-day and To-morrow* (Ed. H. R. Willoughby), Chicago, 1947, p. 94, *The Old Testament against its Environment*, SBT¹, ii, 1950, p. 26.

[21] B. Maisler, 'The Historical Background of the Samaria Ostraca', *JPOS*, xxi, 1948, pp. 117 ff.

[22] J. W. Crowfoot, K. M. Kenyon, E. L. Subenik, *The Buildings at Samaria*, *Samaria-Sebaste Reports*, i, London, 1942, p. 8; Albright, 'The Excavations of Tell Beit Mirsim III', *AASOR*, xxi-xxii, 1941/3, p. 59, *From the Stone Age to Christianity*, p. 314, *Archaeology and the Religion of Israel*, pp. 41, 122, 141, 160, 214, 220; ANET, p. 321; Gray, *Archaeology and the Old Testament World*, p. 151. These ostraka were at first mistakenly dated to the reign of Ahab (Jack, *Samaria in Ahab's Time*, Edinburgh, 1929, p. 145). But it was later recognized that the room in which they were found could have been used until the fall of Samaria (DOTT, p. 204).

[23] Ibid., p. 206. On the form יו, cf. Winton Thomas, 'The Lachish Letters', *JTS*, xl, 1940, pp. 14 f.

[24] Skinner, *Genesis*, p. 531; W. C. Wood, 'The Religion of Canaan from the Earliest Times to the Hebrew Conquest', *JBL*, xxxv, 1916, p. 241; Meek, *AJSL*, xxxvii, pp. 122 f. [25] Obbink, *ZAW*, N.F., vi, p. 272.

[26] There would seem to be no evidence to support Pfeiffer's contention ('Images of Yahweh', *JBL*, xlv, 1926, pp. 216 f.) that Hosea's attacks on the bull images were anti-

Accordingly it would seem reasonable to suppose that the expansion of the second commandment with its preoccupation with images from nature which could be understood as images of foreign gods, specifically had in mind such objects as the bull images. Confirmation of this fact is received from Exod. 34:17, for it is clear that in its present literary context this verse is intended to refer to the golden calf of Exod. 32.

Thus Exod. 34:10 ff. cannot be understood in isolation from the preceding material, namely the story of the golden calf. What was probably originally written as a favourable aetiological account is now used for a polemical attack on Jeroboam's bulls, though the artificality of this treatment can be recognized from the inability of the author to condemn Aaron himself. The account is clearly dependent on 1 Kgs. 12:28 f., as the use of the plural 'gods' confirms, for in fact only one calf was made.[27] Further the treatment of the Levites in Exod. 32:25 ff. may reflect the contention that Jeroboam appointed non-Levitical priests for his royal sanctuaries (1 Kgs. 12:31; 13:33).[28]

Samaritan glosses. In Pfeiffer's view ('The Polemic against Idolatry in the old Testament', ibid., xliii, 1924, pp. 229 ff.) there was no protest against idolatry until Josiah's reform, all the relevant legislation being dated after 621.   [27] Noth, *Exodus*, pp. 246 ff.

[28] Cf. Brinker, *The Influence of Sanctuaries in Early Israel*, pp. 171 f.; Nicholson, *Deuteronomy and Tradition*, pp. 74 f. Noth argues that Judg. 17 f. is a polemical account attributable to Jeroboam I with the intent of discrediting the original Danite sanctuary and its Levitical priesthood ('The Background of Judges 17–18', *Israel's Prophetic Heritage* (Eds. Anderson and Harrelson), London, 1962, pp. 68 ff.). While Noth (cf. J. Bewer, 'The Composition of Judges, Chaps. 17, 18', *AJSL*, xxix, 1912/13, pp. 261 ff.) is right to point out that the account is very much more of a unity than has often been allowed (cf. G. F. Moore, *Judges*, ICC, 1895, pp. 365 ff.; Burney, *The Book of Judges*[2], London, 1930, pp. 408 ff.; C. A. Simpson, *Composition of the Book of Judges*, Oxford, 1957, pp. 63 ff.; A. Murtonen, 'Some Thoughts on Judges xvii. sq.', *VT*, i, 1951, pp. 223 f.), it none the less seems that the sudden transition from the story of the origin of the graven image in Judg. 17:2 ff. to that of the making of the *'ephod* and *teraphim* in verse 5 shows that the former was not originally part of the narrative. Thus Judg. 17:1, 5 ff. described the origin of the first legitimate Danite sanctuary, and concluded with the statement that Jonathan, the descendant of Moses, and his sons were priests at Dan as long as the ark was at Shiloh, there being no mention of the graven image. Probably ארון ('ark') should be read for ארץ ('land') in Judg. 18:30 (Bewer, op. cit., pp. 282 f.; Burney, op. cit., p. 415). Later the graven image was deliberately inserted into this old legend, and the account of the theft of the silver from which it was made created in order to indicate that even the original Danite sanctuary was apostate. The introduction of מסכה must be understood as a later correction. There is therefore no reason for accepting Noth's argument that the pro-monarchial notes Judg. 17:6; 18:1 are original to Judg. 17 f., but not to Judg. 19 ff. In both instances they are probably the work of the Deuteronomic historian, who in Judg. 17:6 shows his disapproval not only of the graven image, but also of the *'ephod* and *teraphim*, which, following Josiah's reform, had become idolatrous (see above, pp. 58, 60 ff.). Accordingly, Judg. 17 f. cannot be used to prove that ancient Israel possessed images of Yahweh (see above, p. 50).

Who then was the author, and what was he attempting to do? It is submitted that he was the JE redactor who following the fall of Samaria, and the bringing of the traditions of the northern kingdom to the south, sought to re-write the Sinai pericope in the light of Hezekiah's reform. Thus he attributes the fall of the northern kingdom to Yahweh's irrevocable breach of the covenant relationship because of Israel's apostasy through syncretism with Canaanite religion. This is brought out in his account by narrating the breaking of the tablets of the law as a result of the people's idolatry with the golden calf, in which animal, through the adaptation of the original aetiological story, the reader is made to recognize Jeroboam's bulls (1 Kgs. 12:28 f.).[29]

By his reference to the breaking of the tablets, the author is again using the suzerainty treaty form, for such a treaty only continued in force while the document recording it remained in existence. If this was destroyed, it had to be replaced, or the treaty would be deemed to be at an end.[30] Thus in order to signify that the covenant relationship was still in force with *Judah*, the JE redactor created the second set of tablets. Since Exod. 34 is intended to record the re-enactment of the covenant at Sinai, naturally the suzerainty treaty form is used.[31] Thus Exod. 34:10 f. constitutes the historical prologue, which is followed by the covenant stipulations (Exod. 34:12 ff.). These are again referred to by the technical term 'words', and are written down on the two new tablets of the law (Exod. 34:27 f.). Further, in order to make clear that what had gone before was intended to be understood as a substitute for the Decalogue, the JE redactor deliberately described the words of the re-enacted covenant as ten (Ex. 34:28b), a phrase which the Deuteronomists were to take over (Deut. 4:13; 10:4). No one later could possibly have used such a phrase to describe the legislation contained in Exod. 34:10 ff. But contrary to tradition elsewhere (Exod. 24:12; 31:18; 34:1; Deut. 4:13; 5:22; 9:10; 10:4), it is not God, but Moses himself who does the writing. In this figure of Moses the reader is intended to recognize Hezekiah who through Judah's syncretism with Canaan is himself threatened with punishment, but can yet save his people through his reform (Exod. 32:30 ff.).[32]

---

[29] 1 Kgs. 12:28 f. is itself probably to be attributed to the JE redactor, and formed part of the pre-Deuteronomic book of Kings (cf. Eissfeldt, *Introduction*, pp. 297 ff.). Jeroboam's words are intended to act as a direct parody of the historical prologue to the Decalogue. It is also probable that it was the JE redactor who introduced the graven image into Judg. 17 f. in order to discredit even the original Danite sanctuary.

[30] Baltzer, *Das Bundesformular*, p. 27; Beyerlin, *Origins and History*, p. 55; Kapelrud, *ST*, xviii, p. 87.

[31] Thompson, *Ancient Near Eastern Treaties*, pp. 33 f.   [32] See above, p. 43.

But since Exod. 34:10 ff. was intended by the JE redactor to be the climax of his rewritten Sinai narrative, he had to make sure that all law earlier than Hezekiah's reform preceded it. Thus he transferred the Book of the Covenant from Josh. 24 to its present position after the Decalogue, rearranging Exod. 20:18 ff. in the process.[33] In addition the JE redactor took the opportunity of adding a preface to the Book of the Covenant specifically designed to reflect Hezekiah's reform, namely the law prohibiting the manufacture of gods of silver or gold (Exod. 20:23) and what is probably an ancient law concerning the structure of an altar (Exod. 20:24 ff.). Further, he concluded the Book of the Covenant with a sermonic epilogue (Exod. 23:20 ff.) in which he again warned against contact with the six indigenous peoples and their gods. It is also probable that Exod. 23:13 is to be attributed to him. This is clearly an addition,[34] and is designed to prevent names of Canaanite gods being used in personal names.[35] This may again reflect Hosea's prophecy (2:19). As a result of this measure, the name Baal came to be replaced by *bosheth* ('shame') (Jer. 3:24; 11:13).[36]

But there has as yet been no discussion of the remaining legislation in Exod. 34, namely verses 18–26. How can this passage be understood to reflect Hezekiah's reform?

Exod. 34:18–26 repeats most of the positive injunctions at the conclusion of the Book of the Covenant by enjoining the keeping of the three agricultural feasts, together with the sabbath and the law of the first-born. Now it has been recognized that Exod. 23:14 ff. is in fact an ancient annual feast calendar, which authorizes the celebration in Israel of what were originally Canaanite agricultural feasts.[37] These were taken over by Israel with the conversion of Canaan and were specifically transformed into feasts to Yahweh, being celebrated at the local sanctuaries. The ordinance that all males should appear before Yahweh three times in the year could only refer to these sanctuaries, appearance at the central shrine of the amphictyony being utterly impracticable.[38] Originally there were probably no fixed dates for these feasts, these being dependent on the state of the crops.

Almost nothing is known about the cultus of the central amphictyonic shrine, though reference has been made to the seven year coven-

---

[33] It is possible that the phrase אל־קנוא הוא ('he is a jealous God') was inserted in Josh. 24:19 by the JE redactor, since this is how he describes Yahweh elsewhere (Exod. 20:5; 34:14). The phrase certainly has the appearance of a later note on the clause כי־אלהים קדשים הוא ('for he is a holy God').

[34] Noth, *Exodus*, p. 190.

[35] Vriezen, *Religion*, p. 169.

[36] Eichrodt, *Theology*, i, pp. 201 f.

[37] Kosmala, *ASTI*, i, pp. 38 ff.

[38] Noth, *History*, pp. 97 f., *Exodus*, p. 190.

ant festival. It is, however, probable that this shrine was particularly associated with the traditions and practices of the covenant community inherited from Kadesh in contrast to the new traditions and practices acquired after the spread of Yahwism into Canaan. Thus initially it would seem that the originally Canaanite agricultural feasts would have been kept distinct from the early covenant traditions, and that at first the Passover brought by Yahwism into Canaan would have been celebrated collectively by all Israel at the central amphictyonic shrine.[39] This would appear to be confirmed by Josh. 5:10 ff., which records that immediately after entering Canaan, Israel collectively celebrated the Passover,[40] and 2 Kgs. 23:22 which states that no Passover like Josiah's had been held since the period of the Judges, again signifying that then the Passover was collectively celebrated by all Israel at one sanctuary. Further it is possible that the legislation in Deut. 16:7 may reflect the earlier situation, an echo of which may also be found in Hos. 12:10.[41]

When the Passover became associated with the feast of Unleavened Bread remains uncertain. Although this may have happened earlier due to the inconvenience of celebrating two festivals at roughly the same time in two different places, it is more probable that it did not occur until after the destruction of Shiloh, the end of the period of the Judges (2 Kgs. 23:22). Certainly by the time the Book of the Covenant was issued, the Passover had been merged with the feast of Unleavened Bread as is shown by the dating in Exod. 23:15,[42] and the recognition that Exod. 23:18 f. constitutes a coda to the calendar, the first two injunctions, and probably the last two, being supplementary Passover provisions.[43]

The incorporation of this calendar together with its coda into the Book of the Covenant indicates that it became part of the law of the united kingdom. Thus Solomon himself officiated at the three festivals

[39] Cazelles, *Code de l'Alliance*, p. 143; de Vaux, *Ancient Israel*, p. 488.

[40] The feast of Unleavened Bread is not referred to here.

[41] Pedersen, *Israel*, iii–iv, E.T., London and Copenhagen, 1940, p. 388.

[42] Ibid., pp. 385; Kosmala, op. cit., pp. 39 f. Originally unleavened bread may have had no connection with the Passover at all (Pedersen, op. cit., p. 400). It would seem that the Passover was celebrated by semi-nomadic peoples prior to the exodus events (Noth, *Exodus*, p. 91; de Vaux, *Ancient Israel*, p. 489). For a discussion of the slaughter of a young animal and the use of a plant held to have beneficial powers elsewhere in the ancient world, cf. Mendenhall, *BASOR*, cxxxiii, pp. 26 ff., who points out that in Exod. 12:21 ff. (assigned to J, as Noth, op. cit., p. 93) there is no indication that the animal was to be eaten, but that the main idea is one of protection. He suggests that the Passover might be a continuation of an ancient custom connected with the establishment of a covenant relationship.

[43] Kosmala, op. cit., pp. 45 ff.

in Jerusalem (1 Kgs. 9:25; 2 Chr. 8:13). But there is no indication that they were only to be celebrated there.

There would have been no point in repeating the feast calendar in Exod. 34 unless it was intended to revise the existing law. Thus the significance of Exod. 34:18 ff. must be found in the additions to the previous concise provisions of Exod. 23:14 ff., which unlike the coda of Exod. 23:18 f. are inserted into the main body of the legislation. This more sophisticated method of amending existing law confirms that Exod. 34:18 ff. is the later piece of legislation.[44]

In the first place the law of the first-born is inserted after the injunction to keep the feast of Unleavened Bread (Exod. 34:19 f.), thereby severing the final clause of Exod. 23:15 from its context. This law is itself derived from the Book of the Covenant (Exod. 22:28b–29), Exod. 34:20 being a subsequent expansion dealing with the ass which could not be sacrified.[45] Whereas in the Book of the Covenant the law stands on its own without explanation, in Exod. 34 it is deliberately inserted as a supplementary Passover law, the law of the first-born being implicitly connected with the striking of the Egyptian first-born, though it originally had nothing to do with the Passover.[46] This connection is fully developed in Exod. 13. That the compiler of Exod. 34 was intending to stress the Passover law is confirmed by the use of the word itself in Exod. 34:25.

Secondly, Exod. 34:21 repeats the sabbath commandment set out in a different form in Exod. 23:12. The use of 'ploughing' and 'harvest' is deliberate, emphasizing that even in the busiest times of the year, obligations demanded by Yahweh must be performed.

Finally, Exod. 34:22 having repeated the earlier legislation about the other feasts with minor variations, the feast of harvest being given its later name of Weeks, Exod. 34:23 f., in contrast to Exod. 23:17, presupposes as far as these festivals are concerned centralization of worship. Is this the distinctive development in Exod. 34:18 ff?

It has already been noted that in addition to his opposition to Canaanite cult objects the Chronicler records that Hezekiah celebrated the Passover festival at the purified temple in Jerusalem, and that men were bidden to attend from all over Judah and even Israel

---

[44] Cf. Daube, *Studies in Biblical Law*, pp. 74 ff.; Kosmala, op. cit., pp. 44 f. Eissfeldt, *Introduction*, pp. 215 f. holds that Exod. 23:14 ff. is dependent on Exod. 34:18 ff., but there is no other instance of law being thus refined. From what follows it will be apparent that Exod. 34:18 ff. has been consciously expanded to meet a new situation. Thus Pfeiffer, 'The Oldest Decalogue', *JBL*, xliii, 1924, p. 305 points out that where Exod. 23 and 34 disagree, later codes are in harmony with Exod. 34.

[45] Noth, *Exodus*, p. 102.   [46] de Vaux, *Ancient Israel*, p. 489.

(2 Chr. 30:5). It would seem that Exod. 34:18 ff. with its stress on the Passover, is to be understood in the light of 2 Chr. 30, thereby reflecting Hezekiah's revolutionary legislation. This must have enacted that the Passover, and, as a result of its identification with the feast of Unleavened Bread, the feast of Weeks and Tabernacles as well, could only be celebrated at the central sanctuary at Jerusalem.[47] But the JE redactor's use of Exod. 20:24 ff. in his preface to the re-positioned Book of the Covenant, which measure implies a plurality of shrines, confirms that Hezekiah did not intend to abolish all sanctuaries. He appears to have envisaged a return to the conditions of the amphictyony in which Jerusalem was to replace Shechem as the amphictyonic centre at which all Israel would gather on the Yahweh festivals, but which permitted other local sanctuaries to exist throughout the land.[48] But because the Passover had been associated with the feast of Unleavened Bread, the other originally Canaanite agricultural feasts were now also to be celebrated at the central shrine, and not merely the Passover, as in the amphictyonic period. It is only by reading Exod. 20:24 ff. in the light of Deuteronomy that a polemic against centralization of worship is discerned, for there is no evidence of any attempt to centralize worship before Hezekiah's reform.

But in view of Josiah's more extensive reform the Deuteronomists have deliberately suppressed Hezekiah's partial centralization of worship. Thus while the JE redactor's account of the golden calf and the breaking of the original tablets of the law was incorporated into Deuteronomy, it was none the less asserted that in contradiction to Exod. 32–34 it was the Decalogue which was again inscribed on the second set of tablets by Yahweh himself (Deut. 10:1 ff.). Similarly while 2 Kgs. 18:4 referred to Hezekiah's abolition of cult objects, it entirely ignored his centralization policy. This caused the Chronicler to miss the point of 2 Kgs. 23:22, and explains why in 2 Chr. 30:26 he refers to Solomon. Knowing from 2 Kgs. 23:22 that no Passover like Josiah's had been held since the period of the Judges, and yet also knowing from his independent material that Hezekiah had already attempted to centralize the Passover in Jerusalem, he imagined that

[47] The Deuteronomic legislation makes Exod. 34:23 f. even more explicit (Deut. 16:5, 16). Hezekiah's innovation in celebrating the Passover in the second month, a detail the Chronicler would never have included if he had not got evidence of it (F. L. Moriarty, 'The Chronicler's Account of Hezekiah's Reform', *CBQ*, xxvii, 1965, pp. 404 ff.), may have led to the priestly law contained in Num. 9:6 ff.
[48] Cf. Vriezen, *Religion*, p. 226, who argues that while the high places were destroyed, the ancient shrines such as Hebron and Beersheba would merely have been purified.

the Deuteronomic historian was concerned to stress the sumptuousness of Josiah's Passover. Thus he himself stressed the enormous offering made by Hezekiah (2 Chr. 30:24), and in effect said that even Solomon with all his wealth could not match such extravagance. He then made Josiah's celebration even more lavish (2 Chr. 35:7), and was able to state that none of the kings of Judah had kept such a magnificent Passover since Samuel, who was evidently regarded as concluding the period of the Judges (2 Chr. 35:18). But the Deuteronomic historian, who made no mention of the lavish offerings, meant that no centralized festival involving all Israel had been held since the period of the Judges.[49]

Only in the Rabshakeh's taunt is there an allusion to this centralization aspect of Hezekiah's reform by the Deuteronomic historian, where an actual injunction of the king may be quoted out of context (2 Kgs. 18:22; Isa. 36:7). The conquering Assyrian could hardly be expected to grasp the nuances of Hezekiah's reform. To him the destruction of so many altars with their cult objects and the centralization of the celebration of the three main feasts at Jerusalem would have looked like a total centralization of worship. But this reference does confirm that Hezekiah did undertake a reform involving some centralization of worship, even though it has been contended that it was partial.

However it is possible that the Chronicler thought that Hezekiah destroyed all shrines throughout Judah (2 Chr. 31:1). Thus in recording the Rabshakeh's taunt he seems to indicate total centralization of worship (2 Chr. 32:12). Having before him the Deuteronomic historian's account, and knowing independently that Hezekiah had centralized the Passover at Jerusalem, he probably imagined that in fact Hezekiah had instituted the same type of reform as Josiah. If this is so, then it is the Deuteronomic historian who is responsible for the Chronicler's misunderstanding of history, and it is in the legislation of Exod. 34:10 ff. that the true nature and extent of Hezekiah's reform can be recovered.[50]

It would seem that the hortatory additions to the third, fourth and fifth commandments are also to be attributed to the JE redactor being in the same preaching style noted both in Exod. 23 and 34. Clearly they are older than the Deuteronomic version as the Deuteronomic

---

[49] That the Deuteronomic historian recognized the importance of Hezekiah's reform is indicated by the high praise which the king is given in 2 Kgs. 18:5. Cf. his remarks on Josiah in 2 Kgs. 23:25.

[50] Mendenhall in his study of the covenant law (*BA*, xvii, pp. 50 ff.) ignores Hezekiah's reform.

insertion in the hortatory addition to the fifth commandment makes plain.[51] Further it would seem that the hortatory addition to the fourth commandment has been directly influenced by Exod. 23:12. Since the JE redactor in effect made the Decalogue act as a prologue to the Book of the Covenant, he evidently felt it necessary to make the sabbath commandment as explicitly comprehensive as Exod. 23:12.[52] It also appears probable that it was the JE redactor who was responsible for the present form of the tenth commandment.[53] While Hezekiah sought a return to the conditions of the amphictyony as far as worship in Judah was concerned, he made no attempt to recover the primitive system of the administration of justice before Jehoshaphat's reform (cf. Isa. 1:21 ff.).[54] He clearly wished to keep it under his own control. But it would seem that in order to justify Hezekiah's retention of Jehoshaphat's reorganization of the administration of justice, the JE redactor created Exod. 18:13 ff. as an aetiological account to give it Mosaic authority, which he then used as a prelude to the Sinai pericope.

Finally it is possible that the JE redactor also created Exod. 34:29 ff. as another aetiological account to conclude his revised Sinai narrative. It has already been argued that this passage refers to the *teraphim*, though because these came to be condemned as a result of Josiah's reform, this word has been changed to מסוה ('covering', 'veil').[55] The JE redactor may well have wanted to confirm that it was only those objects which could be regarded as images of heathen deities which Hezekiah destroyed, and not the legitimate cultic apparatus used in divination, such as the *teraphim*. These would still have been found at the purified shrines.

As a result of this understanding of Exod. 34:10 ff. one can finally dispense with the totally misleading terms 'the ethical Decalogue' and 'the ritual Decalogue'. There never was a ritual Decalogue, and the so-called ethical Decalogue is in fact the Sinai Decalogue, obedience to which determined Israel's existence.

---

[51] See above, p. 82.
[52] See above, p. 69.
[53] See above, pp. 151 f.
[54] See above, pp. 18 ff.
[55] See above, p. 61.

CHAPTER SEVENTEEN

THE DEUTERONOMIC REFORM

Contrary to the impression gained from 2 Kgs., it would appear that Josiah's reform took place in at least two stages.[1] In the twelfth year of his reign (2 Chr. 34:3), because of the political weakness of Assyria, Josiah was able to renounce the latter's suzerainty, and to purge his country of apostate shrines and images, as Hezekiah had done earlier, extending his activity to include part of the former northern kingdom (2 Chr. 34:6). There is, however, no indication that at this stage there was any move to centralize even the three major feasts at Jerusalem, let alone all worship. But in the eighteenth year of Josiah's reign (2 Chr. 34:8) a law book was discovered in the temple, which so shocked Josiah that he forthwith embarked on a drastic reformation. It has usually been held that this book was the nucleus of Deuteronomy itself, and that this had been brought from the northern kingdom to Jerusalem after the fall of Samaria. But it has recently been contended on theological grounds that Deuteronomy itself cannot be the product of the northern kingdom, but that it is a Judaean document being a deliberate attempt at reforming and reinterpreting the Jerusalem cult tradition, particularly in relation to the Davidic covenant.[2] In fact an examination of what precisely were the innovations introduced by the Deuteronomic reform settles the case beyond dispute, for when the Deuteronomic legislation is analysed, it becomes clear that there are two main innovations, namely the centralization of *all* worship at Jerusalem and the extension of the covenant relationship to women— both of which ideas are an extension of provisions contained in Exod. 34:11 ff. This can only mean that the law book discovered in the temple was none other that the JE redaction written in the light of Hezekiah's reform, and it was this discovery which prompted Josiah's sudden drastic action and formed the basis for his own much more far-reaching reform contained in the Deuteronomic legislation.

[1] Cf. Cross and D. N. Freedman, 'Josiah's Revolt against Assyria', *JNES*, xii, 1953, pp. 56–8.

[2] Clements, 'Deuteronomy and the Jerusalem Cult Tradition', *VT*, xv, 1965, pp. 300–12.

Thus in direct contradiction to the law of the altar which the JE redactor had used as part of his preface to the Book of the Covenant (Exod. 20:24 ff.), the opening provision of the Deuteronomic legislation centralized at Jerusalem not merely the three major festivals (Exod. 34:23 f.) but all worship (Deut. 12:5, 13 f.),[3] thereby necessitating the destruction of all other shrines, together with their previously legitimate cult objects such as the *'ephod* and *teraphim*,[4] as well as the centralization of the priesthood.

Further, the JE redactor's caution against foreign marriages (Exod. 34:16) now became an absolute prohibition (Deut. 7:3), and women themselves were brought into the covenant relationship as the specific enactments of the Deuteronomic legislation indicate. By these new measures suggested by Hezekiah's reform, Josiah hoped to eradicate once and for all any possibility of apostasy. All Israelites, whether male or female, were now subject to the criminal law, and all worship was brought under his personal control, being centralized at the purified royal shrine at Jerusalem.

It has been recognized that the present book of Deuteronomy— again modelled on the ancient Hittite suzerainty treaty form[5]—acts as the first book of the Deuteronomic history from Moses to the exile contained in the corpus Deuteronomy—2 Kgs., Deut. 1–3 (4) being the introduction to this work.[6] Much discussion has centred on trying to identify the original book of Deuteronomy thought to be present in Deut. 5–26.[7] It would in fact seem that this is to be found by removing from these chapters the passages which use the plural form of address, which passages are to be understood as insertions made by the Deuteronomic historian.[8] The remaining material using the singular form of address constitutes the original book setting out the burden of Josiah's reform. This includes the major portion of the legislation in 12–26, but neither the historical passage Deut. 9:7b–10:11 nor that in which the Decalogue is set (5:1–6:1). Although the Decalogue itself remains

---

[3] It is probable that Deut. 12:1–12 (plural form of address) is an elaboration of Deut. 12:13 ff. (singular form of address) made by the Deuteronomic historian. Both enactments ordain centralization of worship. Cf. Minette de Tillesse, *VT*, xii, 1962, pp. 64 ff.; von Rad, *Deuteronomy*, p. 92; Nicholson, *Deuteronomy and Tradition*, pp. 27 f.

[4] Cf. 2 Kgs. 23:24 and see above, p. 58.

[5] Thompson, *Ancient Near Eastern Treaties*, p. 22; von Rad, op. cit., pp. 21 ff. and cf. R. Frankena, 'The Vassal Treaties of Esarhaddon and the Dating of Deuteronomy', *OTS*, xiv, 1965, pp. 122–54, who regards Josiah's renewal of the Mosaic covenant as a deliberate substitution of the former vassal treaty with the King of Assyria.

[6] Noth, *Überlieferungsgeschichtliche Studien*, i², Tübingen, 1957.

[7] For a recent study of the problems involved, cf. Nicholson, op. cit., pp. 18 ff.

[8] Minette de Tillesse, op. cit., pp. 29 ff.

in the second person singular, it would still seem from its lack of contact with other second person singular passages that it was not in the original book of Deuteronomy,[9] but was deliberately inserted by the Deuteronomic historian with his other material to act as a prologue to the subsequent legislation, as it did in the JE redaction (Exod. 20). But even though the Deuteronomic historian modelled his account on the JE redaction, he none the less tried to suppress Hezekiah's reform because it permitted the existence of sanctuaries other than Jerusalem. Thus he entirely contradicts the JE redactor's account (Exod. 34) of the making of the second set of tablets of the law (Deut. 10:1 ff.). Similarly in 2 Kgs. 22:3 ff. he merges the two stages of Josiah's reform so that the limitation of Josiah's earlier action should not become apparent.[10]

Since Josiah's sole objective was to seek the maintenance of the Mosaic covenant relationship, it is no surprise that the Deuteronomic law is hardly concerned with the civil law at all, but in the main constitutes an expansion of the criminal law of the Decalogue. It was obedience to this covenant law which determined the existence of the state. Further it was because the Deuteronomist recognized that the criminal law had not been enforced that he adopted a deterrent theory of punishment (17:13; 19:20; 21:21). The criminal was no longer to be executed merely to maintain the covenant relationship, but to deter such widespread breach of the law that Yahweh would be forced to intervene to sever that relationship once and for all. Punishment was now looked at from the criminal's or potential criminal's point of view. Similarly, in order to stress the urgency of enforcing the criminal law contained in and derived from the Decalogue itself, the Deuteronomist punctuated his legislation with the phrase (מישראל) ובערת הרע מקרבך ('and you shall purge out the evil from your midst (from Israel)').[11]

However, with Josiah's death the principles of the Mosaic covenant enshrined in the Deuteronomic reform gradually seem to have been abandoned. This probably accounts for Jeremiah's renunciation of the Davidic line (Jer. 36:30), and support of Gedaliah.[12] Though it was not at once realized, with the fall of Jerusalem and the exile in Babylon the Mosaic covenant concept was at an end. It was to be left to those in exile to work out the precise relationship of Yahweh to Israel.[13]

---

[9] Nielsen, *The Ten Commandments*, pp. 47 ff.

[10] See above, pp. 177 f.   [11] Cf. L'Hour, *Bibl.*, xlvi, pp. 1 ff.

[12] M. Sekine, 'Davidsbund und Sinaibund bei Jeremia', *VT*, ix, 1959, pp. 47–57.

[13] The place of the composition of the Deuteronomic historical work remains uncertain, but cf. Ackroyd, *Exile and Restoration*, London, 1968, pp. 65 ff.

CHAPTER EIGHTEEN

THE PRIESTLY LEGISLATION

There is no information as to the administration of justice in Israel following the fall of Jerusalem and the deportation of the upper classes to Babylon. Presumably to some extent the pre-exilic law continued to be enforced, for there is no indication that foreign law was ever introduced. But whatever was the case, the future of Judaism did not lie with those who remained in Israel, but with the exiles, who were forced in their remote situation to reassess the covenant concept.

Thus the prophets of the exile did not attempt to return to the conditions of the Sinai covenant even though they proclaimed a new exodus (Ezek. 20:35 ff.; Isa. 54:9 f.; 55:3 ff. Cf. Jer. 31:31 ff.).[1] Judgement under that covenant had taken place, and they looked forward to a nation reborn entirely through Yahweh's grace (Ezek. 37). This is the theme of the priestly work, which replaces the idea of the covenant based on one historic act at Sinai by the concept of divine election, which in the inauguration of the sabbath as an act of creation (Gen. 2:2 f.) is traced back to the very beginning of time. The covenant made with Abraham, now seen in the context of primeval history, becomes the basis of Israel's relationship with Yahweh. The Sinai event is not thought of as another covenant but as the disclosure of the appropriate legislation which makes possible the fulfilment of the promise made to Abraham.[2] Thus Israel's existence is attributed to no merit of her own, but to the timeless and continuing election of Yahweh. It is through this that she reappears not as a political group, but as a worshipping community whose *raison d'être* is her central sanctuary and cult in which Yahweh's presence might be made real.

Thus whereas under the Sinai covenant Yahweh's relationship with Israel, and so his presence in the temple, was conditional on Israel's obedience to the law, the priestly work ensured that this relationship should exist irrespective of the law. It recognized that failure was

---

[1] Zimmerli, *The Law and the Prophets*, pp. 79 ff.
[2] Zimmerli, 'Sinaibund and Abrahambund', *TZ*, xvi, 1960, pp. 275 ff., *The Law and the Prophets*, pp. 90 f.

inherent in man, and, through the cult, with its Day of Atonement (Lev. 16:1 ff.), provided the means whereby Israel might ever renew and reform herself, and thus be in continual communion with Yahweh.[3] The priestly legislation was therefore designed to ensure the proper ordering and purity of the cult, from which the offender had to be excluded (Ezek. 20:35 ff.). It therefore protected an existing and permanent relationship from abuse, rather than created and determined its duration.

Although there was initially some hope that the Davidic monarchy might be restored, with the rebuilding of the temple this soon ceased.[4] Instead of the king, the people had become the possessors of the promise made to Abraham. There was no need for the return of the monarch, for the cult alone now effectively secured the God-man relationship. Thus although the high priest fulfilled the king's functions as head of the community, both religious and legal, he was never a party to a covenant with Yahweh.

The substitution of the concept of the Mosaic covenant by election had far reaching effects on the law. In the first place, since Israel no longer traced her existence to the Sinai covenant, the criminal law ceased to be based on the covenant stipulations of the Sinai Decalogue. New crimes could therefore be developed. Thus it is at this point that failure to circumcise is designated a criminal offence (Gen. 17:9 ff.). Whereas this had formerly marked entrance into adult life, and consequently came to signify membership of the covenant community, with the abandonment of the Mosaic covenant concept, the priestly legislation transferred the rite to the eighth day after birth, thus using it to signify membership of the elect community of Israel into which one was born (Lev. 12:3; Gen. 17:12; 21:4).[5]

Secondly, as the cult itself provided the community with the means of propitiating Yahweh through the Day of Atonement, there was now no reason to execute the criminal. Thus it has already been recognized

---

[3] It is not known when the Day of Atonement as described in Lev. 16 was instituted in Israel, but there is no reason why it should not have been devised in the exile as part of the reassessment of Israel's relations with Yahweh, and to have been instituted with the rebuilding of the temple. Ezek. 45:19 f. reflects this reassessment. Particular elements of the ritual in Lev. 16 appear to be old, but originally would only have involved the priesthood.

[4] It should, however, be noted that both Haggai and Zechariah are more interested in the building of the temple, and the inauguration of a new divine age, rather than the possibility of the restoration of the Davidic monarchy. Further there is no indication that Darius ever had to intervene in Israel in connection with any attempt to establish Zerubbabel as an independent Davidic ruler (*Peake*, pp. 645 f.).

[5] Köhler, *Hebrew Man*, p. 38.

that, save in the case of murder, the death penalty was abandoned in favour of the priestly punishment of excommunication, such excommunication being irrevocable.[6]

Thirdly, as the cult and not the Mosaic covenant ensured the God-man relationship, providing in itself the means for dealing with failure, divine judgement on the elect community, as opposed to the individual, ceased to be thought of as a possibility, providing the purity of the cult was maintained. The priestly legislation therefore realized the prophecies of Jer. 31:29 f. and Ezek. 18:1 ff. that an individual would only be liable for his own acts, and not for the acts of others by virtue of his membership of the community. That the moral standpoint of human punishment under Israel's pre-exilic criminal law, which prohibited the execution of anyone other than the actual criminal (Deut. 24:16), could now be applied to divine punishment was thus directly due to the abandonment of the Mosaic covenant concept with its reliance on both individual *and* communal liability.[7]

The date of the introduction of the priestly legislation into Israel remains uncertain for there is no precise information concerning life there from the rebuilding of the temple to the arrival of Nehemiah and Ezra.[8] Although it is possible that later material was added, there would, however, seem no reason to suppose that with the actual rebuilding of the temple, the priestly legislation including the Holiness Code, which would appear to be a product of the early exilic situation,[9] could not have been introduced. Further, by selecting excommunication as the penalty for breach of this legislation, even if initially this was only from the temple, the restored community had the means of enforcing it, whether or not it was generally accepted. Thus it must not be assumed that the priestly legislation as a whole could only have come into force with the reform of Ezra.[10] Indeed, it is entirely probable that his law, which is nowhere supposed to be new legislation (Ezra 7:14), comprised the Pentateuch.[11] Certainly this must have been accepted as authoritative sometime before the Samaritan schism. The dating of the schism is itself uncertain, but in view of the fact that only

[6] See above, pp. 28 ff.
[7] See above, pp. 32 ff.
[8] It is not necessary here to discuss the various views as to the dating of Ezra's mission, but it would seem most likely that Ezra followed Nehemiah, probably arriving in Jerusalem in 397. Cf. Rowley, 'Nehemiah's Mission and its Background', *BJRL*, xxxvii, 1954/5, pp. 548 ff.; Bright, *History*, pp. 375 ff.
[9] Cf. Weiser, *Introduction*, p. 140; Eissfeldt, *Introduction*, pp. 236 ff.
[10] Ibid., pp. 207 f.; Kapelrud, 'The Date of the Priestly Code (P)', *ASTI*, iii, 1964, pp. 58–64; Ackroyd, *Exile and Restoration*, pp. 84 ff.
[11] Weiser, *Introduction*, pp. 138 ff.; Eissfeldt, *Introduction*, pp. 556 f.

the Pentateuch was accepted by the Samaritans, that the Chronicler, who must have written in the Persian period, records Israel's history in the light of the schism, and that the Samaritans focus their hostility directly on Ezra, it would seem that this schism must have occurred shortly after the latter's mission.[12] Therefore, the priestly legislation is unlikely to have been introduced by Ezra, for the Samaritans would hardly have taken over for their scriptures a new work whose introduction in Israel was attributed to the subject of their hostility. The scriptures which they did accept must already have achieved authoritative recognition. Thus it would seem most likely that the priestly legislation was introduced in Israel following the rebuilding of the temple, and that in the period prior to Ezra the Pentateuch was formed, thus allowing it time to become authoritative before the dispute which led to the Samaritan schism. The importance of Nehemiah and Ezra was that they gained the Persian king's authority to enforce already existing law, and by making it state law, could make the ideal of the priestly legislation a reality. This was in fact what Ezra was commissioned to do (Ezra 7:25 f.). Now excommunication from the state itself, and not just the cult, could be enforced.

As part of their measures for the proper ordering of the worship of the post-exilic temple, it would appear that the priests drew up entrance liturgies directed at those seeking admittance to the temple, two of which are probably preserved in Ps. 15,[13] to which the postexilic passage Isa 33:14 ff. is closely related,[14] and Ps. 24:3 ff.[15] These do not demand external observance of the law as such, but a general overriding ethical standpoint, which governs both the thoughts and actions of the intending worshipper. Law here has been replaced by an individual purity which no law can enforce. While Pss. 15 and 24 have often been thought pre-exilic, there is in fact no trace of the existence of these entrance liturgies in pre-exilic legal or historical texts (cf. Jer. 7:2).[16] Indeed it appears that even those who were

---

[12] Rowley, 'Sanballat and the Samaritan Schism', *BJRL*, xxxviii, 1955/6, pp. 190 ff.

[13] There would seem no grounds for the contention of J. L. Koole, 'Psalm xv—eine königliche Einzugsliturgie?', *OTS*, xiii, 1963, pp. 98–111 that the psalm is to be connected with the coronation of the Davidic king. Cf. Clements, *Prophecy and Covenant*, p. 83. On the interpretation of verse 4, cf. M. J. Dahood, 'A Note on Psalm 15, 4 (14, 4)', *CBQ*, xvi, 1954, p. 302.

[14] M. Buttenwieser, *The Psalms*, Chicago, 1938, pp. 203 ff., who, however, holds that Isa. 33:14 ff. is dependent on Ps. 15, which he regards as pre-exilic.

[15] There is no need here to discuss the unity of Ps. 24, but it may be noted that both Kissane, *Psalms*, i, p. 106 and Weiser, *Psalms*, pp. 234 ff. reject the view that verses 7 ff. refer to the procession of the ark to the temple. Cf. Ezek. 43:4.

[16] Cf. Ps. 50 which, while it deplores the presence in the temple of those described in verses 18 ff., likewise gives no indication of any entrance liturgy.

known to have broken the *covenant* law, and therefore should have been executed as criminals, had little difficulty in gaining access to the temple (Jer. 7:8 ff.).[17] But in fact the purpose of these post-exilic priestly liturgies was not to prevent entry into the temple, and so debar the sinner from the means of forgiveness, for the cult existed in order to maintain the God-man relationship. Their aim was rather to impress upon the intending worshipper the seriousness of the undertaking upon which he was engaged, and thereby to encourage a proper confession to be followed by the rendering of the appropriate sin offering. Thus these liturgies are not directed at the *criminal*, who would have been excluded from the cult by excommunication, but at those who could expect to enter it. This explains the absence of any specific criminal offences.[18]

For this reason it would seem that in Ps. 24:4 נפשׁו ('himself') should be read rather than נפשׁי ('my soul'), which would appear to allude to the third commandment since נפשׁ ('soul,' 'self') can be used as a synonym for שׁם ('name') (Amos 6:8), the name being the equivalent of the self in Hebrew thought. The clause refers quite generally to any worthless conduct.[19] It can be readily understood how under the influence of Exod. 20:7 נפשׁי was later inserted in the MT. The LXX reads τὴν ψυχὴν αὐτοῦ (LXXᴬ μοῦ).

But in contrast, the final clause of Ps. 24:4 does seem to have a specific situation in mind, namely a false oath in a property dispute case. It has already been noted that this was a particular concern of the priestly legislator who sought to encourage voluntary confession by persons who had sworn such an oath (Lev. 5:21 ff.; Num. 5:5 ff.).[20] These oaths were not criminal, and so did not involve excommunication from the cult, which explains why they find a place in an entrance liturgy. Naturally the presence in the temple of someone who had sworn such an oath was considered highly undesirable.

Another instance of the same post-exilic priestly concern for the purity of the cult would appear to be the cursing liturgy contained in Deut. 27:15 ff. This does not form part of the original book of Deuteronomy itself for the expected blessings and curses in accordance with

[17] Clements, op. cit., pp. 84 f. notes that these entrance liturgies seem to have had little effect during the monarchy, but he does not consider the possibility that they might in fact be a post-exilic innovation. Mic. 6:6 ff. may be another example of an entrance liturgy, but it is probable that this passage is also post-exilic (cf. J. M. P. Smith, *Micah*, ICC, 1912, pp. 15 f., 124).

[18] This explains why on no account could the Sinai Decalogue be understood as an entrance liturgy (cf. Mowinckel, *Le Décalogue*, pp. 141 ff., *Psalms*, i, pp. 177 ff.).

[19] Thus Weiser, *Psalms*, p. 232 translates: 'who does not direct his thoughts to wrong doing'.   [20] See above, pp. 137 f.

the suzerainty treaty form are in fact set out in Deut. 28. The curses in Deut. 27:15 ff. consist of a miscellaneous collection of offences, whose common factor is their secret nature. In subject matter they are closely related to the Holiness Code, upon which they appear to be dependent,[21] since they would hardly have been incorporated into a liturgy, had they not already been prohibited by legislation. Some of these curses relate to crimes which demanded permanent excommunication from the cult, but others would appear to concern civil and moral offences (Deut. 27:17, 18, 19, 25) which must only have involved temporary exclusion until the offender had made his confession and given the requisite sin offering. This cursing liturgy may have been recited before admission to the temple as a variant form of entrance liturgy, but it is perhaps more likely that it was spoken after the act of worship had been completed. While the aim of entrance liturgies was to encourage a proper self-examination and subsequent confession by the man who anticipated entering the temple, the cursing liturgy would seem to envisage the possibility of someone having fraudulently taken part in temple worship, namely the unknown criminal who should on no account have been granted admission, or the man who had secretly broken the civil or moral law, and had not disclosed this. Thus it is probable that at the conclusion of the act of worship this cursing liturgy was recited, to which the congregation had to assent. In so doing, the secret offender who had acted fraudulently would condemn himself by his self-imprecation. This would explain why in the entrance liturgies general ethical demands are made, but in Deut. 27:15 ff. specific offences are envisaged. In any event the liturgy undoubtedly acted as a deterrent measure to prevent secret offenders from dishonestly taking part in the temple worship. Thus Deut. 27:15 ff. represents a very late addition to Deuteronomy, perhaps at the time that the Pentateuch was formed. Once again in discussing this passage scholars have let form rather than content determine their conclusions.[22]

[21] Eissfeldt, *Introduction*, p. 212. Cf. the stress on sexual offences in Ezek. 22:10 f.; Lev. 18:6 ff.; 20:10 ff., and compare Deut. 27:18 with Lev. 19:14. While Ezek. 22:10 f. does not take into account any relative outside those normally found in a man's house, Deut. 27:22 f. refers both to a half-sister through a common mother, and a mother-in-law. This direct reference to the new priestly legislation would seem to confirm the contention that Deut. 27:15 ff. is a post-exilic composition (see above, pp. 124 ff.).

[22] However, Daube, *Oxford Society of Historical Theology*, 1944/5, pp. 39 ff. does find in Lev. 11, 13, 20 and Num. 35 a peculiar form of legislation attributable to the priestly legislator. This sets out the concrete situation, which is then reduced to its essence, from which follows the appropriate judgement. As Daube points out, the second stage is superfluous.

But while there is thus clear evidence that the priestly legislation continued to distinguish crimes, that is offences which the community proscribed and which it punished in its name, there is, apart from Lev. 5:21 ff.,[23] no precise information concerning torts. This again reflects the very great importance of the criminal law in contrast to the civil law. The priestly legislators were not concerned with suits which one Israelite might bring against another, but with maintaining the purity of the cult by making sure that persons who had committed certain acts should be irrevocably excommunicated.

Finally it may be noted that while it was through the particularism and exclusiveness of the priestly legislation that Israel, although denuded of political power, was able to survive as a nation, this did not mean that her law ceased to contemplate the incorporation of non-Jews into her cult community. Just as the Sinai Decalogue had both created and defined Israel, and yet permitted anyone who had not been present at Sinai to be incorporated into the community by acceptance of the covenant stipulations, so the priestly legislation by making acceptance of the law the criterion for membership of Israel, enabled anyone, no matter of what race, to become a member of the elect community.

This brief discussion of the immediate post-exilic period completes this study of ancient Israel's criminal law. Its aim has been to show that ancient Israel clearly understood the technical concept 'crime', and to isolate her criminal law from all other types of law. For the pre-exilic period the study has sought to argue that the stipulations of the Sinai Decalogue constituted ancient Israel's criminal law code, obedience to which determined the covenant relationship. Even after the covenant was irrevocably broken, the necessity of continuing to distinguish Israel's criminal law in the post-exilic period has been shown, for though the cult then guaranteed the relationship of Yahweh with Israel, it was obedience to the criminal law which determined membership of the elect community. Ancient Israel's criminal law throughout the period covered by this study is thus directly related to her understanding of her relationship with Yahweh. Consequently the recognition of the concept of crime is of the utmost importance in the proper interpretation of the Old Testament material.

---

[23] But this provision was not primarily concerned with the appropriation of property as such, but with encouraging a man to confess to having sworn a false oath (see above, p. 138).

ABBREVIATIONS

AASOR	*Annual of the American Schools of Oriental Research*
AJSL	*American Journal of Semitic Languages and Literatures*
AJT	*American Journal of Theology*
AL	G. R. Driver, Sir J. C. Miles, *The Assyrian Laws*, Oxford, 1935
ALUOS	*Annual of Leeds University Oriental Society*
ANET	J. B. Pritchard (Ed.), *Ancient Near Eastern Texts Relating to the Old Testament*[2], Princeton, 1955
ArOr	*Archiv Orientâlni*
ASTI	*Annual of the Swedish Theological Institute*
BA	*The Biblical Archaeologist*
BASOR	*Bulletin of the American Schools of Oriental Research*
BDB	F. Brown, S. R. Driver, C. A. Briggs (Eds.), *A Hebrew and English Lexicon of the Old Testament* (reprint), Oxford, 1959
BH	R. Kittel (Ed.), *Biblica Hebraica*
Bibl.	*Biblica*
BJRL	*Bulletin of the John Rylands Library*
BL	G. R. Driver, Sir J. C. Miles, *The Babylonian Laws*, i, Oxford, 1952; ii, Oxford, 1955
BT	*The Bible Translator*
BWANT	*Beiträge zur Wissenschaft vom Alten und Neuen Testament*
BZ	*Biblische Zeitschrift*
BZAW	*Beihefte zur Zeitschrift für die Alttestamentliche Wissenschaft*
CBQ	*Catholic Biblical Quarterly*
CH	The Code of Hammurabi
CV	*Communio Viatorum*
DOTT	D. Winton Thomas (Ed.), *Documents from Old Testament Times*, London, 1958
ET	*The Expository Times*
E.T.	English Translation
HL	The Hittite Laws
HTS	*Harvard Theological Studies*
HUCA	*Hebrew Union College Annual*
ICC	*The International Critical Commentary*
IDB	*The Interpreter's Dictionary of the Bible*, New York—Nashville, 1962

Interpr.	*Interpretation*
JAOS	*Journal of the American Oriental Society*
JBL	*Journal of Biblical Literature*
JBR	*Journal of Bible and Religion*
JJP	*Journal of Juristic Papyrology*
JJS	*Journal of Jewish Studies*
JNES	*Journal of Near Eastern Studies*
JPhil	*Journal of Philology*
JPOS	*Journal of the Palestine Oriental Society*
JQR	*Jewish Quarterly Review*
JSS	*Journal of Semitic Studies*
JTS	*Journal of Theological Studies*
K-B	L. Köhler, W. Baumgartner, *Lexicon in Veteris Testamenti Libros*, Leiden, 1953
LE	The Laws of Eshnunna
LXX	The Septuagint
MAL	The Middle Assyrian Laws
MT	The Massoretic Text
N-BL	The Neo-Babylonian Laws
OTS	*Oudtestamentische Studiën*
PEQ	*Palestine Exploration Quarterly*
RA	*Revue d'Assyriologie et d'Archéologie Orientale*
RB	*Revue Biblique*
RHA	*Revue Hittite et Asianique*
RIDA	*Revue Internationale des Droits de l'Antiquité*
RSV	Revised Standard Version
SBT	Studies in Biblical Theology
ST	*Studia Theologica*
TLZ	*Theologische Literaturzeitung*
TQ	*Theologische Quartalschrift*
TR	*Theologische Rundschau*
TZ	*Theologische Zeitschrift*
UUÅ	*Uppsala Universitets Årrskrift*
VT	*Vetus Testamentum*
VTS	*Vetus Testamentum Supplement*
WD	*Wort und Dienst*
WMANT	Wissenschaftliche Monographien zum Alten und Neuen Testament
WO	*Die Welt des Orients*
ZAW	*Zeitschrift für die Alttestamentliche Wissenschaft*
ZDPV	*Zeitschrift des Deutschen Palastina-Vereins*

BIBLIOGRAPHY

Ackroyd, P. R. 'The Teraphim', *ET*, lxii, 1950/1, pp. 378–80.
— *Exile and Restoration*, London, 1968.
Albright, W. F. 'Are the Ephod and the Teraphim Mentioned in Ugaritic Literature?', *BASOR*, lxxxiii, 1941, pp. 39–42.
— 'Anath and the Dragon', ibid., lxxxiv, 1941, pp. 14–17.
— 'The Excavations of Tell Beit Mirsim III', *AASOR*, xxi–xxii, 1941/3, pp. 1–229.
— *From the Stone Age to Christianity*², Baltimore, 1946.
— 'The Judicial Reform of Jehoshaphat', *Alexander Marx Jubilee Volume* (Ed. S. Lieberman), New York, 1950, pp. 61–82.
— 'The Hebrew Expression for "Making a Covenant" in pre-Israelite Documents', *BASOR*, cxxi, 1951, pp. 21–2.
— *Archaeology and the Religion of Israel*³, Baltimore, 1955.
Alt, A. 'Die phönikischen Inschriften von Karatepe', *WO*, i, 1949, pp. 272–287.
— '*Zu hit'ammēr*', *VT*, ii, 1952, pp. 153–9.
— 'Die Wallfahrt von Sichem nach Bethel', *Kleine Schriften zur Geschichte des Volkes Israel*, i, München, 1953, pp. 79–88.
— 'Das Verbot des Diebstahls im Dekalog', ibid., pp. 333–40.
— 'Zur Talionsformel', ibid., pp. 341–4.
— 'The Origins of Israelite Law', *Essays on Old Testament History and Religion*, E.T., Oxford, 1966, pp. 81–132.
— 'The Monarchy in the Kingdoms of Israel and Judah', ibid., pp. 241–59.
Andersen, F. I. 'The Socio-judicial Background of the Naboth Incident', *JBL*, lxxxv, 1966, pp. 46–57.
Andrew, M. E. 'Using God', *ET*, lxxiv, 1962/3, pp. 304–7.
— 'Falsehood and Truth', *Interpr.*, xvii, 1963, pp. 425–38.
— See also Stamm, J. J.
Arnold, W. R. *Ephod and Ark*, HTS, iii, 1917.
Baltzer, K. *Das Bundesformular*, WMANT, iv, 1960.
Bardtke, H. Review: *Mowinckel-Festschrift*, *TLZ*, lxxxiii, 1958, cols. 105–7.
Barnes, W. E. 'Prophecy and the Sabbath', *JTS*, xxix, 1927/8, pp. 386–90.
— 'Teraphim', ibid., xxx, 1928/9, pp. 177–9.
Begrich, J. 'Berit', *ZAW*, N.F., xix, 1944, pp. 1–11.
Bentzen, A. *Introduction to the Old Testament*⁴, i–ii, Copenhagen, 1958.

Berry, G. R. 'The Hebrew Word נוּחַ', *JBL*, l, 1931, pp. 207–10.
Bewer, J. 'The Composition of Judges, Chaps. 17, 18', *AJSL*, xxix, 1912/13, pp. 261–83.
Beyerlin, W. *Origins and History of the Oldest Sinaitic Traditions*, E.T., Oxford, 1965.
Black, M. (Ed.) *Peake's Commentary on the Bible²*, London, 1962 (with Rowley, H. H.).
Blank, S. H. 'The Curse, Blasphemy, the Spell and the Oath', *HUCA*, xxiii. i, 1950/1, pp. 73–95.
Botterweck, G. J. 'Der Sabbat im Alten Testamente', *TQ*, cxxxiv, 1953, pp. 134–47, 448–57.
Brekelmans, Chr. H. W. 'Exodus xviii and the Origins of Yahwism in Israel', *OTS*, x, 1954, pp. 215–24.
Brichto, H. C. *The Problem of 'Curse' in the Hebrew Bible*, *JBL* Monograph Series, xiii, Philadelphia, 1963.
Bright, J. *Early Israel in Recent History Writing*, SBT¹, xix, 1956.
— *A History of Israel*, London, 1960.
Brinker, R. *The Influence of Sanctuaries in Early Israel*, Manchester, 1946.
Brownlee, W. H. 'Exorcising the Souls from Ezekiel 13:17–23', *JBL*, lxix, 1950, pp. 367–73.
Budde, K. *Religion of Israel to the Exile*, London, 1899.
— 'The Sabbath and the Week', *JTS*, xxx, 1928/9, pp. 1–15.
— 'Antwort auf Johannes Meinholds "Zur Sabbathfrage" ', *ZAW*, N.F., vii, 1930, pp. 138–45.
Burney, C. F. *Notes on the Hebrew Text of the Books of Kings*, Oxford, 1903.
— *The Book of Judges²*, London, 1930.
Burrows, M. *The Basis of Israelite Marriage*, *JAOS* Monograph, xv, 1938.
— *What Mean These Stones?*, New York, 1941.
Buttenwieser, M. *The Psalms*, Chicago, 1938.
Cannon, W. W. 'The Weekly Sabbath', *ZAW*, N.F., viii, 1931, pp. 325–7.
Cazelles, H. *Études sur le code de l'Alliance*, Paris, 1946.
— 'David's Monarchy and the Gibeonites Claim', *PEQ*, lxxxvii, 1955, pp. 165–75.
Clements, R. E. *God and Temple*, Oxford, 1965.
— *Prophecy and Covenant*, SBT¹, xliii, 1965.
— 'Deuteronomy and the Jerusalem Cult Tradition', *VT*, xv, 1965, pp. 300–312.
— *Abraham and David*, SBT², v, 1967.
— *God's Chosen People*, London, 1968.
Coates, J. R. 'Thou shalt not covet', *ZAW*, N.F., xi, 1934, pp. 238–9.
Cohen, B. 'Self Help in Jewish and Roman Law', *RIDA³*, ii, 1955, pp. 107–133.
Cook, S.A., *The Laws of Moses and the Code of Hammurabi*, London, 1903.
Cowley, A. *Aramaic Papyri of the Fifth Century B.C.*, Oxford, 1923.

Cross, F. M. Jnr. 'Josiah's Revolt against Assyria', *JNES*, xii, 1953, pp. 56–58 (with Freedman, D. N.).

— *Scrolls from the Wilderness of the Dead Sea* (Catalogue), Norwich, 1965.

Crowfoot, J. W. *The Buildings at Samaria, Samaria-Sebaste Reports*, i, London, 1942 (with Kenyon, K. M. and Subenik, E. L.).

Dahood, M. J. 'A Note on Psalm 15,4 (14,4)', *CBQ*, xvi, 1954, p. 302.

Daube, D. 'Some Forms of Old Testament Legislation', *Oxford Society of Historical Theology*, 1944/5, pp. 36–46.

— *Studies in Biblical Law*, Cambridge, 1947.

— 'Error and Accident in the Bible', *RIDA²*, ii, 1949, pp. 189–213.

— 'Concerning Methods of Bible-Criticism', *ArOr*, xvii, 1949, pp. 89–99.

— 'Direct and Indirect Causation in Biblical Law', *VT*, xi, 1961, pp. 246–69.

— *The Exodus Pattern in the Bible*, London, 1963.

David, M. 'The Manumission of Slaves under Zedekiah', *OTS*, v, 1948, pp. 63–79.

— 'The Codex Hammurabi and Its Relation to the Provisions of Law in Exodus', ibid., vii, 1950, pp. 149–78.

— '*hit'āmēr* (Deut. xxi. 14; xxiv. 7)', *VT*, i, 1951, pp. 219–21.

— 'Die Bestimmungen über die Asylstädte in Josua xx', *OTS*, ix, 1951, pp. 30–48.

Davidson, R. *The Old Testament*, London, 1964.

Diamond, A. S. 'An Eye for an Eye', *Iraq*, xix, 1957, pp. 151–5.

Dinur, B. 'The Religious Character of the Cities of Refuge and the Ceremony of Admission into them', *Eretz-Israel*, iii, 1954, pp. 135–46.

Donner, H. *Israel unter den Völkern*, VTS, xi, 1964.

Draffkorn, A. E. 'Ilāni/Elohim', *JBL*, lxxvi, 1957, pp. 216–24.

Driver, G. R. *The Assyrian Laws*, Oxford, 1935 (with Miles, Sir J. C.).

— 'Problems in the Hebrew Text of Proverbs', *Bibl.*, xxxii, 1951, pp. 173–197.

— *The Babylonian Laws*, i, Oxford, 1952; ii, Oxford, 1955 (with Miles, Sir J. C.).

— 'Three Notes', *VT*, ii, 1952, pp. 356–7.

— 'Babylonian and Hebrew Notes', *WO*, ii, 1954, pp. 19–26.

— *Canaanite Myths and Legends*, Old Testament Studies, iii, Edinburgh, 1956.

— 'Two Problems in the Old Testament Examined in the Light of Assyriology', *Syria*, xxxiii, 1956, pp. 70–8.

Driver, S. R. *Deuteronomy³*, ICC, 1902.

— *Notes on the Hebrew Text and the Topography of the Books of Samuel²*, Oxford, 1913.

Dus, J. 'Das zweite Gebot', *CV*, iv, 1961, pp. 37–50.

Eerdmans, B. D. 'Der Sabbath', *Marti-Festschrift*, BZAW, xli, 1925, pp. 79–83.

Eichrodt, W. 'The Law and the Gospel', *Interpr.*, xi, 1957, pp. 23–40.

— *Theology of the Old Testament*, i, E.T., London, 1961.

Eichrodt, W. 'Covenant and Law', *Interpr.*, xx, 1966, pp. 302–21.

Eissfeldt, O. *Molk als Opferbegriff im Punischen und Hebräischen und das Ende des Gottes Molech*, Beiträge zur Geschichte des Altertums, iii, Haale a. Saale, 1935.

— *Introduction to the Old Testament*, E.T., Oxford, 1965.

Elliger, K. 'Das Gesetz Leviticus 18', *ZAW*, N.F., xxvi, 1955, pp. 1–25.

Elliott-Binns, L. E. 'Some Problems of the Holiness Code', ibid., pp. 26–40.

Evans, G. ' "Coming" and "Going" at the City Gate—a Discussion of Professor Speiser's Paper', *BASOR*, cl, 1958, pp. 28–33.

Falk, Z. W. 'Ex. xxi. 6', *VT*, ix, 1959, pp. 86–8.

— *Hebrew Law in Biblical Times*, Jerusalem, 1964.

Fensham, F. C. 'New Light on Exodus 21[6] and 22[7] from the Laws of Eshnunna', *JBL*, lxxviii, 1959, pp. 160–1.

— 'Exodus xxi. 18–19 in the Light of the Hittite Law § 10', *VT*, x, 1960, pp. 333–5.

— 'The Possibility of the Presence of Casuistic Legal Material at the Making of the Covenant at Sinai', *PEQ*, xciii, 1961, pp. 143–6.

— ' '*d* in Exodus xxii. 12', *VT*, xii, 1962, pp. 337–9.

— 'Malediction and Benediction in the Ancient Near Eastern Treaties and in the Old Testament', *ZAW*, N.F., xxxiii, 1962, pp. 1–9.

— 'Common Trends in Curses of the Near Eastern Treaties and *kudurru*-Inscriptions Compared with Maledictions of Amos and Isaiah', ibid., N.F., xxxiv, 1963, pp. 155–75.

— 'Clauses of Protection in Hittite Vassal-Treaties and the Old Testament', *VT*, xiii, 1963, pp. 133–43.

— 'The Treaty between Israel and the Gibeonites', *BA*, xxvii, 1964, pp. 96–100.

Fichtner, J. 'Der Begriff des "Nächsten" im Alten Testament', *WD*, iv, 1955, pp. 23–52.

Fitzmyer, J. A. 'The Aramaic Suzerainty Treaty from Sefire in the Museum of Beirut', *CBQ*, xx, 1958, pp. 444–76.

Flusser, D. ' "Do not Commit Adultery", "Do not Murder" ', *Textus*, iv, 1964, pp. 220–4.

Frankena, R. 'The Vassal-Treaties of Esarhaddon and the Dating of Deuteronomy', *OTS*, xiv, 1965, pp. 122–54.

Freedman, D. N. See Cross, F. M. Jnr.

Gadd, C. J. 'Tablets from Kirkuk', *RA*, xxiii, 1926, pp. 49–161.

Gehman, H. S. See Montgomery, J. A.

Gemser, B. 'The *Rîb* or Controversy Pattern in Hebrew Mentality', *Wisdom in Israel and in the Ancient Near East*, Rowley-Festschrift (Eds. M. Noth and D. Winton Thomas), VTS, iii, 1955, pp. 120–37.

Gerstenberger, E. 'Covenant and Commandment', *JBL*, lxxxiv, 1965, pp. 38–51.

— *Wesen und Herkunft des 'Apodiktischen Rechts'*, WMANT, xx, 1965.

Gevirtz, S. 'West Semitic Curses and the Problem of the Origins of Hebrew Law', *VT*, xi, 1961, pp. 137–58.
— 'A New Look at an Old Crux: Amos 5:26', *JBL*, lxxxvii, 1968, pp. 267–276.
Goetze, A. 'The Laws of Eshnunna', *AASOR*, xxxi, 1956.
Goldman, S. *The Ten Commandments*, Chicago, 1956.
Good, E. M. 'Capital Punishment and Its Alternatives in Ancient Near Eastern Law', *Stanford Law Review*, xix, 1967, pp. 947–77.
Gordon, C. H. 'Parallèles Nouziens aux lois et coutumes de l'ancien Testament', *RB*, xliv, 1935, pp. 34–41.
— 'אלהים in Its Reputed Meaning of Rulers, Judges', *JBL*, liv, 1935, pp. 139–44.
— 'Hos. 2.4–5 in the Light of New Semitic Inscriptions', *ZAW*, N.F., xiii, 1936, pp. 277–80.
— 'An Akkadian Parallel to Deuteronomy 21:1 ff.', *RA*, xxxii, 1936, pp. 1–6.
— 'Biblical Customs and the Nuzu Tablets', *BA*, iii, 1940, pp. 1–12.
— 'A Note on the Tenth Commandment', *JBR*, xxxi, 1963, pp. 208–9.
— 'The Ten Commandments', *Christianity To-day*, viii, 1964, pp. 625–8.
Gottstein, H. M. 'Du sollst nicht stehlen', *TZ*, ix, 1953, pp. 394–5.
Graham, W. C. *Culture and Conscience*, Chicago, 1936 (with May, H. G.).
Gray, G. B. *Numbers*, ICC, 1903.
Gray, J. 'The Desert Sojourn of the Hebrews and the Sinai-Horeb Tradition', *VT*, iv, 1954, pp. 148–54.
— *The Legacy of Canaan*, VTS, v, 1957.
— *Archaeology and the Old Testament World*, London, 1962.
— *I and II Kings*, London, 1964.
Greenberg, M. 'The Biblical Concept of Asylum', *JBL*, lxxviii, 1959, pp. 125–32.
— 'Some Postulates of Biblical Criminal Law', *Yehezkel Kaufmann Jubilee Volume* (Ed. M. Haran), Jerusalem, 1960.
— 'Witness', IDB, iv, 1962, p. 864.
— 'Another Look at Rachel's Theft of the Teraphim', *JBL*, lxxxi, 1962, pp. 239–48.
Gressmann, H. *Mose und seine Zeit*, Göttingen, 1913.
— *Die Anfänge Israels*, Göttingen, 1914.
Gunneweg, A. H. J. 'Sinaibund und Davidsbund', *VT*, x, 1960, pp. 335–41.
Harper, W. R. *Amos and Hosea*, ICC, 1905.
Hauer, C. J. 'Who was Zadok?', *JBL*, lxxxii, 1963, pp. 89–94.
Herrmann, J. 'Das zehnte Gebot', *Sellin-Festschrift*, Leipzig, 1927, pp. 69–82.
Hertzberg, H. W. 'Die kleinen Richter', *TLZ*, lxxix, 1954, cols. 285–90.
— *I and II Samuel*, E.T., London, 1964.
Hillers, D. R. *Treaty Curses and the Old Testament Prophets*, Biblica et Orientalia, xvi, Rome, 1964.

Hoffner, H. A. 'Second Millennium Antecedents to the Hebrew 'ÔB', *JBL*, lxxxvi, 1967, pp. 385–401.

Huffmon, H. B. 'The Covenant Lawsuit in the Prophets', ibid., lxxviii, 1959, pp. 285–95.

— 'The Exodus, Sinai and the Credo', *CBQ*, xxvii, 1965, pp. 101–13.

Hyatt, J. P. 'Moses and the Ethical Decalogue', *Encounter*, xxvi, 1965, pp. 199–206.

Iwry, S. 'The Qumrân Isaiah and the End of the Dial of Ahaz', *BASOR*, cxlvii, 1957, pp. 27–33.

Jack, J. W. *Samaria in Ahab's Time*, Edinburgh, 1929.

— 'Recent Biblical Archaeology', *ET*, xlviii, 1936/7, pp. 549–51.

Jacob, B. 'The Decalogue', *JQR*, N.S., xiv, 1923/4, pp. 141–87.

Jacob, E. *Theology of the Old Testament*, E.T., London, 1958.

Jastrow, M. 'The Original Character of the Hebrew Sabbath', *AJT*, ii, 1898, pp. 312–52.

Jepsen, A. 'Berith. Ein Beitrag zur Theologie der Exilszeit', *Verbannung und Heimkehr, Rudolph-Festschrift*, Tübingen, 1961, pp. 161–80.

Jirku, A. 'Die Gesichtsmaske des Mose', *ZDPV*, lxvii, 1944/5, pp. 43–5.

— 'Die Mimation in den Nordzemitischen Sprachen und einige Bezeichnungen der Altisraelitischen Mantik', *Bibl.*, xxxiv, 1953, pp. 78–80.

Johnson, A. R. *The One and the Many in the Israelite Conception of God*, Cardiff, 1942.

— 'The Primary Meaning of √גאל', VTS, i, 1953, pp. 67–77.

— *The Vitality of the Individual in the Thought of Ancient Israel²*, Cardiff, 1964.

— *Sacral Kingship in Ancient Israel²*, Cardiff, 1967.

Kapelrud, A. S. 'King and Fertility: A Discussion of 2 Sam. 21,1–14', *Mowinckel-Festschrift*, Oslo, 1955, pp. 113–22.

— 'König David und die Söhne des Saul', *ZAW*, N.F., xxvi, 1955, pp. 198–205.

— 'Some Recent Points of View on the Time and Origin of the Decalogue', *ST*, xviii, 1964, pp. 81–90.

— 'The Date of the Priestly Code (P)', *ASTI*, iii, 1964, pp. 58–64.

Kennett, R. H. 'The Origin of the Aaronite Priesthood', *JTS*, vi, 1904/5, pp. 161–86.

— *Deuteronomy and the Decalogue*, Cambridge, 1920.

— *The Church of Israel*, Cambridge, 1933.

Kenyon, K. M. See Crowfoot, J. W.

Keszler, W. 'Die literarische, historische und theologische Problematik des Dekalogs', *VT*, vii, 1957, pp. 1–16.

Kilian, R. 'Apodiktisches und kasuistisches Recht im Licht ägyptischer Analogien', *BZ*, vii, 1963, pp. 185–202.

Kissane, E. J. *The Book of Psalms*, i–ii, Dublin, 1953.

Kline, M. G. *Treaty of the Great King. The Covenant Structure of Deuteronomy*, Grand Rapids, 1963.

Klopfenstein, M. A. *Die Lüge nach dem Alten Testament*, Zürich, 1964.

Knierim, R. 'Exodus 18 und die Neuordnung der Mosaischen Gerichtsbarkeit', *ZAW*, N.F., xxxii, 1961, pp. 146–71.

— 'Das erste Gebot', ibid., N.F., xxxvi, 1965, pp. 20–39.

Koch, K. 'Der Spruch "sein Blut bleibe auf seinem Haupt" und die israelitische Auffassung vom vergossenen Blut', *VT*, xii, 1962, pp. 396–416.

Köhler, L. 'Der Dekalog', *TR*, N.F., i, 1929, pp. 161–84.

— *Hebrew Man*, E.T., London, 1956.

— *Old Testament Theology*, E.T., London, 1957.

Koole, J. L. 'Psalm xv—eine königliche Einzugsliturgie?', *OTS*, xiii, 1963, pp. 98–111.

Kopf, L. 'Arabische Etymologien und Parallelen zum Bibelwörterbuch', *VT*, viii, 1958, pp. 161–215.

Kornfeld, W. 'L'adultère dans L'Orient Antique', *RB*, lvii, 1950, pp. 92–109.

Kosmala, H. 'The So-Called Ritual Decalogue', *ASTI*, i, 1962, pp. 31–61.

Kraeling, E. G. 'The Present State of the Sabbath Question', *AJSL*, xlix, 1932/3, pp. 218–28.

Kramer, S. N. *From the Tablets of Sumer*, Indian Hills, Colorado, 1956.

Kraus, H.-J. *Worship in Israel*, E.T., Oxford, 1966.

Labuschagne, C. J. 'Teraphim—a New Proposal for Its Etymology', *VT*, xvi, 1966, pp. 115–17.

Landsberger, B. 'Die babylonischen Termini für Gesetz und Recht', *Symbolae ad iura orientis—Paulo Koschaker dedicatae*, Leiden, 1939, pp. 219–34.

Langdon, S. *Babylonian Menologies and the Semitic Calendar*, Schweich Lectures, 1933, London, 1935.

Leslie, E. A. *The Psalms*, New York, 1949.

Lewy, I. 'Auerbachs neuester Beweis für den Mosaischen Ursprung der Zehngebote Widerlegt', *VT*, iv, 1954, pp. 313–16.

— 'Dating of Covenant Code Sections on Humaneness and Righteousness', ibid., vii, 1957, pp. 322–6.

L'Hour, J. 'Une législation criminelle dans le Deutéronome', *Bibl.*, xliv, 1963, pp. 1–28.

Lohfink, N. J. 'Zur Dekalogfassung von Dt 5', *BZ*, N.F., ix, 1965, pp. 17–32.

Loretz, O. 'Exod. 21,6; 22,8 und angebliche Nuzi-Parallelen', *Bibl.*, xli, 1960, pp. 167–75.

McCarthy, D. J. *Treaty and Covenant*, Analecta Biblica, xxi, Rome, 1963.

— 'Covenant in the Old Testament: the Present State of the Inquiry', *CBQ*, xxvii, 1965, pp. 217–40.

— 'II Samuel 7 and the Structure of the Deuteronomic History', *JBL*, lxxxiv, 1965, pp. 131–8.

— *Der Gottesbund im Alten Testament*, Stuttgart, 1966.

McKenzie, D. A. 'The Judge of Israel', *VT*, xvii, 1967, pp. 118–21.

o

McKenzie, J. L. 'The Elders in the Old Testament', *Bibl.*, xl, 1959, pp. 522–540.

MacLaurin, E. C. B. *The Figure of Religious Adultery in the Old Testament*, Leeds University Oriental Society Monograph, vi, 1964.

Maisler, B. 'The Historical Background of the Samaria Ostraca', *JPOS*, xxi, 1948, pp. 117–33.

Malamat, A. 'Doctrines of Causality in Hittite and Biblical Historiography: A Parallel', *VT*, v, 1955, pp. 1–12.

May, H. G. 'A Key to the Interpretation of Zechariah's Visions', *JBL*, lvii, 1938, pp. 173–84.

— 'Individual Responsibility and Retribution', *HUCA*, xxxii, 1961, pp. 107–120.

— See also Graham, W. C.

Meek, T. J. 'The Sabbath in the Old Testament', *JBL*, xxxiii, 1914, pp. 201–212.

— 'Some Religious Origins of the Hebrews', *AJSL*, xxxvii, 1920/1, pp. 101–131.

— 'Lapses of Old Testament Translators', *JAOS*, lviii, 1938, pp. 122–9.

— 'A New Interpretation of the Code of Hammurabi §117–119', *JNES*, vii, 1948, pp. 180–3.

— *Hebrew Origins*[2], New York, 1950.

Meinhold, J. 'Zur Sabbathfrage', *ZAW*, N.F., vii, 1930, pp. 121–38.

Mendelsohn, I. 'Slavery in the Ancient Near East', *BA*, ix, 1946, pp. 74–88.

— *Slavery in the Ancient Near East*, New York, 1949.

— *Religions of the Ancient Near East*, New York, 1955.

Mendenhall, G. E. 'Ancient Oriental and Biblical Law', *BA*, xvii, 1954, pp. 26–46.

— 'Covenant Forms in Israelite Tradition', ibid., pp. 50–76.

— 'Puppy and Lettuce in Northwest-Semitic Covenant Making', *BASOR*, cxxxiii, 1954, pp. 26–30.

— 'The Hebrew Conquest of Palestine', *BA*, xxv, 1962, pp. 66–87.

— 'Covenant', IDB, i, 1962, pp. 714–23.

Miles, Sir J. C. See Driver, G. R.

Minette de Tillesse, G., 'Sections "tu" et sections "vous" dans le Deutéronome', *VT*, xii, 1962, pp. 29–88.

Modrzejewski, J. 'Les Juifs et le droit hellénistique: Divorce et égalité des époux (CPJud. 144)', *Jura*, xii, 1961, pp. 162–93.

Montgomery, J. A. *The Books of Kings*, ICC, 1951 (with Gehman, H. S.).

Moore, G. F. *Judges*, ICC, 1895.

Moran, W. L. 'The Scandal of the "Great Sin" at Ugarit', *JNES*, xviii, 1959, pp. 280–1.

Morgenstern, J. 'The Book of the Covenant—Part II', *HUCA*, vii, 1930, pp. 19–258.

— 'The Book of the Covenant—Part III', ibid., viii, 1931, pp. 1–150.

— 'The Book of the Covenant—Part IV', ibid., xxxiii, 1962, pp. 59–105.

Moriarty, F. L. 'The Chronicler's Account of Hezekiah's Reform', *CBQ*, xxvii, 1965, pp. 399–406.

Mowinckel, S. O. P. *Psalmenstudien*, i, Kristiania, 1921.

— *Le Décalogue*, Paris, 1927.

— *He That Cometh*, E.T., Oxford, 1956.

— *The Psalms in Israel's Worship*, i–ii, E.T., Oxford, 1962.

Muilenburg, J. 'The Form and Structure of the Covenantal Formulations', *VT*, ix, 1959, pp. 347–65.

Murtonen, A. 'Some Thoughts on Judges xvii sq.', ibid., i, 1951, pp. 223–4.

Nahmani, H. S. *Human Rights in the Old Testament*, Tel Aviv, 1964.

Nemoy, L. 'A Tenth Century Disquisition on Suicide According to Old Testament Law', *JBL*, lvii, 1938, pp. 411–20.

Neufeld, E. *Ancient Hebrew Marriage Laws*, London, 1944.

— *The Hittite Laws*, London, 1951.

Newman, M. L. 'The Prophetic Call of Samuel', *Israel's Prophetic Heritage, Essays in Honor of James Muilenburg* (Eds. B. W. Anderson and W. Harrelson), London, 1962, pp. 86–97.

— *The People of the Covenant*, London, 1965.

Nicholson, E. W. *Deuteronomy and Tradition*, Oxford, 1967.

Nicolsky, N. M. 'Das Asylrecht in Israel', *ZAW*, N.F., vii, 1930, pp. 146–75.

Nielsen, E. *The Ten Commandments in New Perspective*, SBT², vii, 1968.

North, R. 'The Derivation of the Sabbath', *Bibl.*, xxxvi, 1955, pp. 182–201.

Noth, M. *Das System der zwölf Stämme Israels*, BWANT, iv. i, 1930.

— 'Das Amt des "Richters Israels" ', *Bertholet-Festschrift* (Eds. W. Baumgartner et al.), Tübingen, 1950, pp. 404–17.

— *Überlieferungsgeschichtliche Studien*, i², Tübingen, 1957.

— *The History of Israel²*, E.T., London, 1960.

— 'The Background of Judges 17–18', *Israel's Prophetic Heritage, Essays in Honor of James Muilenburg* (Eds. B. W. Anderson and W. Harrelson), London, 1962, pp. 68–85.

— *Exodus*, E.T., London, 1962.

— *Leviticus*, E.T., London, 1965.

— 'Old Testament Covenant-Making in the Light of a Text from Mari', *The Laws in the Pentateuch and Other Essays*, E.T., Edinburgh, 1966, pp. 108–17.

— *Numbers*, E.T., London, 1968.

Obbink, H. Th. 'Jahwebilder', *ZAW*, N.F., vi, 1929, pp. 264–74.

Oesterley, W. O. E. *The Psalms* (reprint), London, 1955.

Östborn, G. *Tōrā in the Old Testament*, Lund, 1945.

Pedersen, J. *Israel: Its Life and Culture*, i–ii, E.T., London and Copenhagen, 1926; iii–iv, E.T., London and Copenhagen, 1940.

Petuchowski, J. J. 'A Note on W. Kessler's "Problematik des Dekalogs" ', *VT*, vii, 1957, pp. 397–8.

Pfeiffer, R. H. 'The Polemic against Idolatry in the Old Testament', *JBL*, xliii, 1924, pp. 229–40.
— 'The Oldest Decalogue', ibid., pp. 294–310.
— 'Images of Yahweh', ibid., xlv, 1926, pp. 211–22.
— *Introduction to the Old Testament* (Rev. ed.), London, 1952.
Phillips, A. 'The Interpretation of 2 Samuel xii. 5–6', *VT*, xvi, 1966, pp. 242–4.
— 'The Ecstatics' Father', *Words and Meanings, Essays Presented to D. Winton Thomas* (Eds. P. R. Ackroyd and B. Lindars), Cambridge, 1968, pp. 183–94.
— 'The Case of the Woodgatherer Reconsidered', *VT*, xix, 1969, pp. 125–8.
van der Ploeg, J. 'Les chefs du peuple d'Israël et leurs titres', *RB*, lvii, 1950, pp. 40–61.
— 'Studies in Hebrew Law', *CBQ*, xii, 1950, pp. 248–59, 416–27; ibid., xiii, 1951, pp. 28–43, 164–71, 296–307.
— 'Les šoṭᵉrim d'Israël', *OTS*, x, 1954, pp. 185–96.
Porter, J. R. *Moses and Monarchy*, Oxford, 1963.
— 'The Legal Aspects of the Concept of "Corporate Personality" in the Old Testament', *VT*, xv, 1965, pp. 361–80.
— *The Extended Family in the Old Testament*, Occasional Papers in Social and Economic Administration, vi, London, 1967.
Press, R. 'Das Ordal im alten Israel', *ZAW*, N.F., x, 1933, pp. 121–40, 224–255.
Pritchard, J. B. (Ed.) *Ancient Near Eastern Texts Relating to the Old Testament*[2], Princeton, 1955.
Rabinowitz, J. J. 'The "Great Sin" in Ancient Egyptian Marriage Contracts', *JNES*, xviii, 1959, p. 73.
— 'Neo-Babylonian Legal Documents and Jewish Law', *JJP*, xiii, 1961, pp. 131–75.
von Rad, G. *Old Testament Theology*, i, E.T., Edinburgh, 1962; ii, E.T., Edinburgh, 1965.
— *Genesis*[2], E.T., London, 1963.
— *Deuteronomy*, E.T., London, 1966.
— 'The Form-Critical Problem of the Hexateuch', *The Problem of the Hexateuch and Other Essays*, E.T., Edinburgh, 1966, pp. 1–78.
— 'The Royal Ritual in Judah', ibid., pp. 222–31.
Rapaport, I. 'The Origins of Hebrew Law', *PEQ*, lxxiii, 1941, pp. 158–67.
Reventlow, H. Graf. *Gebot und Predigt im Dekalog*, Gütersloh, 1962.
Rin, S. 'The מות of Grandeur', *VT*, ix, 1959, pp. 324–5.
Ringgren, H. *Israelite Religion*, E.T., London, 1966.
Rodd, C. S. 'The Family in the Old Testament', *BT*, xviii, 1967, pp. 19–26.
Rost, L. 'Sinaibund und Davidsbund', *TLZ*, lxxii, 1947, cols. 129–34.
Rowley, H. H. 'Zadok and Nehushtan', *JBL*, lviii, 1939, pp. 113–41.
— *From Joseph to Joshua*, Schweich Lectures, 1948, London, 1950.

— 'Melchizedek and Zadok (Gen. 14 and Ps. 110)', *Bertholet-Festschrift* (Eds. W. Baumgartner et al.), Tübingen, 1950, pp. 461–72.

— (Ed.) *The Old Testament and Modern Study*, Oxford, 1951.

— 'Moses and the Decalogue', *BJRL*, xxxiv, 1951/2, pp. 81–118.

— 'Nehemiah's Mission and Its Background', ibid., xxxvii, 1954/5, pp. 528–561.

— 'Sanballet and the Samaritan Schism', ibid., xxxviii, 1955/6, pp. 166–98.

— 'Hezekiah's Reform and Rebellion', ibid., xliv, 1961/2, pp. 395–431.

— See also Black, M.

Schmidt, H. 'אוב', *Marti-Festschrift*, BZAW, xli, 1925, pp. 253–61.

Schmidt, W. H. *Die Schöpfungsgeschichte der Priesterschrift*, WMANT, xvii, 1964.

Schofield, J. N. 'Some Archaeological Sites and the Old Testament', *ET*, lxvi, 1954/5, pp. 315–18.

Schreiner, J. *Die zehn Gebote im Leben des Gottesvolkes*, München, 1966.

Segal, M. H. 'The Pentateuch', *The Pentateuch and Other Biblical Studies*, Jerusalem, 1967, pp. 1–170.

Segert, S. 'Bis in das dritte und vierte Glied', *CV*, i, 1958, pp. 37–9.

Sekine, M. 'Davidsbund und Sinaibund bei Jeremia', *VT*, ix, 1959, pp. 47–57.

van Selms, A. 'The Goring Ox in Babylonian and Biblical Law', *ArOr*, xviii, 1950, pp. 321–30.

Simpson, C. A. *Composition of the Book of Judges*, Oxford, 1957.

Skinner, J. *Genesis*, ICC, 1910.

Smith, J. M. P. *Micah*, ICC, 1912.

— *The Origin and History of Hebrew Law*, Chicago, 1931.

Smith, S. 'What were the Teraphim?', *JTS*, xxxiii, 1931/2, pp. 33–6.

Smith, W. Robertson. 'On the Forms of Divination and Magic Enumerated in Deut. xviii, 10, 11', *JPhil*, xiii, 1885, pp. 273–87; ibid., xiv, 1886, pp. 113–28.

— *Kinship and Marriage in Early Arabia* (new ed.), London, 1903.

— *Lectures on the Religion of the Semites*[3], London, 1927.

Snaith, N. H. *The Jewish New Year Festival: Its Origins and Development*, London, 1947.

— 'The Hebrew Root G'L (I)', *ALUOS*, iii, 1961/2, pp. 60–7.

— 'The Cult of Molech', *VT*, xvi, 1966, pp. 123–4.

Speiser, E. A. ' "Coming" and "Going" at the City Gate', *BASOR*, cxliv, 1956, pp. 20–3.

— 'Census and Ritual Expiation in Mari and Israel', ibid., cxlix, 1958, pp. 17–25.

— 'Leviticus and the Critics', *Yehezkel Kaufmann Jubilee Volume* (Ed. M. Haran), Jerusalem, 1960, pp. 29–45.

— 'An Angelic "Curse": Exodus 14:20', *JAOS*, lxxx, 1960, pp. 198–200.

— 'The Stem PLL in Hebrew', *JBL*, lxxxii, 1963, pp. 301–6.

Speiser, E. A. 'Background and Function of the Biblical Nāśî', *CBQ*, xxv, 1963, pp. 111–117.

Stamm, J. J. 'Sprachliche Erwägungen zum Gebot "Du sollst nicht töten" ', *TZ*, i, 1945, pp. 81–90.

— 'Dreissig Jahre Dekalogforschung', *TR*, N.F., xxvii, 1961, pp. 189–239, 281–305.

— *The Ten Commandments in Recent Research*, SBT², ii, 1967 (with Andrew, M. E.).

Staples, W. E. 'The Third Commandment', *JBL*, lviii, 1939, pp. 325–9.

Subenik, E. L. See Crowfoot, J. W.

Sulzberger, M. *The Am Ha-aretz: the Ancient Hebrew Parliament*, Philadelphia, 1909.

— *The Ancient Hebrew Law of Homicide*, Philadelphia, 1915.

Thomas, D. Winton. 'The Lachish Letters', *JTS*, xl, 1940, pp. 1–15.

— 'A Consideration of Some Unusual Ways of Expressing the Superlative in Hebrew', *VT*, iii, 1953, pp. 209–24.

— (Ed.) *Documents from Old Testament Times*, London, 1958.

— (Ed.) *Archaeology and Old Testament Study*, Oxford, 1967.

— 'Some Further Remarks on Unusual Ways of Expressing the Superlative in Hebrew', *VT*, xviii, 1968, pp. 120–4.

Thompson, J. A. *The Ancient Near Eastern Treaties and the Old Testament*, London, 1964.

Tsevat, M. 'Marriage and Monarchical Legitimacy in Ugarit and Israel', *JSS*, iii, 1958, pp. 237–43.

— 'Studies in the Book of Samuel', *HUCA*, xxxii, 1961, pp. 191–216.

Tucker, G. M. 'Covenant Forms and Contract Forms', *VT*, xv, 1965, pp. 487–503.

de Vaux, R. *Ancient Israel: Its Life and Institutions*, E.T., London, 1961.

— *Studies in Old Testament Sacrifice*, Cardiff, 1964.

— 'Le Roi D'Israël, Vassal De Yahvé', *Mélanges Eugène Tisserant*, i, Città del Vaticano, 1964, pp. 119–33.

Verdam, P. J. ' "On ne fera point mourir les enfants pour les pères" en droit biblique', *RIDA²*, iii, 1949, pp. 393–416.

Vieyra, M. 'Les noms du "mundus" en hittite et en assyrien et la pythonisse d'Endor', *RHA*, xix, 1961, pp. 47–55.

Vriezen, Th. C. *The Religion of Ancient Israel*, E.T., London, 1967.

Wallis, G. 'Eine Parallele zu Richter 19:29 ff. und 1 Sam. 11:5 ff. aus dem Briefarchiv von Mari', *ZAW*, N.F., xxiii, 1952, pp. 57–61.

Wallis, L. *Sociological Study of the Bible*, Chicago, 1912.

Waterman, L. 'Bull Worship in Israel', *AJSL*, xxxi, 1914/15, pp. 229–55.

Watts, J. D. W. 'Infinitive Absolute as Imperative and the Interpretation of Exodus 20⁸', *ZAW*, N.F., xxxiii, 1962, pp. 141–5.

Weingreen, J. 'The Case of the Woodgatherer (Numbers xv. 32–36)', *VT*, xvi, 1966, pp. 361–4.

— 'The Case of the Daughters of Zelophchad', ibid., pp. 518–22.

Weiser, A. *Introduction to the Old Testament*, E.T., London, 1961.

— *The Psalms*, E.T., London, 1962.

Weiss, M. 'Some Problems of the Biblical "Doctrine of Retribution" ', *Tarbiz*, xxxi, 1961/2, pp. 236–63.

Westermann, C. *Basic Forms of Prophetic Speech*, E.T., London, 1967.

Wevers, J. W. 'A Study in the Form Criticism of Individual Complaint Psalms', *VT*, vi, 1956, pp. 80–96.

Whitley, C. F. 'Covenant and Commandment in Israel', *JNES*, xxii, 1963, pp. 37–48.

Widengren, G. 'The Ascension of the Apostle and the Heavenly Book', *UUÅ*, 1950.7, pp. 7–76.

— 'King and Covenant', *JSS*, ii, 1957, pp. 1–32.

Willesen, F. 'Die Eselsöhne von Sichem als Bundesgenossen', *VT*, iv, 1954, pp. 216–17.

Wiseman, D. J. 'The Vassal Treaties of Esarhaddon', *Iraq*, xx, 1958, pp. 1–99.

— 'The Laws of Hammurabi Again', *JSS*, vii, 1962, pp. 161–72.

Wolf, C. U. 'Terminology of Israel's Tribal Organisation', *JBL*, lxv, 1946, pp. 45–9.

— 'Traces of Primitive Democracy in Ancient Israel', *JNES*, vi, 1947, pp. 98–108.

Wolff, H. W., 'Jahwe als Bundesvermittler', *VT*, vi, 1956, pp. 316–20.

Wood, W. C. 'The Religion of Canaan from the Earliest Times to the Hebrew Conquest', *JBL*, xxxv, 1916, pp. 1–279.

Wright, G. E. 'The Present State of Biblical Archaeology', *The Study of the Bible To-day and To-morrow* (Ed. H. R. Willoughby), Chicago, 1947.

— *The Old Testament Against Its Environment*, SBT[1], ii, 1950.

— *Shechem*, London, 1965.

Yaron, R. 'On Divorce in Old Testament Times', *RIDA*[3], iv, 1957, pp. 117–128.

— *Introduction to the Law of the Aramaic Papyri*, Oxford, 1961.

— 'CPJud 144 et Alia', *Jura*, xiii, 1962, pp. 170–5.

— 'Forms in the Laws of Eshnunna', *RIDA*[3], ix, 1962, pp. 137–53.

— 'Matrimonial Mishaps at Eshnunna', *JSS*, viii, 1963, pp. 1–16.

Zimmerli, W. 'Das zweite Gebot', *Bertholet-Festschrift* (Eds. W. Baumgartner et al.), Tübingen, 1950, pp. 550–63.

— 'Ich bin Jahwe', *Geschichte und Alten Testament, Alt-Festschrift*, Tübingen, 1953, pp. 179–209.

— 'Die Eigenart der prophetischen Rede des Ezechiel', *ZAW*, N.F., xxv, 1954, pp. 1–26.

— 'Sinaibund und Abrahambund', *TZ*, xvi, 1960, pp. 268–80.

— *The Law and the Prophets*, Oxford, 1965.

REFERENCE INDEX

INDEX OF AUTHORS